"Three Cheers for the Derrys!"

A History of the
10th Royal Inniskilling Fusiliers
in the 1914-18 War

by

Gardiner S. Mitchell

Acknowledgement is due to the:
Imperial War Museum for inclusion of prints of illustrations.
These are for sale on application to Photograph Archive, Lambeth Road, London SE16HZ.

First Published in 1991
Second Edition Published in 2008
by YES! Publications
www.yespublications.org
10-12 Bishop Street
Derry/Londonderry
BT48 6PW
Tel: 028 71261941
www.yespublications.org

ISBN: 978-1-873832-33-2 (softback edition)
ISBN: 978-1-873832-34-9 (hardback edition)

Front Cover Design: J.P. Cunningham

For Sophie & James

Contents

Foreword

When I was growing up, and learning history at school, it always seemed to be about dates. I now realise that history is really about people.

That is what makes this book so compelling. It contains first hand accounts from a period of history which has slipped over the horizon of living memory. There are now no veterans of The Great War alive in Ireland.

But there is an insatiable appetite for the period. It is on the school curriculum. And, today's generation can, with ease, trace their family history to the early part of the twentieth century.

My great uncle, Donald Clark, from Belfast, fought at the Somme. He was a member of the 14th battalion of the Royal Irish Rifles, the same battalion as William McFadzean, who won the first Victoria Cross on the first day of The Battle of the Somme, July 1st 1916. He also lived long enough to know that it was not "the great war to end all wars."

His medals are a treasured possession.

My own industry, television, has given new life to flickering black and white images from The First World War. But this book is in technicolour, because the stories are told in detail by those who "were there."

The second edition of "Three Cheers for the Derrys!" is timely, and we have new information – an interview with a veteran from the battalion, who was not known to the author, at the time of the first edition. And there are new photographs to illustrate the revised text. But the story remains the same.

The First World War still fascinates, because there had never been a war like it; and there has never been a war like it since. It was a conflict where nineteenth century methods of fighting met twentieth century technology. And, caught in the middle were the soldiers, brave men like those in the Derrys.

And lest you think that history is something from the past. It lives today. The Great War may have ended ninety years ago, but we are still reaping the whirlwind even now. For a start, it spawned many social changes. It brought about communism – and fascism. Without the First World War, there would not have been a Second World War; or the Cold War, which followed that.

I commend this book at another level. All history is local. The Great War was an event on a world stage, but it resonated in the fields and by ways here in Ireland. These survivors – all dead now – have come to life again through their words. Read their stories, but also remember those who "…shall grow not old."

Paul Clark   UTV

"I recall the deeds of the 36th Ulster Division, which have more than fulfilled the high opinion formed by me on inspecting that force on the eve of its departure for the front. Through the long years of struggle, which have now so gloriously ended, the men of Ulster have proved how nobly they fight and die."

KING GEORGE V

"The record of the 36th Division will ever be the pride of Ulster."

WINSTON CHURCHILL

CHARGE OF THE 36th ULSTER DIVISION

Somme, 1st July 1916. Painted by James Prinset Beadle R.A.

Jim Donaghy MBE (1991)

Leslie Bell (1991)

Preface

As a six-year-old sitting at Sunday School in a room in the Victoria Hall, Londonderry, I gazed, week after week, at a striking picture above the hearth. It was the "Charge of the Ulster Division" on July 1st, 1916. Every week, staring at the advancing soldiers and the exploding shells, I saw something different. As time went by and I became slightly older I realized this was a very special event - away back in history.

At church my mother would point out to me my Great Uncle, Jim Donaghy, and I was told that he had fought at the Battle of the Somme. I was fascinated that he had been there, and always looked at him in awe.

It was many years later that I visited him and we started to talk about the First World War. It was still as vivid to him as if it had happened yesterday. Names of comrades, dates and events came flooding back. They were imprinted in his memory just as they had occurred in his teenage years and on checking with the official war diaries of the Royal Inniskilling Fusiliers, his recollections proved to be incredibly accurate. Hearing those stories whetted my appetite to find out more about the battalion in which he served. I was fortunate in being able to talk to another of the handful of remaining veterans, Mr Leslie Bell from Moneymore, who also proved to have an extremely sharp memory.

This book is about a tightly knit group of young men, who before the war went to the same schools, played on the same streets, visited each other's homes and knew each other's families. Brothers, fathers and sons and many friends enlisted together. Throughout the War they saw the men of their community, many of whom had never left Ireland before, slaughtered and maimed in a war which had little or nothing to do with them.

I decided to write this book as I feel that these last veterans' stories should be recorded to let the people of my generation, and those beyond, have a glimpse of the suffering, hardship, comradeship and bravery of this band of young men who were known as "The 10th (Derry) Battalion Royal Inniskilling Fusiliers"

or

"The Derrys".

Jim Donaghy (1918)

Chapter 1
Enlisting

Jim Donaghy:-

"My father died in June of 1914 when there was talk of Home Rule and then War. War was finally declared on the 4th of August 1914. During that first week I was made redundant at the linen mill where I worked, as orders for the continent had been cancelled. I decided to enlist, but due to the recent death of my father, my mother wouldn't let me go. I was offered a job in the Ebrington shirt factory in Londonderry, where my father had worked, but I didn't want to work there – I wanted to enlist. It was in May 1915 that my mother finally conceded to let me go.

Two of my friends decided they would join up as well. We arranged to meet at Ebrington Barracks to enlist but on the day only one showed up — wee Joe Curry. Joe was 17, I was 18. The minimum age for joining up was 19 but we had no trouble in enlisting. We chose the 10th Royal Inniskilling Fusiliers (Derry Volunteers) as our battalion as they were mainly recruited from the City and County of Londonderry. The battalion at this time had just finished its basic training at Finner Camp on the west coast of Donegal and was now on the long march to Randalstown for further training.

On the day that we had been told to report back to the barracks, before being sent to Enniskillen for our recruits' course, we watched with pride the 10th Inniskillings — our battalion, march through the streets of the city."

Londonderry had been waiting in anticipation for the arrival of their men. It had been eight months since they had gone away but now they were returning. The children were given the day off school and the streets and houses were decorated with flags. Led by their flute band, the Battalion had left Finner on May 8th, 1915 and had marched through the towns and villages of Donegal. The locals had turned out to wish them luck as they marched past in the blazing sun with full kit. On May 11th they left Strabane at 6am to march the fourteen miles to the city. That morning they were elated at the thought of marching through their home City and County. The day started off dry and cool but soon a thick haze set in which developed into a heavy drizzle – the first bad weather they had encountered since leaving Finner camp.

The brass band of the 3rd Battalion Royal Inniskilling Fusiliers, stationed at Ebrington, marched out to Prehen on the city boundary to meet their comrades. Shortly after 11am the fifes and drums of the battalion band could be heard playing a brisk march and soon the marching column came into view. At the head was the distinguished figure of Lieutenant Colonel Ross Smyth, Commanding Officer of the Derrys, mounted on his horse. He was accompanied by Major Kinhard and Captain Toker. The brass band of the 3rd Battalion took the lead and marched the men into the city in spectacular style. The streets were lined with cheering crowds and the windows of the houses had their full complement of children and ladies waving

Colonel Ross Smyth leads the 10th Royal Inniskilling Fusiliers on the march to Londonderry, May 1915.

Photo: Bobby Kilgore

The Derrys marching through Coleraine on their way to Randalstown.

Photo: Northern Newspaper Group

miniature Union Flags and shouting greetings to the soldiers. These were their fathers, uncles, brothers and sons whom they had last seen in the autumn of 1914 and they looked magnificent in their uniforms.

They marched to the Polo Field on Clooney Road where the band of the 3rd Battalion dropped out and the lead was retaken by the Tenth's own band who positioned themselves in the centre of the field. They struck up 'The British Grenadiers' as the men were marched past and dismissed. The battalion was camping overnight in the city. The unfortunate men from County Derry were billeted in huts in the field but most of the City men went home.

Next day the Battalion left the Polo Field at 10am and set off across the bridge, again accompanied by the band, to recruit others into the Battalion. Crowds thronged the streets. It was the 'Rabble Day', the hiring fair, when many farm-labourers and farmers were looking for employers and employees respectively. The Recruiting Sergeants were busy and, at the end of the day, sixty more men had enlisted.

The next day, May 13th, the 10th Battalion marched past their families and friends for the last time as a Battalion. They were now soldiers on their way to the War, untouched, innocent and naïve to the horrors they would endure over the next three years, and oblivious to the awful reality that many would never return to see their city, families or friends again.

Company Sergeant-Major Henry Allen with his expectant wife. Their son was born in March 1916.
CSM Allen was killed on July 1st 1916 and never saw his son. His wife was left to bring up a family of eight.

TO THE MEMBERS

OF THE

ULSTER VOLUNTEER FORCE

I greatly appreciate the action of our Volunteers in rallying so enthusiastically to my call for Defenders of the Empire. To those who have not already responded to that call and are eligible and can go, I say—QUIT YOURSELVES LIKE MEN AND COMPLY WITH YOUR COUNTRY'S DEMAND.

Enlist at once for the Ulster Division in Lord Kitchener's Army for the period of the War.

You were formed to defend our citizenship in the United Kingdom and the Empire, and so preserve our civil and religious liberty. Now the United Kingdom and the Empire are threatened we must fight with our fellow-Britishers until victory is assured.

To those Loyalists who are not eligible or cannot go I appeal that they shall fill up the vacancies in the U.V.F. ranks caused by those going to the Front, so that we may maintain in fullest efficiency the Ulster Volunteer Force to protect your homes and hearths—that is a duty we owe to the Volunteers who go abroad to fight the country's battles. Let every Loyalist be faithful to the trust, and by each one doing his duty our country will be saved and our own interests preserved.

NO SURRENDER.

GOD SAVE THE KING.

EDWARD CARSON.

Old Town Hall, Belfast,
7th September, 1914.

Article from Londonderry Sentinel recruiting UVF for the Ulster Division September 1914.

Chapter 2
The Formation of the Battalion

No Home Rule postcard.
Linenhall Library.

The 10th Battalion Royal Inniskilling Fusiliers was formed at Finner Camp on August 15th, 1914. The men of County Londonderry had been preparing to fight a civil war against Home Rule in the summer of 1914 as had the rest of the Unionists in Ulster. They had been formed into units of the Ulster Volunteer Force (UVF) and were trained in the use of firearms. Once war was declared they were quick to show how loyal they were to Britain and many of these units signed up together. Such was the 10th Inniskillings.

A section of City of Derry UVF at a training camp.

Photo: Bobby Kilgore

The battalion was made up of four companies which consisted mainly of men from the following areas:-

A Company:-
Londonderry City.
(Company Commander, Major Macrory).

B Company:-
Londonderry City.
(Company Commander, Major Waring Smyth).

C Company:-
Coleraine, Limavady and other County districts.
(Company Commander, Major Trench).

D Company:-
The last to be formed. These men came from the rural districts and smaller villages and hamlets of the County.
(Company Commander, Captain Miller).

Officers of the UVF on the steps of Drenagh House, Limavady before the war.
The motor cyclist is Major Macrory and Lt. Drennan is standing next to him.

Photo: The late Willie Wilson

Leslie Bell came from Moneymore and was one of the first to enlist with the Inniskillings.

"I was an Ulster Volunteer as were nearly all of the original officers and men of the battalion. I was sixteen and a half and decided to join up for the fun and excitement. Quare fun it turned out to be! My parents didn't like it when I told them that I was joining up.

Leslie Bell

On 5th of September 1914 myself and twenty-two others left Moneymore to enlist at Finner Camp. We caught the train to Ballyshannon arriving at 3pm and walked the few miles up to Finner Camp, arriving around 4pm. At that stage it didn't look like an army camp. It was mainly bell tents and groups of about a dozen of us slept in these. There were no rifles either. All weapon training, other than shooting, was with wooden guns. Every day from reveille at 6am until 8am we had physical training and for the rest of the day usually square bashing."

A postcard of Harry Wilson's showing Finner Camp in late 1914. The men are training in civilian clothes under the watchful eye of Colonel Ross Smyth.

A large group of 10th Inniskillings at Finner Camp, Maj. Macrory and Lt. McClure are seated in the centre, Bugler Downs is in the centre of the front row.

Photo: Bobby Kilgore

A reporter from the Londonderry Sentinel newspaper describes the training programme for the average day:-

6am	Reveille, dress then tidy tent
6.45-7.45am	Drill
8-9am	Breakfast consisting of tea, half a pound of bread with butter or jam, with occasionally tinned fish, bully beef or bacon
9-10am	Drill
10.15-11.30am	Drill
11.30-12pm	Rest
12-12.45pm	Drill
12.45-1.45pm	Dinner, consisting of potatoes, soup and a pound of beef, usually boiled
2-3.15pm	Drill and 15 mins rest
3.15-4.45pm	Drill
	Tea consisting of bread, butter and jam (Occasionally tinned meat)

Thereafter the men are free except on Wednesdays and Fridays when night attacks are carried out. The drill is varied by occasional route marches, which average from 10-12 miles. As a rule the bulk of the men visit Bundoran each evening. The men are due in camp at 9pm. The last post is sounded at 9.30pm and lights out is at 9.45pm.

A group learning semaphore signalling using flags.

Photo: Helen Colhoun

The Derrys were part of the 36th Ulster Division. The Division was made up of three brigades, 107, 108, and 109. Tenth Inniskillings belonged to 109 Brigade and in the autumn of 1914 the whole brigade was training at Finner Camp. It consisted of the following units:-

9th Royal Inniskilling Fusiliers
(Tyrone Volunteers)

10th Royal Inniskilling Fusiliers
(Derry Volunteers)

11th Royal Inniskilling Fusiliers
(Donegal and Fermanagh Volunteers)

14th Royal Irish Rifles
(Young Citizens Volunteers, Belfast)

Training at the start was treated as a bit of a lark. Men being instructed without proper military uniform and equipment, dressed in different clothes and headdress ranging from flat caps to bowler hats, could not really produce good results. Some of the Non Commissioned Officers (NCOs), who didn't have uniforms, wore armbands to identify their rank. How could they behave like soldiers when they didn't look or feel like soldiers?

Leslie Bell:-

"We didn't think the War would last long enough for us to get to France. We thought it would be over by Christmas as the stalemate of the trenches hadn't set in yet."

COMMANDING OFFICER OF THE
10TH ROYAL INNISKILLING FUSILIERS

Lieutenant Colonel Ross Acheson Smyth JP was born on September 3rd, 1862. He entered the Royal Irish Regiment on May 23rd 1885 and received his baptism of fire in the Chin-Lushai Expedition in 1889-90 and for this was awarded the Indian General Service Medal with bar. He served with the mounted infantry in the Boer War and was slightly wounded in that campaign. For his services, which were Mentioned in Despatches, he was awarded the brevet of Major and the Queen's Medal with five bars.

He retired on half pay in 1903, and lived at his home in Ardmore, near Drumahoe, just outside Londonderry. He was heavily involved in the formation of the Ulster Volunteer Force in the Londonderry area. On the raising of the Ulster Division, he was given the command of the 10th (Service) Battalion, Royal Inniskilling Fusiliers, with the temporary rank of Lieutenant-Colonel.

Jim Donaghy:-

"I knew Colonel Ross Smyth before I joined up. His house at Ardmore was only a short distance from Drumahoe. I used to work as an assistant gardener to him before I got a job at the Bleach Green Mill. When his son, Master Johnny, came home from college, he used to sneak down the garden to me to get a crafty smoke on the sly. Many a great

wrestling match we had in the rose garden, much to the annoyance of old Dixon the gardener. Master Johnny enlisted as an officer cadet and joined his father's old regiment. He was killed in his first action when the battalion of the Royal Irish Regiment he was serving in, was almost wiped out when they took the village of Le Pilly, near Aubers Ridge, not long after the war started."

2/Lt John Ross Smyth was killed on October 20th, 1914 and has no known grave. He was 18 and was Colonel Ross Smyth's only son.

Jim Donaghy:-

"Ross Smyth looked every bit a Colonel and was always on his great big horse. He had a fine word of command and when we were tired or slowing down you could hear his voice thundering, 'Come on the Tenth Inniskillings!"

Lt Col Ross Atcheson Smyth, Officer Commanding the 10th Royal Inniskilling Fusiliers.
(The Colonel was nicknamed 'Rossie' by the other ranks.)

Photo: Author

OFFICERS 10th BATTALION ROYAL INNISKILLING FUSILIERS

BACK:- 2/Lt J.W. Drennan, 2/Lt W.A. Gaussen, 2/Lt W.A. Stevens, 2/Lt K.A. Mackenzie, 2/Lt E. Crawley, 2/Lt H.F. Chillington, 2/Lt W.J.K. Moon, Lt. E. McClure, 2/Lt J. Douglas.

MIDDLE:- Lt J.M. Wilton, 2/Lt J. Shannon, Lt McConachie, Lt. C.L.N. Stronge, Lt R. Shaw, Lt A.F Cook, 2/Lt A.W. Wakley, 2/Lt I.B. Barrett, 2/Lt J.N. McCleane, Lt G.E.Austin.

FRONT:- Capt Waring Smyth, Capt R.S. Knox, Capt J. Proctor, Capt R . Toker, Maj. F. Macrory, Lt:Col R. Smyth, Maj. F. Trench, Lt F. Boyd, Capt J. Miller, Capt M. Robertson, Capt. E. Barton.

Photo: Royal Inniskilling Fusiliers Regimental Museum.

Photo: Author

WARRANT OFFICERS & SERGEANTS (RANDALSTOWN JUNE 1915)

Back Row: Sgt Ferris (D), Sgt Moore (D), Sgt Irwin (B), Sgt Davidson (B), L/Sgt Arbuckle (B), Sgt Porter (B), Sgt Sloan (C), L/Sgt Adams (D), L/Sgt Montgomery (C), L/Sgt Brangham (C).

2nd Row: Sgt Kennedy (B), Sgt Jameson (B), Sgt Given (B), Sgt Graham (C), Sgt Baird (C), Sgt Grundle (C), L/Sgt McMenemy (A), Sgt O'Brien (A) Sgt McElroy (D), L/Sgt Doherty (D), Sgt Shields (Pioneer), Sgt Macky (D).

3rd Row: L/Sgt Hunter (C), L/Sgt Logue (A), Sgt Bogle (B), Sgt Black (A), Sgt McGahey (A), Sgt Bailey (A), Sgt Allan (A), Sgt Jameson (A), Sgt McCombe (D), Sgt Harley (tailor), Sgt Spooner (A), Sgt Weir (D), Sgt Scott (D).

Front Row:- Sgt Matthews (A), CSM Bracken (B), CQMS Bosworth (B), CQMS Synnott (A), Lt Boyd, Lt. Col R. Smyth, BSM Kensdale, QMS Cox, CSM Brannagh (C), CQMS Hutchman (C), CSM Campbell (D), CSM White (A).

23

THE BATTALION BAND

The band was made up mainly from members of the Marquis of Hamilton Flute Band, Londonderry, more commonly known as 'The Hamilton Band'. Its ranks were augmented with members from other bands, such as the Maiden City (Rosemount), 'No Surrender' flute band (Londonderry City), the Burnside flute band (Portstewart), Parke flute band (Coleraine) and the Limavady flute band.

The bandsmen had two main tasks – firstly, to supply the battalion with music when it was on the march or on parade and, secondly, to act as stretcher-bearers and assistant medics when in action, two members being assigned to each platoon.

Jim Donaghy:-
> *"The first leader was Drum Sergeant Matthews, an old soldier from London. He was given the task of bringing the band up to military standard. He was affectionately known to all as 'Drummie' and went to France with the battalion, even though he was well over the age for military service."*

The band was composed mainly of fifes and drums but also had buglers and four pipers. The drums were emblazoned with the badge of the castle of Enniskillen and the battalion scroll. The battalion march was the stirring 'British Grenadiers' but the local tunes of 'The Sash' and 'Derry Walls' were just as popular.

The bandsmen were non-combatant and did not carry firearms. Nevertheless their duties would be every bit as, if not even more, harrowing than that of any other members of the battalion. Much of their time would be spent in frantic frustration, trying to help the horrifically wounded and the dying, many of whom would be in excruciating pain. They would always be in the thick of the action and spend much more of their time in the role of medical assistants than they could ever have imagined.

SQUARE BASHING

It was a difficult transition from being members of the UVF to the higher discipline and seemingly endless drilling, or 'square bashing' as it was called, of a British army unit. Training was carried out by NCOs and Warrant Officers from England, most of whom had seen service in the Boer War some thirteen years before.

RSM Kensdale

Jim Donaghy:-
> *"The first Regimental Sergeant Major had one eye and we called him the one eyed gunner."*

Skill at arms and other training requiring the use of firearms, other than shooting, was carried out using wooden guns, much to the frustration of men who had previously used real rifles in the UVF. Most units received their rifles in October and November. These were old Lee Metford models, left over from the Boer War.

The Battalion Band. 'Drummie' Matthews is positioned to the right of the bass drum.

Many of the Ulster born drill instructors had their own methods of teaching and words of command that wouldn't be found in any British Army training manual.

Jim Donaghy:-
"Old Sergeant McGahey taught us how to march. Once we were falling into shape he would shout in time to our step:
> *Left, right,*
> *Left, right,*
> *Now you have it!*
> *See you keep it!"*

Sergeant Porter was another drill instructor. He originally came from Londonderry but had emigrated to Canada, but as soon as he heard that war was declared he returned to enlist with the Derrys. He was known as 'Fadeaway Porter' as he used to replace the word of command, 'Fall Out' with 'Fade away boys!'"

Conditions at Finner were far from good. Food was cooked in field canteens and beef and other foods proved to be inedible as they were frequently undercooked. The Orderly Officer was inundated with complaints as he did his rounds. The substandard food was substituted on such occasions with something they were to be tired of eating over the next few years – bully beef. A tin of 'bully' and a loaf of bread were distributed and divided between every four men.

A group photographed at Finner Camp in 1914.
The gentleman on the right is Mr. Bigger who owned a big pork processing operation in Foyle St.
Londonderry. Supplying Finner Camp would have been a lucrative contract.

Photo: Arthur Nutter

Photo: Helen Colhoun

Members of No. 5 Platoon from B Coy.

Uniforms were received in mid-October 1914. There were many underage lads in the recruits and it was disappointing and frustrating for them when they were issued with the uniforms for which they had waited so long.

Leslie Bell:-
"The uniform was too big for us. You had to alter it so that it would fit you."

A severely underage recruit from 'B' Company.

The original cap badge of The Ulster Division.

Although the battalion was called the 10th Royal Inniskilling Fusiliers they did not wear the Inniskillings badge at that stage, but instead wore the Carson's army 'Dixie Badge'. This was a badge showing the Red Hand of Ulster with three drops of blood coming from the wrist. Later the badge was replaced with the Royal Inniskilling Fusiliers' grenade and castle badge.

During the autumn of 1914, the weather was very windy, wet and miserable. One night there was a severe storm which flattened most of the tents in the camp. Some of the Derrys went with Lieutenant Stronge down to the range. They sheltered for the night in the shed where the targets and other equipment were kept. The rest of the battalion, along with the rest of the 109 Brigade, had to lie with the flattened tents drawn around them for shelter from the torrential rain. All, that was, except for the Young Citizen Volunteers. They went with their officers to hotels and accommodation in Ballyshannon.

The YCVs were from the more affluent families of Belfast and there was a certain degree of antagonism between them and the men from the west of Ulster, many of whom were from very poor homes. It would take a long time before they were fully accepted by the rest of the Brigade as the true friends, comrades and excellent fighting unit they would prove to be.

As more equipment arrived and more training was carried out, the battalion was slowly licked into shape along with the rest of the Brigade. The tents were replaced with wooden huts and early in 1915, the 9th and 11th Inniskillings, along with 14th Rifles, were moved to Shane's Castle, Randalstown, County Antrim, for further training, leaving the Tenth in Finner.

A group of Young Citizen Volunteers (14th Royal Irish Rifles) at Randalstown.

Photo: Noel Jenkins

1914

An unidentified group at Finner Camp from B Coy.

Photo: Helen Colhoun

A group of Derrys, proud with their new weapons.

Photo: Bobby Kilgore

In the late spring of 1915 the battalion had 1204 officers and men, not counting three officers and 99 NCOs and men sent to Enniskillen to help form the nucleus of a reserve battalion. Eventually, on May 8th, 1915, the 10th Inniskillings packed up and left Finner on the long march (over 120 miles) to Randalstown in County Antrim. They had learned by now that nothing, not even a long march like this, was simple in the army. Before leaving Finner, each man had a considerable weight of waste iron punchings from the shipyard in Londonderry placed in his backpack. The extra weight was to prepare them for the incessant, long route marches with full kit which they would endure in France.

The Derrys marching up Bridge Street Coleraine.

Photo: Northern Newspaper Group

The Derrys crossing Bann Bridge, Coleraine, May 1915.

Recruiting for D. Company in Kilrea on the march to Randalstown, May 1915.

Photo: R.Simpson

Chapter 3
"Come on You Chocolate Soldiers!"

When the 10th Inniskillings left Londonderry on May 13th, 1915 they marched through some of the main towns in County Derry. They reached Limavady on the 13th and left the next day en route for Coleraine. After a stop there, the final leg was through Kilrea on the 18th and Castledawson on the 19th, before reaching Randalstown the same day. Throughout the journey the battalion was given a tremendous reception by the locals. They were suntanned and a lot fitter than they had been when they left Finner. Many were a lot lighter too, as some of the iron punchings that had to be carried in their packs had been discarded at each stop!

Leslie Bell:-

"I enjoyed the march, although it was tough going. Even though we were carrying full packs, very few had blisters. We were all hardy lads that were used walking.

One morning, marching past a farmyard, a farmer had left a big can with about ten gallon of milk in it waiting to go to the creamery. Being hungry and dry we sampled it and eventually emptied the can. We were afraid that we would be reported but he was decent enough and didn't. A few days later we were going past the same place. There was a lady there with a couple or three children with her. As soon as she saw us coming, she shouted, 'Johnny son, bring in the dog's dinner, there's the soldiers coming!'

We camped at Shane's Castle in Randalstown. The camp was more sheltered than windswept Finner but when it rained the main areas were really muddy and as a result it was hell keeping your kit clean.

Marching into Limavady on the way to Randalstown.

Photo: Benn Hunter

We had fixed bayonet practice here. This was treated at the start as a bit of a lark, charging dummies and yelling our heads off. We never had a notion that we would ever have to use it but we thought that it was more good training for Carson's men. In the event of Home Rule, we'd be fit to hold our own."

The area around Randalstown was used for training. From June 9th-11th, 109 Brigade took part in manoeuvres in the areas of Douglas Top and Brae Hill, in the Antrim Hills overlooking Larne. It was a lengthy march to those areas. The soldiers camped overnight and were attacked the following day by other units of the 36th Division. After the exercise everyone was tired. The YCVs were adamant that they were not going to march back but wanted to return to Randalstown by train! Their Colonel, Spencer Chichester from Dungiven, arranged it. The Derrys marched back as did the rest of 109 Brigade. That night the gates of the camp were lined with tired and annoyed soldiers waiting to give the returning YCVs a piece of their mind. As the YCVs entered the camp they received a hot reception of jeering, wise cracks and shouts of 'Come on you Chocolate Soldiers!'

On July 6th, 1915 the 10th Inniskillings left Randalstown by train, travelling to Dublin for the crossing of the Irish Sea to Holyhead. The Derrymen were in great form.

Leslie Bell:-
"Before leaving we had been issued with full kit and even ammunition, whatever the reasoning for it was. By the time we reached Dublin we had most of the roof shot off the train! What could they do to us anyway we thought? Sure we're going to France. They never issued us with ammunition again until we were abroad."

Most of the men in the Battalion had never travelled outside Ulster before and this was turning into a great adventure for many of them.

Leslie Bell:-
"Leaving Ireland never cost us a thought. We had been in camps for the last few months doing the same old things and were just relieved to get moving at last."

The journey over to the mainland was certainly not a pleasure cruise for men who had never been on a boat before. They were packed on tightly and many were violently seasick. The journey was also hazardous as they faced the possibility of enemy attack for the first time – there were reports of German submarines operating in the area.

The battalion boarded a train and travelled on the long journey through Wales and England to Seaford, near Brighton, on the south coast, where they spent most of the summer of 1915 with the rest of the Ulster Division.

Officers and men eat together at meal time, Randalstown.

Photo: R.Simpson

After extensive research of over 20 years a photograph of 'A' COMPANY has never been traced.

'B' COMPANY
10th Inniskilling Fusiliers
Randalstown
May 1915

Photo: Author

Photo: D. Darragh

'C' COMPANY
10th Inniskilling Fusiliers
Randalstown
May 1915

'D' COMPANY
10th Inniskilling Fusiliers
Randalstown
May 1915

Photo: James Kingham

Chapter 4
Jim at Finner

Jim Donaghy:-

"Myself, Joe Curry and the recruits that had enlisted on Rabble Day were escorted to the Great Northern Station by Lance-Corporal Kane. We caught a train to Enniskillen, the depot of the Inniskilling Fusiliers and were billeted in the jail in the town. We had our meals there and slept in the cells, but the doors were left open! Every day we made our way to the main barracks for drill and PT. We found that another of our close friends, wee Jack Cochrane, had joined up at the same time but at a different location. We spent approximately three weeks at Enniskillen before travelling to Finner camp for further training.

Finner was cold and wet. The west coast must have disagreed with me as I was always unwell and had a bad time healthwise. One Sunday, after church parade, my two best friends Jack Cochrane and Joe Curry went a few miles down the coast to Bundoran for the day. As I was feeling unwell again they left me behind. Later in the day the Orderly Sergeant asked for volunteers for those wanting to join the next draft going to the battalion in England. I volunteered as I had had enough of Finner. When my pals returned later that night they were most upset at not being able to go, as we all wanted to stay together."

The Depot at Enniskillen which is now the Regimental Museum of the Inniskilling Fusiliers.

Photo: Author

Officers and men taking a break from the long march.

Best part of the day - meal time.

Chapter 5
Training in England

Jim arrived in the seaside town of Seaford, near Brighton in the south of England in mid September. He was excited as he approached the camp as it was there that he would meet the rest of the Derry Battalion for the first time.

Jim Donaghy:-

"Seaford was a lovely camp. It was a great sight for me to see the whole of the 36th Division for the first time. All that was except for the 9th Inniskillings as they had measles and were in quarantine back in Ulster. It was a great place compared to Finner Camp."

It was there that the Division was visited by Sir Edward Carson and Lord Kitchener in July. Kitchener was delighted with what he saw and wanted the Division in France as soon as possible.

The men were more impressed with their old leader, Carson. They cheered him and his wife as they came round to chat to them.

Leslie Bell:-

"Carson got a great reception during his visit, but if he had visited us nine months later in France, many would have killed him. They felt that it was he who had got them into their predicament."

Sir Edward and Lady Carson

Photo: Linenhall Library

On September 1st, the Battalion was supplied with five hundred of the new Lee Enfield .303 rifles as a result of Lord Kitchener's inspection. The troops were very keen to get possession of these new weapons.

Leslie Bell:-

"These were great rifles, compared with the ones we had in the UVF. There were a few arguments as to who should get one as there wasn't enough to go round. Some people said there was favouritism in the way they were distributed, but I didn't care as I got one. That rifle stayed with you night and day and mine did me for all my war."

Those who had been disappointed did not have to wait too long for the next consignment to arrive on September 3rd when the Derrys entrained and left Seaford for Bramshott and musketry practice. The whole Division was to have its final shooting practices with the new rifles before going to France. Up until this time there had been very little firearms training.

Jim Donaghy:-

"At Bramshott some of the battalions heard that we were going to France soon. There was going to be terrible ructions unless they had a leave before going and demanded forty-eight hours leave. This was granted to all."

For those who survived, it would be nearly two years before the ordinary soldier would be granted leave again.

An unidentified section of 10th Inniskillings with Lee Metford rifles.

Photo: Noel Adair

Chapter 6
France at Last

The battalion marched from Bramshott camp to the railway station where they were to board the train to Folkestone. It was an uneventful journey but the battalion did suffer its first casualties.

Jim Donaghy:-

"As the train was pulling into the station everyone was standing up and gathering their kit. We were packed on to the train. Men had their gas masks at the ready and were holding on to their kit bags and rifles when all of a sudden the train's brakes failed and it crashed into the buffers. Several men were hurt in the collision though none badly, but the Regimental Sergeant Major banged heads with one of the men and cut his face. This proved to be a good source of amusement."

On October 5th, the battalion left Folkestone with the rest of the 109 Brigade. The men travelled on an old steamer for the journey across the Channel.

Leslie Bell:-

"We were packed on it like herrings in a basket. It was a dirty wee boat. All the lights were doused as again there were fears of German submarines. We were in high spirits that we were now arriving in France. We arrived in Boulogne around 1am and we marched through the town and then up the hill to a camp of tents a couple of miles away."

Jim Donaghy:-

"We were very tired and slept soundly. The next morning was a surprise. We were wakened by some little French boys shouting 'England, England, bully beef for me....Ciggie, ciggie for me!"

After this brief introduction to the locals, the battalion then travelled by a very slow train to the village of Coisy, a few miles north of Amiens.

Jim Donaghy:-

"Coisy was a peaceful but dirty wee village well away from the front. We were billeted in the French peasants' cottages, outhouses and barns. During the day we practised attacks, shooting and bomb throwing."

Undoubtedly one of the most unpopular training sessions was that in preparation for gas warfare. On October 17th, the battalion was given a practical demonstration in the use of gas helmets and gas by Third Army's Gas Adviser. Those early gas masks were foul smelling and restricted the wearer in his breathing, causing discomfort at the best of times. Soldiers were expected to fight in them and during the course of the training, when A Company was first to undergo this unpleasant task, some soldiers were sick. After their masks had been 'cleaned' they were passed to B Company. Due to numerous complaints C and D companies did not have to wear them during that training session.

10th Inniskillings in practice trenches at Coisy. Notice lack of steel helmets and the man looking over the parapet of the trench. The reality of the first trenches in the front line would be a big shock.

Photo: Capt. McKenzie Collection

"Why wasn't I born a girl?"

A postcard sent home by one of the 10th Inniskillings, not impressed by their introduction to the trenches.

On October 20th, the 10th Royal Inniskilling Fusiliers moved to the village of Beauval.

Jim Donaghy:-
"This was a nice village and we spent our time building huts, cleaning and repairing for the next unit to arrive."

Leslie Bell:-
"The closer we moved to the front, the louder we heard the guns. It was then we started to get worried."

The guns got very loud as they neared the village of Hebuterne on October 27th, 1915.

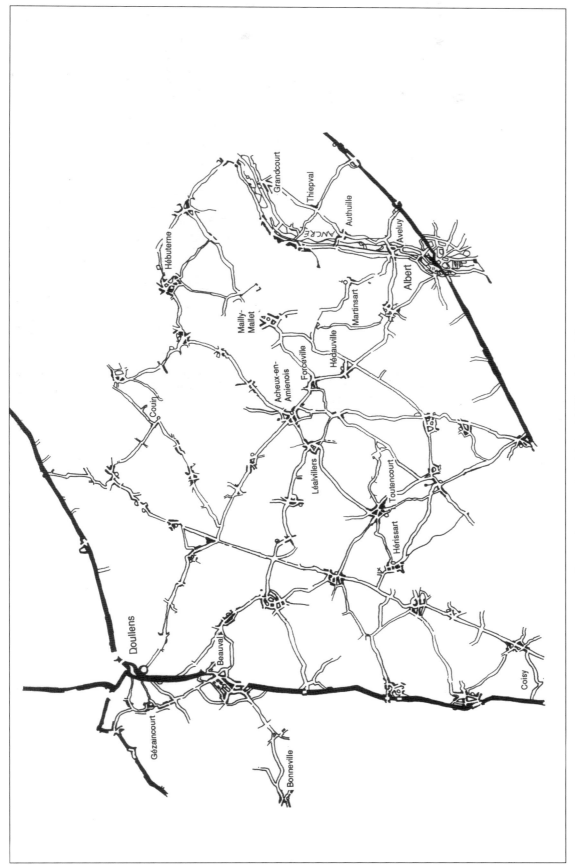

Villages visited by the 10th Inniskillings in the Albert area.

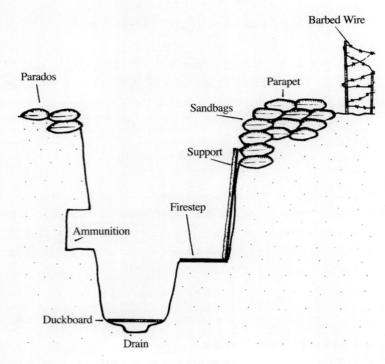

Construction of a typical British trench

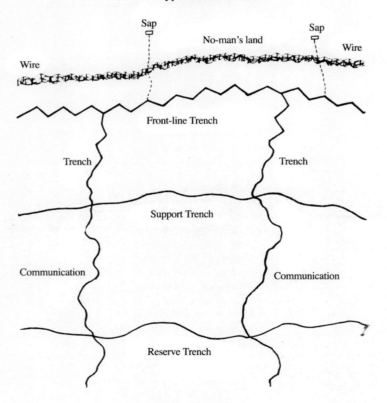

The trench network

Chapter 7
"Welcome to Rat-Run Hall"

The Derrys were eager to get to the front and into action. On October 27th, 1915 the news that they were to do a stint in the front line trenches near Hebuterne was received enthusiastically. They were disappointed, however, when they found they were to be split into platoons and mixed with the Dorsets for training in holding the front line. The Dorsets were by that time old hands in trench warfare.

Jim Donaghy:-

"We were nearly killed the first time we were going up to the trenches with Colonel Ross Smyth. He made us carry two extra blankets and extra ammunition. This was far too much to carry. We were weighed down like pack mules and as we slipped and slid on our way through the trenches we were lucky we didn't have any casualties as Jerry was shelling. It was so tough going that the Brigade-Major gave him a slating for over-burdening us.

When we got into the trenches we were surprised by the state of them. They were not too bad compared with trenches we would have to man later but they were damp and rat infested. The dug-out we were first in had a sign post outside it, 'Welcome to Rat-Run Hall.' At first we saw no sign of rats but we decided to hang the emergency rations we had brought with us in a string bag from the roof to stop the rats getting at them. As soon as it was dark we noticed shadows moving around the bag, and then it started to swing. The rats were clambering over and swinging on the rations trying to get at them. My mate, Bobby Taylor got up, grabbed his bayonet and swiped at them, cutting one in half."

Pumping water out of the trenches at Hebuterne, August 1915

Photo: Imperial War Museum, Q56800

The men brought some food to last them the seven days they were in the trenches. That was usually bully beef and biscuits known as 'Iron Rations.'

Jim Donaghy:-

"The biscuits were rock hard. You could hardly have broken them. We used to soften them in cold tea. The food was nearly always cold. There was no cooking as such in the trenches. Sometimes a ration carrier would bring us something hot, perhaps soup."

Soldiers devised ways of heating a cup of tea with a candle. After a long period of time it may have become lukewarm.

Jim Donaghy:-

"Every day, rain, hail or snow, every available man had to 'Stand To.' This meant everyone standing in the trench with their rifles at the ready to repel a possible enemy attack. It was a favourite practice to mount early morning raids under the cover of the poor, misty light of the first rays of dawn or the approach of night."

'Stand to' would be a daily feature of their routine in the front line, until the end of the war.

The stress of sentry duty also told on the men, standing out in all weather conditions to observe no-man's-land and the enemy trenches. A sentry had four hours on duty and two hours off. Sergeant Bogle sent a letter home describing his first sentry duty of Hebuterne.

"We had almost a month dodging about here in different parts before we got our first experience of the Germans. We were put into the first line trenches with an English regiment for instruction in trench warfare, and afterwards we had a section of trenches to ourselves. I remember well how I was shook up (I was asleep in the dugout) and told to take my section and relieve the Englishmen in a sap[1]. It was a wet, dark, miserable night: a strong wind was driving the rain into our faces. How cold we all were as we felt our way along the winding trench. After handing over to me his instructions, the N.C.O. in charge told me the story of the famous black dog that is so well known in this part of the fighting line. This dog, it appears, always accompanies the enemy patrols and acts as a sort of scout for them when their parties are out on an expedition in the 'No Man's Land' between the trenches. It is, of course, credited with extraordinary sagacity, and, despite dozens of claims made by alert sentries to have laid it out, it turns up with aggravating persistence at intervals. Naturally I kept a very sharp lookout on that night, but saw nothing of this strange dog. That night impressed me very much: the crack of the snipers' rifles broke the stillness now and again as they carried on their everlasting duel, the utter darkness, then a whisper from the waiting man. 'Sentry over on the left has heard something suspicious amongst the wires on his front.' I go over there, hear the sentry's report, listen, and strain my eyes in the direction pointed out. Just then a rocket shoots up from the German trenches and bursts into a ball of light, rendering everything as clear as day for a few seconds, then fades away rapidly, leaving the darkness blacker than before. I am satisfied it may possibly have been rats the sentry heard, and perhaps his nerves have been a little upset, for no human being can be seen in the vicinity of those wires. I return to my post, and ponder why shouldn't a sentry's nerves be a little*

unstrung on such a night. Down on the right, about sixty yards away, by a little clump of bushes, lie the decomposed bodies of three Germans, one an officer, shot one night by a patrol from the regiment lying next us. The enemy had never made any attempt to take

away these bodies or to bury them. I wondered why, for I knew had the corpses been British they would not have lain two hours after dark. I afterwards learned that 'Old Fritz' (The English Tommies' term for the Germans) had placed powerful bombs on top of the remains, so that any souvenir-hunting British soldier would be blown to fragments if he touched them. How glad I felt when the dawn appeared and the time for my section's relief drew near, when I could go to the dugout for twelve hours' rest. In the section of trenches defended by my company were a number of dugouts, some of them spacious enough to hold quite twenty men; others accommodated as little as ten. Each of these dugouts had its name inscribed on a piece of biscuit box, placed in a conspicuous position above it. One rejoiced in the very suggestive title, 'Fleabite Lodge.' The next one was known
as 'Vermin Villa.' Others were 'Rats' Home' and 'Mouse Mansion.' A few more were recognised by such high-sounding names as 'Hotel Metropole,' 'Mount Royal,' and 'Grand Hotel.' The dugouts are dry and have plenty of straw in them, so that the men can sleep more or less comfortably, chiefly less, though, I dare say, in time one could get used to such little discomfort as, say, a rat suddenly executing a few steps of a dance on your face or starting a miniature landslide from the roof over your unconscious head. And the mice are such cheeky little beggars! They have developed quite a habit of losing their foothold, falling down on top of you, then scurrying away with excited squeakings as if in glee at your discomfiture and your startled attempts of self defence. I dare say new hands in the trenches feel rather glad than otherwise when a sharp voice is heard. 'Now, then, time the other section on duty was relieved.'

Except for the odd shell and burst of machine-gun fire the first stay in the trenches was uneventful, but the men encountered an unforeseen enemy – boredom.

To relieve the tedium, the soldiers had some sport with the vermin that lived with them and on them. One of these games was called 'The Staff of Life, on the Point of Death'.

Jim Donaghy:-
"We shot the rats in the front and reserve trenches. When you were on sentry duty at night, you put a wee bit of food on the point of the bayonet on the end of your rifle and rested it on the parapet. You soon saw the two pink eyes and heard the sniffs of it as it

shuffled its way up to the food. Sometimes there was a group of them and when they reached for the bait, you pulled the trigger. As time went on we weren't allowed to shoot them as some of our men had been hurt in the process."

Another great pastime was the collecting of lice from uniforms.

Leslie Bell:-

"The lice were desperate. They kept you going all the time. The best way of getting them was to take off your shirt and to run the end of your cigarette up the seam and that's how you got the boyos.

We had been issued with sheepskin and goatskin jerkins for the winter as it was bitterly cold. You just wore them over the top of your tunic and boys but were they full of lice. Not only that, I had a goatskin and the smell of it would have killed you!"

TIME OUT OF THE TRENCHES

Jim Donaghy:-

"Our platoon billeted in a barn, stacked with sheaves of wheat. There was a big orchard behind and the surrounding outhouses were jam packed with cooking apples. If you opened the door out rolled apples there were so many. When we came out of the trenches we used to wash our uniforms when we could, as they were infested with lice. We boiled them in old petrol cans which we had cut in half. On this particular Sunday we were sitting around the fire outside our barn after we had hung our clothes up to dry. Someone decided that we should make a stew out of the apples as it would be a change from our normal rations. We needed a saucepan, so we all harangued a quiet big chap called Harry to call at the French woman who lived in the house nearby and ask her for a saucepan.

'What will I say to her?' he asked.

'Just ask her if she could lend us a saucepan'.

We walked up with him and watched while he knocked politely on the door. When the woman appeared he politely asked her, 'Madame, Madame,....voulez vous,' he hesitated and then hurriedly blurted out...

'Voulez vous give me a wee black saucepan?'

Everyone laughed their heads off, but she knew what we wanted, smiled and got us one.

Photo of French Woman taken by Captain Proctor

We peeled the apples and started to cook them. Someone emptied a tin of jam in as well. It made the most beautiful smell and as we were only used to army rations it attracted men from other platoons. Men passing would ask, 'Hey boys, that's a great smell. What's that you have? Give us some of that!'

They were told to, 'Get away a that!' and after some time Bobby Taylor tasted it and decided it was ready. We got our dixies out, ready for the stew. Other men were watching Bobby Reid lifting the saucepan – and the bottom fell out of it. Everybody was in fits, laughing. We had to club together and buy a new saucepan from a wee shop in the village for the woman."

Leslie Bell and Duncan Jordan were bombers in Thirteen Platoon. On one occasion they found a novel way of scrounging a drink from a wee French canteen run by a girl and her father.

Leslie Bell:-

"One time when we had no money, Duncan Jordan said, 'We'll get a drink, no matter where it comes from.'
'How are we going to get it?' says I.
'You stand there to you see!'
Next thing I knew, he went behind the canteen, pulled the pin out of a Mills bomb and let it rip off! The shout went up inside, 'The Allemands coming, Allemands, Allemands!' and they all cleared to the cellar. Duncan went in, lifted two bottles of brandy and away we cleared."

Duncan Jordan (left) and a mate from 13 Platoon D Coy

The battalion normally spent seven days in the trenches and seven out. During this time they acted as support to the battalion which was in the front trenches. The soldiers didn't have this as free time; there was extra training, inspections and lots of working parties both in the reserve and front lines. Sometimes the working parties would be simple and safe, cleaning up an area or helping to build accommodation huts at the rear. Ammunition for the artillery was unloaded at the rear. Often it would have to be carried up to the guns or the front by working parties, a very dangerous and stressful exercise. Frequently the work was in the the front trenches, repairing shell damage to parapets and dug-outs. Undoubtedly one of the most loathed and dangerous duties was the wiring party. Shrapnel from exploding shells and bombs, small arms fire and corrosion damaged the barbed wire defences in front of the British trenches. This had to be continually repaired and reinforced.

Leslie Bell:-

"You were working and knocked hell for leather during the day and then out doing working parties at night. Putting up wire was the worst job. It was no joke going up on a winter's night with a big freezing roll of barbed wire on your back, laden down like a pack mule. Then out over the trenches out to your wire in no-man's-land. The slightest noise could have got the German machine-gunners to open up. At least in the trenches you knew what you were doing and you had some protection."

GORENFLOS
November 1915 – 6th January 1916

It was December 18th, 1915. Nothing of importance in the French calendar but a special day to the men of the Derry Battalion. It was the 246th anniversary of the shutting of the gates of the City of Londonderry in the face of hostile soldiers of the Catholic King James II by thirteen Protestant apprentices. In commemoration of this event an organisation had been formed called 'The Apprentice Boys of Derry' and one of their ceremonies was the burning of an effigy of Governor Lundy of the city, who had tried to betray the inhabitants. Just because they were in France this year didn't mean that the men were going to break with tradition.

Jim Donaghy:-

*"An eight foot effigy of the traditional pattern had been made by Sergeant Bomber Dan Gillen who was in charge of the bombing section[*2]. It was hung from a big beech tree in the centre of the little village, opposite a big crucifix. We had the battalion band, kegs of beer and a great party was in full swing when Gillen produced a bomb made from a jam tin filled with gun powder. He had decided that this year we wouldn't burn Lundy – we'd blow him up! We eventually talked him out of his plan but during the burning ceremony he lit the bomb and threw it into the pond in the centre of the village. Well - it went off - and blew most of the windows in. He wasn't too popular as we had to pay for the damage."*

Sketch of the burning of Lundy in Gorenflos,
18th December, 1915.

D. Hannah 1991.

The morning after the celebration
of burning Lundy.
The remnants were still
hanging from the tree.

CHRISTMAS 1915

Jim Donaghy:-

"Christmas 1915 was spent in a nice wee barn in Gorenflos. We had been billeted in a farm belonging to a French woman. She lived with her old father and her two children. Her husband was away fighting in the French army so the old man had to carry out the

heavier farm work. One morning we woke up to a strange rhythmical sound. We looked outside and saw the old man threshing the wheat by using hand flails. We had never seen this before and decided to have a go and give him a hand. It didn't take us long to pick up the technique. We got quite friendly, helping out where we could and the woman invited us home to her house for Christmas dinner. We had a great meal. She roasted a pig and we had vegetables, beer and wine."

Photo of snow covered village of Gorenflos in December 1915, taken by Captain McKenzie.

Chateau guarded by Leslie Bell and Duncan Jordan. This was the Officers' Mess.

Photo: Captain McKenzie Collection

Leslie Bell was not so lucky:

"My chum Duncan Jordan and myself were taken out of the trenches on Christmas Eve to go and guard a chateau where the officers were having a big do. It was sleeting and snowing. The officers were inside and we were outside. During our guard duty Duncan would walk round one side of the castle, I'd walk round the other and we'd meet in the middle. A couple of lorries of ladies arrived and they were all having a great do. Around midnight you could hear the champagne corks flying. We were cold and wet and never got as much as a cup of tea the whole night. I said to Jordan, 'What could the like of you and me do if the Germans would happen to come over and attack these people that we're supposed to be guarding?'

'I know what we can do!' says Jordan. 'We can hide – and let them blow them to Hell if they like!'"

Many of the men were quite annoyed at the difference in the treatment, conditions and duties between officers and men.

Leslie Bell:-

"After all, we were all volunteers. Sometimes we made sure we got our own back. On those long route marches the senior officers rode horses. Poor old Captain Miller, our platoon officer, wasn't much of a horseman. In fact you'd have thought that he had never seen a horse in his life. He used to get on the horse, just sit on it and it would follow the rest of the battalion. I was in the first section of Thirteen Platoon, directly behind him and when you got the Sergeant-Major away back behind, making sure there were no stragglers, we used to tickle the horse between the legs with a bit of a whin bush and away she'd go. After the oul Captain had been thrown over its head a few times, eventually he would just walk it with the rest of us."

Capt J.T.E. Miller Officer Commanding
D Company.
Photo: Author

Capt. Barton takes a break from the saddle.
Photo: Captain Proctor

One particular officer wore a protective jacket under his tunic. Ordinary soldiers would not have been allowed to do this even had they been able to afford one.

On December 31st, A and B Companies were sent with Major Macrory to the village of Gasincourt. They had been detailed for duties with the Royal Engineers with the job of repairing and reconstructing the badly damaged village. The men also helped with farmwork and many enjoyed it as it took their minds away from the war and reminded them of home. The Derrys impressed the local inhabitants so much by their hard work and friendliness that when it was time for them to leave it was a sad farewell. The battalion had grown to like the peaceful little village and had made many good friends. When they departed on February 2nd, the Mayor wrote the following letter.

To Brigadier-General T.E. Hickman,
36th Division,
B.E.F.

5th February 1916

Dear Sir,

The 10th Battalion of the Royal Inniskilling Fusiliers, Major Macrory, Officer Commanding, have been billeted with us for a month, and we were painfully surprised to learn of their departure on Wednesday evening the 2nd inst. Permit me to say dear sir, that we shall retain the most pleasant memory of this regiment, for, during all the duration of its sojourn in the commune, the conduct of both officers and men was of the most exemplary character. Not only was there not a single complaint lodged against them, but we established with them the truest of friendship, a state of affairs that was heartily reciprocated by them. May I also be permitted to make to Major Macrory the just tribute of gratitude we owe him. With the greatest courtesy and zeal he always welcomed any requests made to him, and put his men at our disposal for the threshing of the harvest. He is a worthy commander, surrounded by good soldiers and seconded by good officers, who, under any circumstance, would know, I am certain, to defend the common cause. I shall be very grateful if you will authorise this letter to be read to the entire battalion, and if you will express to them in our name our admiration and affection.

> Believe me,
> Your most respectful servant,
> Gambier.
> (Mayor of Gasincourt)

The Divisional Commander replied that he was delighted to receive this report and the Brigadier-General wrote to the battalion in reply:
   "Well done, Derrys! I am very pleased."

The battalion was marched up to the village of Acheux just behind the front line. Most of the 36th Division was there and it presented a very different scene to peaceful, clean, Gasincourt.

Jim Donaghy:-
   "Boys, but Acheux was a dirty wee hole. There was thick slimy mud everywhere and you were just plastered in it."

The battalion was billeted in tents and every day for two weeks five hundred men from the battalion were detailed for duty with 109 Railway Company, Royal Engineers. Their job was to construct a railway line at Acheux and Lealvillers. There were numerous fatigues for those not on railway duties.

Divisional football matches took place during recreation time and the Derrys produced a fine team. Undoubtedly the star was Sergeant Alfie Bogle who as always produced his usual 'Very hot shots'. In one game they beat 9th Inniskillings 7-0, two goals being scored by the ever popular Lieutenant Ernest McClure.

A group of 10th Inniskilling footballers.

Photo: S. McCafferty

On February 12th, A and B Companies were relieved from the heavy labour of railway construction. They were to go up to the front trenches at Mailly-Maillet for four days and, this time, were to be instructed by half of the 15th Battalion Royal Irish Rifles.

Jim Donaghy:-

"As we left Acheux the battalion was in battle order and moving in extended line across open country. The pheasants and hares couldn't get past the lines of men and they ran in front of us. There were partridges getting up beside you and flying in all directions. The place was thick with game."

As they made their way to the front the soldiers had mixed feelings. Most were glad to get away from the 'navvies work' and fatigues. They had not joined up to do work like that. They were there to fight the Boche. Many others were content in what they had been doing. Things had been all right where they were.

---

[1] A sap was a narrow trench which was dug out into no-man's-land at 90° from the front line trench toward the German line and was used as an observation or listening post for enemy activity by a few men.

[2] Sgt Gillen was a well known ventriloquist back in Ireland and attracted large audiences when he performed. He was also credited with early innovations for propelling bombs and grenades towards the German lines some of which were adopted in general, by the army at that time.

Chapter 8
"Mailly-Maillet... a terrible, terrible place"

Jim Donaghy:-

"Mailly-Maillet has to be one of the worst places we were ever in. The battalion moved here on the 24th of February 1916 for further instruction with the 15th Rifles. The trenches were terrible. We took over a sector which had been captured from the Germans. This position was very, very bad. You were slipping and sliding in mud and water and it was cold too. Very cold. Most times the water was up to the knee, an odd time you had to wade waist deep. Before you went into the trenches, you collected gumboots from a big pile at the end of the communication trench. They weren't much good as they frequently had holes in them and a lot of times the water went over the top. Many of the men were suffering from trench foot. Some of my mates had it so bad they had to spend a long period in hospital. To combat this, officers had orders to inspect their mens' feet daily. In bad trench conditions officers had to apply a grease made out of whale oil on their soldiers' feet.

An officer carries out a foot inspection
(notice the perfect text book trench).
Photo: Imperial War Museum, Q10622

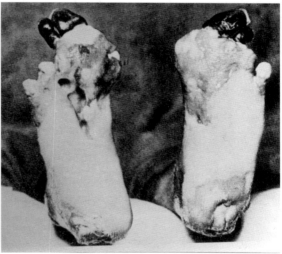

A severe case of trench foot
Photo: Imperial War Museum, Q16317

It was snowing at times and freezing cold and if this wasn't bad enough, Jerry was only a couple of hundred yards away and spent his time sniping at us. Due to the knee deep water in the trenches we would walk on the raised fire step and if you didn't keep your head down you would have got hit. Even if you made a loud noise at night or he heard some men splashing their way down the trench he would immediately have opened up with a quick burst from his machine guns, the bullets whacking into the sandbags a few inches above your head. One night going into the trenches we were making our way along. It was tough going with the mud and water and we had all our kit with us. There was an old trench which had been abandoned as the water in it was several feet deep in the shallowest places. This obstacle had to be crossed by a makeshift bridge made from *a few slippery planks of wood and as Wesley Goodman was crossing, he fell in. We had the greatest difficulty getting him out. We had to lie down in the mud and even though we had to be quiet, men were making wise cracks and laughing when Jerry opened up with machine guns. Luckily no-one was hit. Some were telling him that he had a 'Blighty'[*1]. As for Goodman, he had been hurt and from then he was given light duties further to the rear for the rest of the war."*

The first fatality in the trenches for the 10th Inniskillings happened at Mailly-Maillet when Pte. Duncan Mundell was killed by a shell on February 20th. It was in this action that L/Cpl Garvin from D Coy won the Military Medal, the first for the battalion. Garvin was in charge of the bombing section in the most dangerous part of a fortification called "The Redan" and at 8pm was hit in the side by shrapnel. He refused to leave his post throughout the night… a trench which was knee deep in ice-cold, stagnant water. When he was relieved from his post, he was delirious and in a very poor state.

A few days later curiosity got the better of one man and he fell victim to the ever watchful sniper. It was a hard earned lesson which the rest of the soldiers quickly learned... keep your head down. The place where he died had already seen other soldiers killed here by snipers and had been named "Suicide Corner."

Lance Corporal David McGuire

Photo: Author

H. Wilson:-

"Lance–Corporal David McGuire was the big drummer in the battalion band. He stuck his head over the top of the trench for a quick look… and got one. Everyone was talking about it."

In the front line the men were billeted in dugouts which, like the trenches, were in a poor state. They let water in through the roof and the floors were soaking wet. To add further to the misery, it was there that the Derrys first encountered the German rifle grenades. These were fixed on to the muzzle of the rifle and propelled into the air by firing a blank cartridge. For such a simple device they exploded with devastating effect and the men detested them.

Jim Donaghy:-

"Jerry was an artist with the rifle grenade and used them to great effect dropping them into our trenches. You didn't hear them coming the way you could hear the whine of an artillery shell so you didn't have time to run for cover.

Jerry was also very prominent on raids, always trying to capture the trenches he had lost. Due to the amount of raids he had been carrying out, men had to be sent into positions in no-man's-land at night to listen for the enemy sneaking up on our trenches.

One of the first days we were there a sergeant of the 15th Rifles asked for four volunteers from our Company to man one of these positions. I was one of the volunteers and that night we set out just after dark. We crawled out through our wire to spend the night in a big muddy, wet shell hole. Jerry was strafing (shelling) constantly and we spent a rough, cold night out there. We had strict orders to come back just before first light. You daren't wait till dawn to crawl back those few yards as Jerry would have seen you and cut you to ribbons.

At the end of our first stint in the front trenches with the 15th Rifles we were making our way down the communication trench. It was sleeting again and we were slipping and sliding in the deep mud and water. Jerry must have heard us because he gave us a heavy strafing of five-point-nine inch shells. They were landing all around us. Davy Adams took cover in a dugout which had been cut into the bank, when a shell landed beside it burying Adams alive. We had to go back and start digging him out. Luckily he escaped without injury and we had no serious casualties. Oh, it was powerful altogether, it was a bad, bad place."

The battalion was in high spirits when it heard that it was moving further south. Major Macrory wrote in his diary, 'the battalion was told it was to move to a cushy part of the line.' After a day's march the men arrived in the little village of Martinsart where they were to hold the Thiepval Wood section of the line.

Martinsart had been badly shelled during the course of the previous few months but the barns and outhouses of the surrounding farms in which the men were billeted, were regarded as luxurious compared with the cold, wet, stinking, dugouts of Mailly-Maillet. The trenches they took over again proved to be in a far better state and, with a bit of ingenuity, water could be drained into the little River Ancre which flowed just behind some of the trenches. This area was also less stressful than the previous section of the line as the Germans were not as active on this part of the front.

Lance Corporal Davy Adams with his sisters.
Photo: Author

The men of the Ulster Division had volunteered to come to the aid of France in her fight against Germany. At the start French people had cheered them through the streets as they marched up to the front. People would occasionally ask men to their homes for tea and the men would in turn help with heavy farm work and in other ways as most of the French men were in the army. As the war dragged on and the novelty wore off, the reception the soldiers received became cold and distant. Sometimes the French were even hostile as was made obvious to most of the battalion by the actions of one of the inhabitants of Martinsart.

Jim Donaghy:-

"The water we received with our rations was sometimes undrinkable. It may have been contaminated by petrol, for example. There was a farmhouse at Martinsart and it had a big hand waterpump in the little farmyard. An old woman lived there. Every time the men asked if they could use the pump they were told in no uncertain terms they couldn't and were chased away. One particular evening the men wanted water but they knew they were being watched from within. Willie Braid was the best singer I have ever heard and had the loveliest singing voice. Herbie Andrews was another good singer and the two of them proceeded to fool about outside the farmhouse. Both of them started to sing at the top of their voices and at the same time danced towards the pump. They were just about to touch it, when she dived out of the house and threatened them with a stick. By this time quite a large crowd had gathered so the two dancers, still singing, proceeded to dance around her, making her furious. This caused great amusement to the assembled soldiers who were laughing and shouting. She stormed into the house in a rage and received a loud cheer from all the men. Herbie and Willie danced and sang on, totally unconcerned. That was until she dived out of the door wielding a huge sword, again to the delight of the assembled men. How they laughed and howled at the sight of the two jokers being chased by an old woman."

Leslie Bell remembers the same old woman:-

"I remember her all right because we were unfortunate enough to be billeted in her barn. She eventually chained and padlocked the pump. To one side of the farmyard was a big manure heap. Corporal Rankin from Coleraine, a wee stout chap, got drunk one night and decided to take a shortcut – through the middle of the midden. It took us ages to get him out of it and when we did, you could have smelt him a hundred mile away."

---

[1] A blighty was a wound, severe enough to have the casualty sent back to Britain.

Chapter 9
"Baptism"

'The Lucky Tenth' was the nickname being used by other battalions of the 36th Division in reference to the Derrys at this stage. Their casualties had been very light in relation to the amount of time which they had spent in the front line. Their previous stints in the trenches had been quiet. All that was about to change, however, on a cold Sunday morning, March 10th, at Thiepval Wood.

Jim Donaghy:-

"Myself and several others found ourselves manning a dangerous location called a sap. This was a camouflaged position in no-man's-land, connected to the front line by a narrow trench. Stand-to was over and we were just finishing off our breakfasts of bully beef and biscuits when Sammy Richmond carelessly threw his empty tin over his shoulder. It landed out of the sap in full view of Jerry. Lance Corporal Billy Jackson, our NCO, nearly went mad, barking at Richmond that he had given our position away.

Later Jerry started to find the range of our position with rifle grenades, then with light trench mortars. He ranged all positions until about 3pm when he ended up with a strafe of heavy artillery shells. They came out of the blue blowing trees to matchwood and throwing tons of chalky soil high into the air. I saw Willie Braid, the great singer, run for cover to a dug-out which had steps leading down to it. He had just got inside when it was hit by a big mortar. All that was left were several sandbags."

Most of the men of A and B Companies experienced this heavy shelling. Even Colonel Ross Smyth had a lucky escape. He and two others had been in a dugout which was acting as battalion headquarters when they were blown off their feet by the blast of shells landing only ten yards away.

Jim and the other men in the sap thought all this enemy activity had been caused by the actions of Richmond. The other men of the Battalion who hadn't witnessed the breakfast incident knew that it was almost certainly the German heavy artillery ranging, and once they had found the range, it was only a matter of time before a full-scale bombardment. No-one knew when it would happen. The soldiers spent a tense and uneasy night in the trenches.

Jim Donaghy:-

"Suddenly, before midnight, there were the most almighty screams followed by the explosions of shells. It was terrifying. All around was being devastated. Shells were landing everywhere. After a few minutes our commanding officer, Captain Robertson, came up and called us out of the sap, as it was very exposed. He told us to mix with the other men in the front line trench. I was the last man out and was carrying a box of Mills bombs under my arm. I quickly left them in the fire bay and stood up. We were all standing on the fire step. It was the most awesome fireworks display with men shouting, 'Look at that one! Look at the colour of that one!' There were all different colours of flares shooting up. Men were standing in awe. Then the rifles and machine guns opened

up from the enemy line. The Germans were raiding. We started to pour rapid fire at their lines. Crash! There was a terrific explosion! A massive shell had landed immediately behind us and I was blown out over the front of the trench, on to our wire. I was still clinging to my rifle. I was dazed, but realised that I was in full view of the Germans and frantically clambered back into the trench.

There were dead and injured everywhere. The only thought that I had was to find my pal, wee Jim Boyd. He had been next to me before the explosion. I couldn't find him anywhere. Jim was always easily recognised as we had been issued with sheepskin coats and Jim's was a fancy one, all different colours. Lance Corporal Eddie Donnelly was shouting to me, 'Hey Jim!...Oh God Jim, come on quick!' When I got over to him I saw that he had a great big hole in his leg. Nearly half of it had been ripped away. I got Eddie my emergency field dressing from my tunic and started to fix him up as best as I could. My thoughts were still on Jim Boyd. I couldn't get him out of my mind. When I glanced down in the light of the flares that were lighting up the sky, there in the muddy trench I found I was standing in the remains of my pal. Eddie Donnelly died a short time later.

Jim Boyd
Photo: S. McCafferty

George Stirling had been badly injured by the same shell that killed Jim. His whole back was riddled with shrapnel. We couldn't get him to the rear for proper medical attention as the communication trench had been blocked with trees felled by the barrage. He had to stay with us in the trenches and endure the rest of the shelling which ended around 1.30am. He had three medics with him all night. During that time he endured a living hell. He screamed, writhed in agony – said prayers, sang hymns, laughed in delirium and called for his mother. He died around 7am. Both of us had been in the same infant school. We knew each other so well. It was hard to believe he was dead. He was only twenty."

Leslie Bell and Duncan Jordan were in another sap during the attack.

Leslie Bell:-

"All around us was blew to bits. It was a wonder how we survived. When we eventually made our way back to the front line a sergeant said he never thought he would see us back alive. I replied sarcastically that he was a long time looking for us!"

The ferocity of the intensity of the bombardment on the Tenth's trenches was reported by a padre from the 12th Royal Irish Rifles as; 'Shells coming over at the rate of sixty to a minute.' The Derry's first major action was extensively reported in the Ulster newspapers as letters arrived home from the front. The following letters appeared in the Londonderry Sentinel:-

I am proud, to be able to say that, although the Germans smashed some of the parapets and wrecked a trench, the men of the 10th acted with such steadiness and met the attack with such a withering fire from machine guns and rifles that the Germans were unable to take the trench.

An un-named officer of the 10th Inniskillings

I never saw a splendid lot of heroes as our fellows. I got almost buried myself trying to get ammunition into the fighting line. Our men stood and defied the Huns, and we have some brave officers, who encouraged us greatly and we heard nothing all round but 'No Surrender!'

Bugler W. Teacy

We have had a hot time of it and seven of our men were killed. I went to the support of the bombers with sixty men of the battalion. They stood the great test well and are making an undying name for themselves. We gave them such a bad time of it that they will hardly trouble us for a few days.

Sergeant-Bomber Dan Gillen

The following poem appeared in the Londonderry Sentinel not long after the action:-

10th Inniskilling Fusiliers (Derry Volunteers)
In action March 10th and 11th, 1916

Oh, brave lads of Derry, it makes our hearts merry
To hear of your deeds on a foreign French soil;
On the battlefield gory redounds to your glory,
Though far from your homes on the banks of the Foyle.

The blood thirsty Germans, the vilest of vermin,
Bombarded your lines but alas for their toil!
Like noble defenders you cried 'No Surrender!'
The glorious old watchword you learnt by the Foyle.

Some people traduced you when duty induced you
To answer your King and your Country's call;
You have shown the wild Hun you can handle a gun,
Brave lads from the Bann, the Roe and the Foyle.

Your officers too, showed true grit through and through,
Captains, lieutenants, and NCOs all;
You are sure to be in for the march on Berlin,
Then, Hurrah for the 10th from the banks of the Foyle.

While brave deeds we are singing a sad note is ringing
For your comrades that's parted from all earthly toil;
They have fought their last fight, they have died for the right:
God comfort their friends who mourn by the Foyle.

J.K. Londonderry.

The battalion's casualties were five killed and ten wounded. This was more than the total casualties they had incurred since arriving in France. That night the Tenth had been opposed to the famous Prussian Guards. They had made a determined attack on the Derrys' trenches and but for the troops standing doggedly at their posts returning rapid fire, throwing bombs and exposing the enemy to a continual hail of bullets from the Lewis guns, the trenches would almost certainly have been overrun. This had happened to the south where the trenches of a regular battalion connected to the Tenth's were entered by the Germans and resulted in fierce hand to hand fighting. Over the din of the bombardment the shouts of the Englishmen could be heard.

Although the Derrys were shaken up by the ferocity of the attack and the deaths and injuries of their friends, they felt a sense of achievement at having withstood one of the finest German regular regiments. They were also elated when Sir Douglas Haig honoured them by mentioning them in despatches. General Nugent, Commanding the Ulster Division, wrote a 'Special Order of the Day' for the 36th Division honouring the Battalion. In it he wrote that the 10th Inniskillings had shown extraordinary discipline, pluck and coolness, and it was only their rapid fire, under heavy shelling, which prevented a German advance along the front.

Drummer William Adair (right) and a friend from the band show off their new sheepskins coats in a formal photo to be sent home for a laugh.

Photo: Noel Adair

The Battalion could now hold their heads high. No longer could they be referred to as 'The Lucky Tenth' – they had had their baptism of fire.

The Derrys now found themselves in the grind of trench warfare which, for them, was starting to heat up. There was constant shelling and sniping, which took a small but steady toll of dead and injured, but again the Derrys had light casualties.

Jim Donaghy 17/4/16:-
"After one seven day stretch in the front line, when not one man was killed, we were relieved by the 9th Inniskillings (the Tyrones). We moved back to a position in the reserve trenches in the middle of Thiepval Wood. Here you were out of sight of the German lines and you felt more relaxed. Every time we came out of the trenches the first thing we did was to get a wash, as most times we didn't get our boots or uniforms off in a week. Every time, Willie Graham was the first man to strip off and he invariably

washed himself from head to toe, starting with his head. It was a lovely morning and although we were in good cover, we had orders to wear our steel helmets. Willie started to douse himself and we were all laughing at the way his hair was sticking up. He came over to my Section and started to fool about with the lads. As he turned to go back to his own Section, which was only a few yards from us, a German shell exploded a fair distance away. He put his hand to his head and then fell. He had been hit in the back of the head with a small piece of shrapnel. He was taken to the first aid post at the bottom of the trench and Lieutenant Wilton went with him. He died a short time later.

A Belfast Telegraph newspaper cutting of Pte Willie Graham.

Willie was a great wee chap. Many's a time when some of the men were coarse in their language you would hear Willie saying, 'Ah come on now lads, no need for that.' He was always full of fun and many's a laugh we had with him about his wee problem. He was hen-toed. After rain, which left the chalk covered roads in a white mud, whoever would have been marching in front of Willie would have had the whole back of his uniform covered in white splash-marks, flicked up by the way he marched."

The steel helmet saved many lives. Note the use of sandbags to keep the rifle clean.

Photo: Imperial War Museum, Q1778

The Battalion was now involved in daily working parties. A and B Coys were in the support trenches at Thiepval Wood with C and D Coys positioned further towards the rear where they were arranged in working parties of 175 men and engaged in various maintenance projects. When the men were not in the front line trenches they may have felt somewhat safer, but they were still vulnerable to the effects of long range sniping and machine gun fire.

Men of the 10th Inniskillings at Gordon Castle dugouts in Thiepval Wood.

Photo: Capt McKenzie Collection

Lt. McClure and Capt Barton relax during a quiet period in Thiepval Wood. This area was on the reverse slope of the hill out of sniper view. The roar of an approaching shell would have allowed enough time to scramble into the dugout immediately behind.

Photo: Capt Proctor

THE MAY 7th RAID

The Tenth were in reserve to 1st Dorsets, a unit of the 32nd Division that was manning the front line. The unit next to them were 9th Inniskillings who were planning a night raid. This was to be the first big raid by the Ulster Division. That night the men of the Tenth waited in their billets, just outside Martinsart for the din heralding the start of the attack. It was anticipated that the Germans would retaliate with their artillery so everyone had been warned to take cover.

Jim Donaghy:-

"The 9th Inniskillings were in Thiepval Wood and were going to make a raid. That night we heard the artillery start and we stood at the doors of our billets admiring what we thought was a very heavy shelling that the 9th were giving Jerry. There was the odd shell coming over in our direction in reply from the enemy, then it got very heavy in the Dorsets' sector. We were in reserve to the Dorsets and Captain Robertson and Captain Boyd came running and staggering up the meadow. You could see the red hot shrapnel falling all around them. They gathered my platoon and one other and we followed them up a path, across a meadow and made our way down the sheltered communication trench into Johnston's Post, just to the south of Thiepval Wood. Two platoons of A Company had gone with Major Macrory to reinforce the Dorsets and had arrived there before us. It turned out that Jerry had decided to attack them. Jerry had put in a heavy raid and had entered the Dorsets' trenches. When we arrived in Johnston's Post we found nine big Germans, each of them over six feet tall, lying dead at the cookhouse door."

Lieutenant Douglas in Thiepval Wood.
Photo: Capt Proctor

It had been a heavy raid with approximately 100 hardened German veterans taking part. Not only had the 1st Dorsets suffered casualities but also the reinforcements from A Company of the 10th Inniskillings. Pte. W. Shields was hit in the head by a shell splinter and killed instantly while Pte. R. Collins died shortly after from his wounds with another eight men wounded in fierce hand to hand fighting, before the Germans retreated. The Germans had also taken 25 prisoners from the Dorsets. Unfortunately Cpl. Miller, a member of the Tenth who was assigned to the 109th Machine Gun Section, was in a machine gun post near the Hammerhead sap when it was overrun. After putting up a great fight with his machine gun, eventually both he and his officer were overpowered and in the struggle wouldn't allow themselves be taken prisoner and were then killed by the Germans.

Within several minutes of the end of the German raid, the 9th Inniskillings started their raid which had been planned to commence at 12am. This did not make good military sense as now the element of surprise had been lost and the Germans were on high alert making the mission to try and take prisoners impossible and highly dangerous. However this incident shows one instance of many of the inflexibility of high command to adapt to changing circumstances on the battlefield. The result was that the raiding party ended up being trapped in no-man's-land for several hours due to the heavy German shelling and suffered casualties in the process.

The next day a wire was sent to the Tenth from the General Officer Commanding the 32nd Division.

"The GOC 32nd Division wishes to thank the 109th Brigade for the very prompt and effective support given to his left battalion last night. Please convey his warm appreciation of the services they rendered, to all concerned."

On May 8th the Battalion was withdrawn into Divisional reserve at the village of Lealvillers to practice for the massive summer offensive which the men referred to as 'The Big Push.'

Brigadier General Hickman, commanding 109 Brigade, despatched the following letter to his units:-

"The Brigadier General desires to express to all officers and men of the 109 Brigade his keen appreciation of the behaviour of all ranks whilst in the trenches over the last three months. It is a great pleasure for him to feel that the careful training given to all by their commanding officers had borne such good fruit. Work has been hard and casualties numerous but both have been cheerfully borne, the best sign of gallant spirit, determination and above all good discipline. The Brigadier General hopes that all ranks will enjoy the short period of comparative rest allowed to them, and that when the time comes, they will return to the firing line to do still more valuable work for their country."

A captured German Howitzer at the Inniskillings' Museum in Enniskillen.

Photo: Author

Chapter 10
"The Big Push"

The Allied High Command had decided in the autumn of 1915 that the following summer would be the date of the long awaited offensive. The proposed attack was to have been a joint effort, consisting of some forty-five French and twenty-five British, Commonwealth and Imperial Divisions. Unfortunately the Germans attacked first, in February 1916, in the area around the French fortress of Verdun. It was felt that the loss of this strategic fortification would have ruined French morale so the French generals planned a strategy of holding on to it with dogged resistance. The occupants were subjected to some of the worst bombardments and attacks of the war with the Germans slowly blowing the area and its defenders to pieces with massive siege guns. In the process of defending the area, the French army was being bled white.

By the summer of 1916, with the heavy losses, and the fighting still raging, the French could only produce sixteen Divisions for the offensive. French morale was at its lowest so it was felt that the bulk of the fighting would have to be carried out by the British. General Sir Douglas Haig placed General Sir Henry Rawlinson in charge of the British attack. He was allocated some 520,000 infantry and 2,029 guns – the biggest collection of artillery ever assembled for an attack. The area chosen by the Generals was the front around the River Somme. The British would attack along a fourteen mile section and the French on the left would attack along an eight mile section.

The plan was quite simple. The artillery would pound the German lines for five days before the attack with the greatest bombardment in history. On Z Day the infantry would go 'over the top' attacking the shattered German lines. When these had been broken, the cavalry, which had been waiting in the rear, would push through the gap, attacking the enemy from the flanks and the rear. It was hoped that this would cause the break up of the German lines and the armies would then revert to open warfare, thus ending the stalemate of the trenches.

The whole of 36th Ulster Division was at Lealvillers being trained for the 'Big Push.' Shallow trenches had been dug to represent the German positions they would have to attack so that on the day every man would know exactly what he had to do. Those practice trenches depicted the enemy positions accurately and had been based on reconnaissance photographs taken by the Royal Flying Corps. The different enemy lines and strongpoints which the men would have to take were named after towns in Ulster so that they would be easily remembered – Strabane, Omagh, Lisnaskea, Dungannon and Lurgan.

Up until then the standard method of attack was to soften-up the enemy lines with a short artillery barrage, causing casualties and forcing the defenders to keep their heads down. When the artillery stopped firing, the infantry went over the top and attacked the enemy lines with fixed bayonets. In the time interval between the cessation of the artillery and the soldiers charging, the enemy had time to consolidate, quickly regroup and then intercept the soldiers in no-man's-land where they were attacked with machine-guns, bombs, rifle fire and enemy artillery. The artillery would have already had their guns sighted in on the land between the front line trenches and when they opened fire with salvo after salvo of shells, it caught the soldiers out in the open where they were most vulnerable. The losses were horrific and many thousands had been killed in such attacks.

Going "over the top".

Photo : Imperial War Museum, Q70165.

However, a new artillery technique was to be employed for the first time in the Somme attack. It involved close coordination between artillery and infantry and it was termed a 'creeping barrage.' It differed from the previous method of attack in that the artillery would still bombard the front line, but on this occasion when the infantry were to attack, the artillery would not stop but commence firing on the second enemy line a hundred yards behind. This would not give the same amount of warning that an attack was in progress and would create an element of surprise, thereby helping the infantry to cross no-man's-land with fewer casualties. When the attackers had taken the first line and regrouped, simultaneously the artillery would then start to bombard the third line. When the infantry had taken the second line they would wait again until a predetermined time when they would attack the third line and the artillery would lift onto the fourth line. This would happen until the attacking infantry reached their final objective – the fifth line.

The men continually practised attacking across this mock battlefield under the careful supervision of their officers.

Leslie Bell commented:-

"You could have attacked those positions with your eyes shut we had practised it so much."

LIFE IN LEALVILLERS

The Derrys were in high spirits and enjoyed this clean little village where, between intensive training periods for the big attack, they could relax.

Jim Donaghy:-

"Our platoon was billeted in a big barn filled with sheaves of wheat. Most of the men slept on top of the sheaves. The doors of the barn opened into the street and were left open as it was so hot. My Platoon, No. 6, had some rough nuts in it and there had been two or three fights in the billet. I decided enough was enough and bivouacked in the orchard behind. It wasn't long after this that Sergeant Irwin came out as well saying that he couldn't sleep either with the noise, wisecracks and banter. He set his bivouac up beside mine and for the rest of the time we were there we slept out. Our company commander was billeted near to the other ranks. One night he had enough of it when the 14th Rifles, returning from a 'night out' were making cods of themselves when everyone else was trying to sleep. Sergeant Irwin woke me in time to hear the company commander shouting, 'Will you go to hell's blazes and get to your beds and give us a wink of sleep!'"

BOXING CHAMPIONSHIPS
Friday May 19th, 1916

As the Battalion was now in the comparative safety of the rear lines and 109 Brigade assembled in one place, it was decided that the finals of the Boxing Championships which had been cancelled in Seaford could now be held.

The Derrys held on to their reputations as fine sportsmen.

Jim Donaghy:-

"We had Boxing Championships out in the open air. Most of the 109 Brigade were watching. The Derrys won three out of the four categories. Big Alfie Bogle, the Sergeant of A Company, won the heavyweight championship."

Sgt Alfie Bogle,
Heavy Weight Boxing Champion
of the Ulster Division

In the sports results in the Londonderry Sentinel it was reported:- "In the feather weights Lance-Corporal J. Scott of the Tenth had knocked out his opponents in the early bouts and in the final, when opposed to the much bigger opponent, Sgt. Maultsaid of the Y.C.V., fought the best fight of the day. In the middle weights Lance-Corporal Andrews proved too good for his men in the early bouts, and in the final knocked out his opponent from Y.C.V. In the heavy weights, Sgt. Alfie Bogle knocked Johnston of the Y.C.V. about so much that he gave in during the second round and in the final easily accounted for Private Jeffries of the machine-gun section."

Some rare entertainment for the battalion occurred on the May 29th.

Jim Donaghy:-

"The battalion had a campfire concert in a big orchard behind the barn our platoon was billeted in. Two big bonfires had been lit and nearly all the men were assembled. There were a few barrels of beer and fancy food that we didn't normally get in our rations. Some officers from different battalions of the 109 Brigade had been invited. There were recitations, songs and sketches by both officers and men. One item was a song written by Lieutenant Monard of the 14th Irish Rifles, (Young Citizen Volunteers). It was sung to the tune of the 'The Mountains of Mourne.' I still can remember most of it yet."

'Three Cheers for the Derrys!'

Through no fault of my own I'm here like a coon,
To sing you a song that will be without tune;
But if you don't like it please don't go away,
For there are some others who'd like you to stay.
At least when I asked them that's what they told me;
And when you have heard them I'm sure you'll agree,
But for all this great concert we'd all rather be
Right away back to Ireland where'er it may be.

We've had some great trials since we've been out here,
But the greatest by far is the shortage of beer;
Perhaps you remember we used to get rum,
But that drink is stopped now for some months to come.
As least when I asked them that's what I was told;
And they pinched all the blankets, though nights are so cold;
Soon they'll take off our trousers, and naked we'll be;
Och! What a fine sight for the French folk to see.

A few lucky fellows have got home on leave,
But if you've not had yours there's no need to grieve;
The war won't be over till Derry turns green,
And you're sure to get leave before nineteen-nineteen.
At least when I asked them they seemed very sure;
If you want to know more ask Lieutenant McClure.
All the folks send us comforts as well as they can,
Where the clean streets of Coleraine sweep down to the Bann.

Some good news has just come from old Randalstown,
And it sheds some fresh lustre on Derry's renown,
A fine new battalion is just being trained
What to do on a Sunday if ever it rained.
It's a great thing to think we've all done our bit,
To form a new army it's a big hit;
We'll give fact, face and details whenever we see
All our wives and our sweethearts where'er they may be.

Tomorrow we go to a nice pleasant spot,
Martinsart is its name – do you know it or not?
We shan't sow potatoes or fight the good fight;
No; we'll do working parties from morning till night.
At least when you get there that's what you'll be told,
And you go to the trenches to dig there for gold;
But for all that you'll find there you might as well be
By your own little firesides, where'er they may be.

Three cheers for the 'Derrys,' who took all the starch
From the Germans at Thiepval on the 10th night of March.
Through all the bombardment their feelings were blithe,
Quite right when commanded by Colonel Ross Smyth.
And when in the future they fight the bold Hun
He'll lead us to glory and give us some fun;
And when that is over we'll go back without fuss
To the sweet Irish maid that's just waiting for us.

Lt. Monard 14th Royal Irish Rifles (Y.C.V.)

This song was given rapturous applause and was always popular with the men. There wasn't much in the line of entertainment or recreation, except in the little cafes and bars, many of which were in a dirty and run-down state. The troops made their own innocent fun and, sometimes, not so innocent!

Jim Donaghy:-

"I was a member of the last guard we mounted in Lealvillers. Sergeant Alfie Bogle was in charge that night and during our stint we arrested two of our battalion. They were walking down the main street, blind drunk, singing their hearts out. In front of them they were pushing a barrel of French beer they had liberated, as if they hadn't a care in the world."

Jim Donaghy, Jim Pomeroy & Bobby Taylor

Photo: Author

Chapter 11
Back to the Front

Everyone was sorry when the Battalion left Lealvillers on June 14th and marched up to the Thiepval area again. As they got closer to the front they realised that the date of the attack could not be far away. The roads were congested with other squads, all marching with full kit in the one direction – to the front. Piles of assorted ammunition for the artillery were stacked along the roadsides. Lorries and horsedrawn wagons carried essential stores and working parties were digging assembly trenches in Thiepval Wood where the infantry would gather before the attack. Everyone was busy in some form of work for the 'Big Push.'

As the number of men and the piles of stores increased there was a need to hide their locations and numbers from the Germans. Columns of men and vehicles moved at night, while working parties carried out their multitude of tasks as much as possible under the cover of darkness. The Derrys spent most of their time digging assembly trenches during the day at Thiepval Wood. The weather was extremely hot and the work was strenuous. Steel helmets, which became uncomfortably hot under the summer sun, had to be worn at all times. Uniforms were sweat filled and dust-covered and, as always, lice infested.

Jim Donaghy:-

"When we came out of the front line some of the lads would go down to the River Ancre for a swim. It wasn't too safe as on one occasion, Lance-Corporal Kane, (the NCO who had escorted me up to Enniskillen when I had enlisted) was in bathing and was shot in the head when a German machine-gunner opened up from long range. There were a few other casualties but Kane died on the way to the field hospital." (May 2nd, 1916)

The soldiers had found that the River Ancre had a good stock of both coarse and game fish. Many different methods were employed by the canny Derrymen to try and catch them. Some tried sporting methods of line, hook and worm. Some tried the old traditional methods of poaching and others tried 'the 1916 method.'

Leslie Bell:-

"We used to throw Mills bombs into the river to get the fish. The explosion would kill or stun them and they would float to the surface. I had a go at and got a couple of rare looking things. We didn't know what sort of fish they were but we soon decorated them and made short work of them at tea time. Eventually everyone was at it. More bombs were being thrown at the fish than at the Germans and they got scarce."

Jim Donaghy:-

"There were thousands of soldiers working and sleeping in Thiepval Wood. Jerry shelled it, so for extra

A Mills Bomb
Photo: Author

protection we dug our own little shelters into the sides of a bank or the trench. One night Bobby Reid hung up his watch above his head as he did every time he slept, to protect it from the dirt in the trench. The next morning he found it had been wrecked by shrapnel."

Taking cover in Thiepval Wood

Photo: Imperial War Museum

Death was an ever present threat and many found comfort in religion. They were pleased when the Battalion Padres arrived, Canon King from Derry Cathedral representing the Church of Ireland and the Reverend Patton, the Presbyterian Churches. A few words of fellowship and a chat were welcome on guard duty or at some other lonely time, whether it was in a trench in the middle of the night or when lying wounded at the field hospital.

Jim Donaghy:-

"The two Padres went everywhere with us in the trenches. One night Bill Thornton, Harry Wilson, Bobby Reid and myself were in a wee dugout singing hymns at one o'clock in the morning. The two of them had come around with Captain Austin who was the Orderly Officer. They pulled back the blanket which was acting as a door saying 'Hello boys! Are you enjoying yourselves?' They gave us a packet of five Woodbines. Every Sunday that we were in reserve and could have our service, Canon King read the sermon from the Bible which he always placed on top of the cook-cart."

Padre Patton eventually won the Military Cross with two bars for the gallantry which he displayed in his duties to the Derrys.

Officers inspect the battalion cook-carts in the rear lines.

Photo: J. Robertson

BOMBING RAIDS

One of the duties the infantry feared most of all was a raid on the enemy trenches at night. During their stay in the Thiepval area many raids were organised.

Leslie Bell:-

"Sometimes when things were fairly quiet a staff officer from headquarters would tell our officers that things were too quiet and the enemy had to be kept on his toes and orders would be issued for trench raids to take place. After a raid which may have ended up with maybe two or three of our own men killed or wounded, you might have been told by the same staff officer in the rear lines, 'Oh you put up a jolly good show.' We felt it was a bloody good show! Men lost their lives or got badly wounded in these. He wasn't there to see the wounded in agony. He didn't know the dead."

Jim Donaghy:-

"You were usually picked for these by your platoon sergeant. 'You, you – and you will be coming with me on a raid on Jerry tomorrow night.' Usually six or seven men went out with as little kit as possible, through our wire into no-man's-land, trying to get close enough to Jerry's trenches to throw a bomb or two, or to take a prisoner. One of the worst things you encountered were the Verey lights. These were fired into the air to provide illumination over a wide area at night. It just lasted a few seconds but there you

were – exposed, out in no-man's-land and in that short space of time the Germans could have opened up with their machine-guns and cut us in half. If the Verey lights went up you had to either get down fast or Jerry would have put you down. You sometimes froze and hoped he would mistake you for the debris that was lying everywhere.

It was very hard to get through the belts of German wire and a lot of times we never got near their trenches because of it. You knew their sentries were listening and could call down a barrage on you at any time. To make matters worse they had their raiding parties out at the same time. Usually no-one would volunteer for to take part in a raid and we were grateful the Battalion had its own bombing party. In charge was Lieutenant Spalding. He came from London but he was originally from America. He was a very popular officer with the men, in fact more of a pal. There was no officialness with him and he hand picked all the men in his unit. Boys, but they were game, Spalding quietly leading them out of our trenches at night, through our wire. Most nights they made contact with the enemy and sometimes they would bring back prisoners. Boys, but those lads in the bombing party were a rough and fearless lot."

On Saturday June 24th, the artillery opened up all along the front. The noise was terrific and at times could be heard in England as a low rumble. From now until the attack, the guns would fire night and day at the Germans.

The beautiful, hot, summer weather broke but the big bombardment of the German lines continued. Day after day it rained continuously. Conditions were so bad that the date of the attack had to be postponed for a few days. But orders came from Headquarters for more trench raids.

Jim Donaghy:-
"I was picked by Sergeant Porter, along with my friends Bobby Reid, Bobby Taylor, Jim Knox and Billy Edgar. We were detailed to go with him on a trench raid with the task of collecting information on the effects of the Allied bombardment on the German lines in our sector. That evening we were quiet and sullen. The day had been as gloomy and dismal as we had been. It had rained all day. It was like waiting on a death sentence. A couple of hours before the raid, orders came from Headquarters that it was cancelled due to the weather. We were awfully glad."

The attack had originally been planned for June 28th, but due to the terrible wind and rain it was postponed to July 1st. A special order of the day was issued on June 27th, from Major-General Nugent, general officer commanding the Ulster Division.

SPECIAL ORDER OF THE DAY 27TH JUNE, 1916

On the eve of the offensive for which the Ulster Division has trained and waited for so many months, I wish that every officer and man of the Division should know how absolutely confident I feel that the honour of the British Army and the honour of Ulster are in safe keeping in their hands.

It has been my privilege to command the Division in France during the past nine months, during which time I have had various opportunities of seeing that it has been steadfast in defence and gallant in minor offensives.

The time has now come to show to the world the qualities which fit it for the great offensive about to open.

Much is expected of the Ulster Division and I am certain that the expectations will be fulfilled.

Resolution, self-reliance, discipline and the spirit which knows no surrender and no defeat are present in full measure in every unit of the Division and will bear fruit on the Battlefield that will redound to the credit of our country.

Nine months ago, the King, after his inspection of the Division desired me to write to tell him how it bore itself in its first great encounter with the enemy. I know that I shall be able to write and tell him how the men of the Ulster Division bore themselves like men in the day of battle and did all that was asked of them.

To every officer and man of the Division I wish success and honour.
O.S. Nugent Major-General Cmdg 36th (Ulster) Division

Due to the postponement of the attack the troops were withdrawn from the trenches. It was a terrible strain on them to have to march back the seven miles to Forceville as they were wet, cold and exhausted. Most of them were carrying sixty or seventy pounds of equipment, others even more. As they passed through Martinsart the heavier items of kit; bombs, Lewis guns, extra ammunition, were carefully stacked along the side of the road to be collected as the battalion returned on the eve of the attack.

Jim Donaghy:-
"We were billeted in a wooden hut in Forceville. The whole time we were there a big fifteen inch howitzer was positioned outside the door and it blazed away, night and day at Jerry. Everytime she fired, the hut shook violently. We grabbed what sleep we could, lying on our groundsheets, wrapped in our blankets. The Germans were active too, sending over the odd shell. When we were in Martinsart one of these landed one night a short distance away from where we were. It exploded right in the middle of a squad of the 13th Royal Irish Rifles (Co. Down Volunteers) as they marched along the road up to the front line. Their casualties were horrendous."

The shell caused almost sixty casualties, killing or wounding almost everyone in the group. Fourteen men were killed instantly with a further ten dying of wounds during the night. It is believed that the shell had been fired on the marching troops as a result of information relayed by a German spy who was operating from the spire of a church nearby and directing shelling. The dead and wounded were moved from the site by other units of the Ulster Division. Many soldiers on their way to the assembly trenches would witness the crater and the surrounding area festooned with the blood drenched legacy of the carnage, and for them, it must have been a most disconcerting sight as it brought home the grim reality which lay ahead of them.

Graves of the members of the 13th Royal Irish Rifles who were all killed by the same shell near Martinsart

Photo: Author

The men of the Tenth were waiting in anticipation of the attack. They had been on working parties all day, moving ammunition and stores. At night, in the huts, things were tense and men started to get on each other's nerves.

Jim Donaghy:-

"Some of the lads were gambling, playing cards. A couple of minor fights had broken out. But the night before the 1st of July we had a great tea... a fry. In all the time we had been in France we never had a fry, until then."

A special meal! Everyone felt that tomorrow was going to be a special day – the long awaited 'Big Push.' Many thought it was the beginning of the end of the war and in a matter of weeks they might be in Berlin.

The men in Leslie Bell's platoon were excited but puzzled:-

"One of our officers had just gone on a course. He would miss the big attack. If this was going to end the war tomorrow why was he on a course?"

It was thought by most officers and men that nothing could have survived the seven day bombardment of the German lines. A total of over 1,500,000 shells had been fired. The soldiers had seen it and heard it night and day.

Leslie Bell:-

"Our minds were almost numb with the constant sound and vibration of guns firing and shells exploding."

One officer told his platoon,

"Tomorrow you'll just light your pipes and cigarettes, slope arms and walk across. It'll be like a Sunday stroll. There'll be no opposition."

Chapter 12
"Our Father, Which art in Heaven"

It was a beautiful evening. Just before dusk the men left their billets and assembled in platoons along the road at Forceville. The battalion lined up, 22 officers and 742 other ranks, making final preparations for the attack. It was an impressive sight.

Under cover of darkness the battalion marched out of the village at 9.15pm to take up its positions, marching by platoon to reduce casualties should they come under shellfire. They were on their way to the 'Big Push' at last, filled with mixed emotions. Most were confident that the next day was going to be a great victory, but the closer they got to the front, the more they realised that this was going to be anything but a Sunday stroll.

Jim Donaghy:-
"As we were coming over the hill the sight was incredible. The noise was terrific. You couldn't hear anyone talk to you. There were explosions everywhere and the sky was lit up by huge flashes as Jerry shelled our trenches in front of us. The air was vibrating with shells exploding and the screeching of our shells going over our heads. The air smelled of the smoke of burnt gunpowder."

The route to the trenches was crosscountry and to aid the men as they made their way up to the front, red lights had been placed at suitable intervals to help them on their way to the trenches. A brief stop was made in Martinsart to collect the heavier equipment, stockpiled there from the postponed attack. Each man searched for the kit which he had left there two days previously, while other units marched past on the crowded road. With their full kit on the Battalion marched out of the village and then slipped and slid their way through Aveluy Wood which was pitch black and very muddy, lit up only by the flash from explosions. The heavy packs made walking through the mud difficult. During the attack next day it would make getting up and lying down slow and awkward. It would be almost impossible for them to move at any speed faster than a brisk walk as they were now carrying sixty to seventy pounds on their backs.

Moving through the wood the Battalion found itself under enemy shell-fire. Misfortune struck as Colonel Ross Smyth became one of the Derrys' first casualties as they crossed the River Ancre on structures built by the engineers.

Leslie Bell:-
"Old Colonel Ross Smyth was crossing the Ancre on a pontoon bridge when a shell exploded scaring his horse and he fell off spraining his leg. He was sent back to the rear by ambulance. That was the end of the war for him."

The Battalion was fortunate in escaping without further casualties. Major Macrory from Limavady took command and as they came nearer the trenches instructions were received from guides placed at corners and other reference points to help direct the units to their locations. In the darkness and confusion the Derrys passed another battalion and found it to be their old pals of the 15th Rifles. They quickly exchanged greetings and wished each other the best of luck as they moved to their own section of the assembly trenches. These were so narrow that they found it difficult to turn around with their kit on.

A and B Companies of the Tenth were positioned in the front line trenches and C and D were positioned in the reserve trenches. Immediately behind the Battalion in the support lines were the 14th Rifles, the Young Citizens Volunteers.

Jim Donaghy:-

"As we entered the trenches everything was in commotion. The first thing my Platoon had to do was to move to the side to allow the stretcher-bearers to pass. They were carrying boys down to the first aid post. They were screaming in pain from shell-shock. When they passed we continued on our way up through the communication trench, along the front outer edge of Thiepval Wood into our positions. My Company, B, was to be in the first wave of the attack. The battalion was in position shortly after 1am. The weather was good but we spent an uncomfortable night with the Germans constantly shelling our lines."

The Battalion occupied a section of the trenches with their objective in front of them – the German C line known to the men as Omagh. It included a strong point, the Schwaben Redoubt known as Dungannon, a fearsome system of trenches that were defended by several thick lines of barbed wire and numerous machine-guns. The 14th Rifles were in support to assist the Tenth in holding the C line and then they were to advance on to the fifth German line. The 9th Inniskillings were on the right with the 11th Inniskillings as their support. The 109 Brigade had been given one of the most heavily defended parts of the German front line to attack.

Jim Donaghy:-

"In the darkness, final arrangements for the attack were made. The wire had previously been cut and four gaps were cleared in our wire to allow us easy clearance of our own defences."

Leslie Bell:-

"The sun rose in the east, a very red colour. Someone said it was blood on the sun. Someone else said there would be a lot more on it before it went down."

Jim Donaghy:-

"Around 6am we were all given a tot of rum. Narrow openings were cut through the parapets so we could walk out of the trenches before first light, rather than having to 'go over the top' at zero hour.

At 7am the Stokes (Trench) Mortars started a terrific hurricane bombardment on the German front line. These were capable of firing eight shells into the air before the first one had hit the ground.

The noise was terrific and the Germans now opened up with a heavy bombardment in retaliation, in fact the noise was unbelievable. We had spent most of the night on our knees, with our faces towards the parapet to protect it from shrapnel, our backs getting some protection from our steel helmets and back packs. The noise was terrible. No-one was talking. You couldn't even hear yourself speak. Men had their wee bibles out and were reading them. Others had taken photographs of their mothers, wives and children out of their tunic pockets and were looking at them. Some were making their wills in the back page of their pay books. Just before the first units went out into no-man's-land, my Platoon was one of them, we all said the Lord's prayer – and then we said it again. We sang hymns even though we could hardly hear our own voices."

It was a vision of Hell. They knew that things had not gone according to plan and they were about to be killed. Some set fire to their personal belongings in the trench.

Jim Donaghy:-

"As the bombardment of the British and German guns intensified a young lad, attached to Seven Section, sobbed and cried in the corner of the trench. He had joined recently and this was his first bombardment. Some thirty minutes before we attacked, I watched as the Orderly Corporal came running down from Battalion Headquarters. It was a dangerous journey as he ran through the crowded trenches with the German shells exploding all around. He arrived out of breath and had orders which had been sent from Divisional Headquarters that the wee chap had to be sent back home. He was underage. The corporal took him away." [*1]

One of the many underage lads in the 10th Inniskillings. Almost certainly Reuben Orr who was killed. Joined at 15 and killed aged 17.

Photo : Author

Jim and Leslie Bell were just some of the many lads in the battalion who were underage but did not complain.

Leslie Bell:-

"How could we complain. We had volunteered!"

In the support trenches Leslie Bell's thoughts drifted back to home.

"I was thinking it would be milking time now at my father's farm at Moneymore and everything would be lovely and peaceful."

Leslie Bell and J. McGarvey
from 13 Platoon, D Coy.
Photo : Leslie Bell

It was a beautiful summer morning. At 7.15am, A and B Companies went out by platoons into no-man's-land. No-one shot at them as the German trenches were under intense bombardment.

Jim Donaghy:-
"Our officer signalled that it was time to go out into no-man's-land by blowing his whistle. You didn't hear it. You just saw him doing it. We moved through the cut gaps in the fronts of our trenches and crawled forward until we were about one hundred yards from the German front line. There we lay flat, spaced about three yards apart, and waited. Our front trenches were now taking a battering from the German artillery. As I was lying there I got a feeling of loneliness as I couldn't see anyone else. I looked back over my shoulder and spotted four or five of my Platoon lying behind me to my left. All of a sudden a big six inch shell landed in between them. It ploughed through the ground and came up through the soil, just like a salmon coming out of the water. It lay there with its shiny silver nose pointing upward. We cringed, but it didn't explode! The next thing I knew was Bobby Knox shouting to me that the Corporal in charge of our Platoon was dead."

While A and B Companies moved into 'no-man's-land,' C and D Companies advanced from the assembly trenches in Thiepval Wood into the now almost vacant front-line trenches. They were empty except for the dead, the wounded and the stretcher bearers.

At 7.30am sharp the hurricane bombardment of the trench mortars stopped and from the front trench came the regimental bugle call, followed by the advance. There was a lull in the Allied shelling as the artillery sights were being set on the German communication trenches and second line.

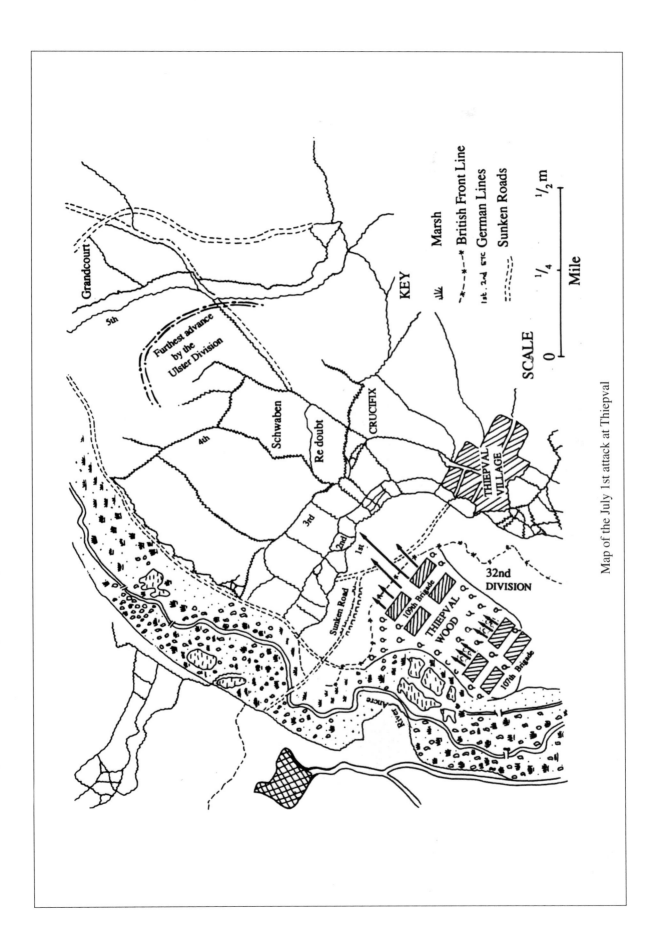

Map of the July 1st attack at Thiepval

Jim Donaghy:-

"We didn't hear the bugle from where I was. The Germans were still shelling. We just watched our officers and NCOs and as they got up, we got up as well and advanced as we had been trained to do."

Commanding officers were not allowed to go with their men as they were deemed too valuable and their role on the day was to organise and implement the advance. Major Macrory, now in charge, wrote in the Battalion's diary:-

"The spectacle of these lines of men moving forward with rifles sloped and the morning sun glistening on their fixed bayonets, keeping their alignment and distance as well as if on ceremonial parade. Unfaltering, unwavering....this spectacle was not only impressive, it was extraordinary. Hardly a man was seen to fall at this stage of the advance.

They seemed for the most part dazed and bewildered by the fury of our bombardment and were only too glad to surrender and throw down their arms. They were sent back under escort to our trenches, about sixteen prisoners to each escorting soldier. The first batches of these prisoners were so anxious to reach the shelter of our trenches that they had outstripped their escort in the dash across the open and meeting our reinforcing lines coming forward were bayoneted by them in the heat of the moment."

10th Inniskillings' War Diary

Pte Stewart Moore
Photo: Ronnie Moore

Little opposition was encountered by A and B Companies as they reached the front German trenches. Pte Stewart Moore and his mate fired at two Germans coming straight at them and shot them both. As he ran past he noticed two items beside his body, an Iron Cross and a hard backed book. The bullet had passed through the dead centre of the German's New Testament[1]. In the support trench directly behind, a large number of prisoners who had been sheltering in deep underground dug-outs were taken. Their numbers and their state of mind caused disaster when they were being escorted back to the British lines.

B line was also taken and here the dug-outs had to be bombed as they were still being held by the Germans who would not surrender. It was there that another of the many tragic incidents of the day happened.

Jim Donaghy:-

"Lieutenant Spalding had went down into one of the dug-outs to clear any remaining Germans out. Another section went past and not knowing he was down there, tossed a few bombs in killing him."

Things were going fairly well for the Derrys and the whole of the Ulster Division, in comparison with the fortunes of the Divisions on either side which were suffering horrendous casualties. They had not crawled into no-man's-land before zero hour and by the time they had gone over the top and advanced at marching pace towards the enemy lines, the Germans had come up from their deep underground bunkers, set up their machine guns and mowed down the advancing troops. Now as the 29th and 32nd Divisions were giving the Germans little to worry about, these machine guns were aimed at the Ulster Division from the flanks. Hell was now about to begin.

The fortified village of Thiepval which was supposed to be taken by the 32nd Division turned its guns on the 9th Inniskillings on the right flank and the Tenth also suffered terrible casualties as a hail of bullets swept through them. At this stage of the advance most casualties were left where they fell, much to the frustration of their comrades.

Jim Donaghy:-
   "Men were falling around you, beside you, but you had to go on."

The men of the support C and D Companies had endured a terrible barrage as they had waited in the trenches and their casualties were pitiful. Duncan Jordan and Leslie Bell crouched in the trench and waited for the order to advance. Leslie's job was to carry the bombs in a canvas bucket and pass them to Duncan for throwing.

Leslie Bell:-

Capt M.A. Robertson
Photo: Author

   "We had no bother getting out of our trenches. The first two lots of dead and wounded were in the trench. You just had to walk out over the top of them. My Platoon got thirty yards when a big shell exploded above us wiping out the whole lot. I was badly hit in the legs and was lying on the ground. Captain Robertson was running up with his Platoon and as he ran past, gave me a kick to see if I was still alive and shouting for me to come on. I was lying on my side and watched him and the others advance, until a shell burst above them and downed him and some of his men."

Leslie Bell watched the battle with men constantly falling as they were hit by the hail of machine-gun bullets or tossed into the air by exploding shells. Captain Miller, D Company's commander, was badly wounded in the face by shrapnel by the same shell that had wounded Leslie. The Captain had been escorted back to the lines but Leslie would have to wait long into the afternoon before he would receive first aid.

As the attack pressed on, the next obstacle was the heavily fortified position, the Schwaben Redoubt. It was said by officers that it was impregnable and could not be taken.

Jim Donaghy:-
   "The Schwaben Redoubt was bristling with machine-guns and fortified with masses of barbed wire. It caused us great problems and many casualties. We were fired on from the front, the left, the right – and behind as dug-outs hadn't been properly cleared of the enemy, as we advanced so quickly behind the artillery barrage."

As the Derry men made their way toward the third line they were again trapped in a hail of bullets. The front wave attacked at such speed that they got caught by the British artillery. More men fell. One of these was Captain Proctor, C Company's commander. He was leading his men towards the 'Crucifix' (which was believed to be towards the front right hand corner of the Schwaben Redoubt) and as he jumped into a German trench, a German officer fired at him point blank and immediately threw his pistol away and held his hands up. Captain Proctor's men refused to accept the surrender after this and speedily avenged their officer.

Capt Proctor poses for a photograph taken with his camera in the front line at Thiepval. Little did he know that a few months later, his body would be lying a few hundred metres away out in no-man's-land.

At about 9am the fire lifted from the third line and the troops advanced fighting fiercely and took that line. The Derrys had taken their objective. Now they had the job of consolidating the trenches they had captured and they set up all available machine guns in defensive positions. At this stage 14th Rifles in support were to have taken over the attack, advancing through the positions captured by the Derrys. As they did, many of the 10th Battalion went with them! They joined the remnants of the other battalions of the Ulster Division which were now mixed together and advanced towards the next line.

Jim Donaghy:-

"At the third line there was a big concealed dug-out and as we approached it shots were fired out of it and some of our men were hit. Sergeant Porter was in charge and worked his way up to it ordering the Germans to come out and surrender. Something happened which caused Porter's men to open fire killing some and wounding others. A young German was lying on the ground, with his hands covering a big wound in his stomach. He was dying and as he looked up at us he kept repeating... 'No bon... No bon.' It really upset us."

About noon confusion reigned and while the wounded Captain Robertson and Lieutenant Wilton were trying to locate their position in C line on a map, they were simultaneously struck by rifle fire, the former being wounded in the chin and shoulder and the latter in the chest. It was at this point that Sergeant Porter tried to get Captain Robertson back to the British lines with the help of Lieutenant Wilton. A shell burst above the rescue party as they dragged him along on a groundsheet. Porter and Roberston were killed, Lieutenant Wilton being wounded again, this time in the shoulder. As he lay there Sergeant Irwin came to his rescue and helped him back to the safety of their own lines. During the process Irwin was wounded, but he undoubtedly saved the life of Lieutenant Wilton.

Sgt James Porter
Photo: Author

Lt J Wilton
Photo: Author

Still the attack pressed on – still the casualties fell.

It was a small band of exhausted men composed of different battalions of 109 Brigade that fought at the German fifth line trenches.

Jim Donaghy:-
"When we were going for the fifth line we could see the heads of the Germans about five hundred yards way. They were standing on top of the parapet, in full view firing at us. We were consolidating ourselves, running from dug-out to dug-out. We had no officers."

Jim Donaghy, Bobby Reid, Alfie Bogle, Alex Millar, Harry Wilson and a few others were all that had made it to the fifth line from the Derrys.

Jim Donaghy:-
"We were very thirsty and the rum that had been given to us didn't make matters any better. I wished I hadn't eaten the onions from the fry we had the night before as they never agreed with me at the best of times. Then, all of a sudden we were caught in the open by a heavy barrage of five-point-nine inch shells [2] The one that wounded me killed or wounded about six others. I was hit twice. Once in the thigh and once in the throat and within seconds lost so much blood that I looked like a red tunicked soldier. When I composed myself, I saw a wee chap from 'The Top of the Hill' [3] He was buried up to his mouth by the shell. I ran over to him and in the middle of the bombardment tried to hack him out with my entrenching tool. I dug like mad to try and get him out. The whole time, his head was moving from side to side and above the terrific noise of the battle I could hear him repeating the Lord's Prayer over and over again. He died before I could dig him out."

Harry Wilson:-

"Alex Millar was killed by a shell. I thought he was still alive. There wasn't a mark or any blood coming from him."

Old newspaper cutting of L/Cpl Alex Millar

As they waited for the expected reinforcements to arrive Sergeant Bogle was hit and wounded. Still they waited. A runner made the hazardous journey with a message, a bitter message, stating that no reinforcements were coming and they should retire. The battered remnants of the Battalion along with the rest of the Division limped and helped each other back towards their own lines. It was at this stage they knew that all had been in vain. These gallant men, with eyes staring, parched tongues and grim faces made their way back over the shambles of the battleground.

Jim Donaghy:-

"When we were coming back the air was filled with all types of shrapnel. The bullets were whizzing past us and hitting the ground beside us. We couldn't even see our own lines as the smoke was like fog, lit up from both sides with blue and yellow flashes of guns and firing and shells exploding. The rattle of the machine-guns never stopped. As we made our way along we spotted a sergeant from C Company lying in a German trench. Beside him lay three dead Germans at a dug-out door. I thought he was dead but he was just conscious and when we looked more closely at him we saw that his arm had been ripped open the whole way down and he was bleeding to death. We got a puttee from someone's ankle and wrapped it around the wound. Then Bobby Reid and myself put him on a groundsheet and dragged him back to our medical orderlies."

As Harry Wilson made his way back he was shot several times in the legs. The long frantic scramble back through the German lines and no-man's-land had been littered with the bodies of the dead and wounded. Some were making their own way back, crawling, and many would die from lack of blood. Others would lie there waiting for help to come. For many it did not as they were in no-man's-land and if they did not die from their wounds they perished from shock, exposure or lack of water.

Jim Donaghy:-

"When we reached our medics Bobby Sterritt took the sergeant from us and we decided to go back for another. I found Willie Campbell. He had been the boss of the cutting room of the shirt factory where my father had worked. He was badly wounded around the head and we helped him back to our lines. We were going out again but were ordered not to. We were exhausted. I was weak from loss of blood and suppose I was a terrible looking case as I was covered in blood. Sergeant Willie McGarvey was helping Lieutenant Wilton back. Wilton had a big gaping hole in his shoulder and was in a bad state.

I was taken to the field dressing station to get my wounds bandaged. There were casualties everywhere... dead and dying. You had to wait your turn. Some didn't get a turn... there was no hope for them."

Not all of the men had retired from the last three German lines. A small band of the Derrys under the command of Lieutenant McClure of C Company were grimly hanging on to the Crucifix on the German C line. There seems to have been confusion in the order to retire from the D line which at one stage was being heavily shelled. An order was given with the intention of retiring a short distance to a safer and more fortified position out of the bombardment area some twenty metres away, but the order was interpreted as a withdrawal to the German A line or Thiepval Wood. Nevertheless this band of men were hanging on to the position, fiercely beating back the German counter-attacks. At approximately 5pm a message arrived at battalion Headquarters from the right flank that ammunition, bombs and water were desperately needed by Lieutenant McClure and his men. A band of stragglers was hastily rallied and sent with Captain Knox, some thirty men in all, with ammunition and bombs. Another party was sent with six four gallon petrol tins filled with water. As they picked their way through the bullet and smoke swept no-man's-land they were heavily shelled and suffered casualties. The surviviors were unable to find Lieutenant McClure's party as the area was under terrific shelling and machine-gun fire. The scene was of utter confusion[*4]. The band of reinforcements handed over the water to men of different battalions in the C line. Many casualties occurred and later in the evening the last remnants of the Battalion made their way into the front trenches they had left in the morning.

Lt Ernest McClure
Photo: Author

These were now being manned by 16th Royal Irish Rifles. As the men of the 10th Inniskillings returned they were sent back to the assembly trenches where they were given water and rations.

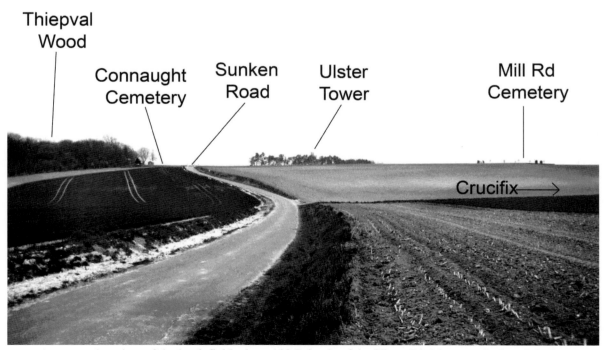

A present day view of the battlefield where 109 Brigade of the Ulster Division attacked on July 1st.

Photo: Author

Leslie Bell received his long awaited help.

"I had pulled myself forward to the shelter of the sunken road and got help around 4pm. I got taken back to our trenches and then to the rear where I was left for another two hours on the grass verge at the side of the road before being taken by ambulance to the field dressing station. It was a great big marquee. I was left outside it on a groundsheet. There was nobody in it that I could see except for the wounded and a wee nurse from Devon. Her apron was covered in blood. People were calling out for their wives and their mothers. She was running round trying to soothe them as best she could. Many's a time I thought, if anyone should have got a VC it was her. She saw more suffering that day than anyone."

The roll call on the evening of July 2nd in Martinsart was described by some of the survivors of the Derrys as the saddest and most moving experience of their lives. After the long list of names was taken at that mournful parade, in spite of it all they still cheered their officers, many of whom had also been killed, badly wounded or were missing in action.

Of the 22 officers and 742 other ranks who went into action on July 1st only ten officers and 336 other ranks returned to roll call at Martinsart on July 2nd, 1916.

They had been to Hell – and back. On July 1st, 1916, the Ulster Division fought their way through the German defences and advanced further than any other division deployed in the attack. If the other divisions had had a similar degree of success the attack would have achieved its aims and resulted in a major breakthrough.

The faded flag carried by the 10th Inniskillings on July 1st 1916, hangs in the United Services Club, Limavady. This was an unofficial flag made out of khaki shirts.

Photo: Author

On July 3rd the Tenth moved to the village of Headauville. The thoughts of how over half of their Battalion were lying dead or injured at Thiepval, and the horrors they had witnessed, must have been driving the survivors insane. This was the first time they had nothing to do since the battle and their innermost fears and emotions were now taking their toll. That night, Padre Patton picked a band of volunteers who returned to Thiepval. They spent the night frantically searching for their comrades out in no-man's-land. What they must have encountered during this search, as they scrabbled and crawled around in the darkness, must have been a dreadful experience. Even the slightest noise could have alerted the enemy to their presence and caused machine gun fire to be directed on them. No-man's–land held unimaginable horrors. Hundreds of mutilated corpses and body parts of their comrades littered the battlefield, many of them lying in huge numbers around the sunken road. Considering they had been lying out in the hot, summer sun for almost three days the smell of death was everywhere as they crawled around and over the blackened and bloated corpses looking for any sign of life.

The vast majority of these dead soldiers would have no known grave and those who took part in the search were very brave individuals.

Over the next few months the gaps in the ranks of the Derrys would be filled with recruits, many of whom had never set foot in Ulster. The close bond of the Battalion as a whole would never be the same. Just as part of the Battalion died that day and it would never be the same, so part of Ulster died. It too would never be the same.

[1] See image of New Testament at end of roll of those who served with the 10th Inniskillings at back of book.
[2] There is confusion as to whether this was a German or the British barrage.
[3] Top of the Hill is the height on the east bank of the Foyle overlooking the city centre of Londonderry.
[4] Lieutenant McClure and his men were never found and have no known graves.

Chapter 13
Aftermath

BATTLE OF THE SOMME.

ALL STILL GOING WELL.

Further Progress on British Front

SUCCESSFUL NIGHT RAIDS.

French Repulse Fierce Attacks.

THE NEW RUSSIAN ADVANCE

Some Striking Gains.

It was not until July 8th that the first massive casualty list appeared in a Londonderry paper. Casualty lists from July 1st were still being published a month later. Those lists included names of people posted as missing who were killed, also names of soldiers 'killed' who were later found to be alive. Jim Donaghy, although wounded and in hospital, was reported as missing, much to the anguish of his mother.

There was hardly a home in Ulster unaffected by the tragedy of July 1st. Whole streets were in mourning. In the 10th Inniskillings there were many cases of brothers, or father and son, being either killed or wounded. This was the case for Harry Wilson. Both he and his father were wounded on July 1st and by coincidence both spent some time in St. Thomas's hospital in London recovering from wounds. They did not know what had happened to the other and even though they travelled home on the same boat and train, it was only when they were crossing the bridge in Londonderry, a few hundred yards from their home in the Fountain estate, that they met[1].

That year the annual July 12th Orange celebrations were cancelled at the request of the Grand Lodge of Ireland. There was nothing to celebrate – Ulster was in mourning. The following items about the 10th Inniskillings appeared in local newspapers shortly after the first casualty lists were published.

They reflect the thoughts of a devastated community – and a devastated Ulster Division.

THE ATTACK OF THE ULSTER DIVISION

The following letter appeared in the Londonderry Sentinel. It was written by Pte Willie Campbell (brought in from no-man's-land by Jim Donaghy) while he was in hospital and sent to a friend:-

> *"I am sorry I did not get far till the Germans got me. I had just advanced 200 yards into no-man's-land when I got hit with a bullet from a machine gun. It struck my helmet and came right through it, leaving a hole as large as a five shilling piece. The bullet was deflected downwards, giving me a three inch lacerated wound above the right eye, but I thank God that my eyesight is safe. I had a very narrow escape on Thursday previous. As five of us were coming down the trench over came a whizzbang and wounded two in*

front of me and two behind me and I escaped uninjured. Later on, however, I was wounded and while in the trench a big shell came over and buried three of us with clay. You should have seen our boys advancing on the July 1st with the Derrys and Tyrones leading. It was a fine sight and like something you would see in a cinema – chaps falling beside you and you going on making for your objective, shrapnel bursting above you and high explosive shells bursting all around and machine guns sweeping the ground. You would wonder how they were able to advance but our boys got the length of the 4th German line but had to retire to the 3rd as there was a danger of them being cut off."

The following poems were printed in the Londonderry Sentinel on the July 15th, 1916 by Fieldcard which was the pen-name of one of the 10th Inniskillings.

IN MEMORY
OF THE ULSTER VOLUNTEERS
WHO FELL ON THE 1ST JULY, 1916

The Summer days are on the wane,
Night shadows early fall;
The green leaf soon to yellow turns,
Soon winter winds will call;
But as the night succeeds the day,
And sunshine follows rain,
The gloom of Winter disappears,
And Summer comes again.

O'er Ulster night has fallen,
There's weeping in the land,
For those who fell in honour's cause,
A brave and fearless band.
But only for a season:
Does not the Old Book say
Weeping will but last the night,
Joy cometh with the Day!

There are lonely homes in Ulster,
Some 'light of life' has shed;
There are many names of loved ones
Among the list of dead.
They fell for God and honour;
Why are ye lonely, when
They answered soon as they were asked,
And fought and died like men!

At the Hospital, 2nd July, 1916.

Come closer, Bill, old comrade, I'm glad to have you here,
It does not seem so hard to die when one we love is near,
For as 'kids' we played together – 'Shot marbles on the Wall'.
And as youths in good old Brandywell we used to kick the ball.
You tell them in the dear old town – old Derry on the Foyle
That the boys who drilled with 'Wooden guns' were worthy of their soil.
But you'll hardly need to tell them, e're now the world has heard,
What hardy Sons of Ulster for their King and Country dared.
How when ordered from the trenches, by just that one word 'Go!'
With the war-cry 'No Surrender' they quickly found the foe,
And onward dashed, from trench to trench, as streams the rushing tide,
The Fountain, Dark Lane, Rosemount, and the lads from Waterside
Went onwards, ever onward, their progress none could stay.
They weren't out 'Goose-stepping' nor singing 'Dolly's Brae.'
But to clear the Earth of him we hate – Lor', how those Germans ran!
They hadn't time to 'wait and see' at 'Omagh' or 'Strabane.'*2
It maybe someone blundered, the fault might've been our own,
But when we reached trench No.5, we found ourselves alone:
Alone and unsupported, amidst a withering fire,
Yet we held our winnings gamely till the order came – 'Retire!'
I cannot, or will any man, the story ever tell.
How caught in that triangle – it seemed the mouth of Hell –
With comrades falling, falling, we formed as on parade:
'You'll fight a rearguard action', was all our leaders said.
And in that rearguard action, Bill, I got the knockout blow;
And now I've go to 'travel' the road that all must go.
When lying faint from loss of blood I heard a brother call,
'We cannot leave him here to die, where one goes go we all.'
It was a chap from Monaghan, a loyal man and true;
He swung me 'cross his shoulders, and said he'd see me through,
'Right, matey,' then another said 'Where one goes go we all,
I'll help you, brother Ulsterman – I'm County Donegal."
The Ulsters fought the rearguard, with many a hearty cheer,
And the next thing I remember was being patched up here.
But I know the efforts useless, I feel I'm going fast
I see the new day breaking, for me will be the last;
I'll ne'er again sit on the Wall on an evening calm and cool
To watch the youngsters playing 'tig' around First Derry School.
I thought of 'Derry Walls Away' when joining in the fight,
I said it was for Ulster, I wanted right-left-right.
You'll tell them in the dear old town – Old Derry on the Foyle –
That the men who guarded Ireland's shore sleep neath a foreign soil:
And when the news of victory comes and the old church joybells ring,
They'll raise a stone for those who fell for Country and their King.

A lettter sent home by Lt. J.W. Shannon, wounded and captured July 1st 1916.

Lt J. W. Shannon
Photo: Author

"A shell dropped into the trench beside us and killed the four men following me, while a fragment of the shell hit me on the right side, almost at the ball of the leg, penetrating through and smashing the bones on both sides, also carrying a section of the shin bone away with it, and leaving two large holes at the entry and exit. I also received three slight shrapnel wounds on the left leg. Unfortunately the mangled bodies of the four poor fellows who were killed fell across my legs and body and pinned me to the ground. I was in this position for half an hour, vainly struggling to release myself and remove the bodies with my hands. However after a time, some passed along the trench and having appealed to several of them, I persuaded one man to lift the bodies off my leg. I can quite understand the younger fellows shying at it as the sight was awful. Later one of the surviving officers of our battalion came along and he lifted me to a clear space further on in the trench and he gave me water. Later still an officer came and bandaged the wounds, putting my legs in temporary splints. There I was, left alone, as the others were making preparations to hold the line some hundred yards away to the right.

There I lay until evening, when to my surprise, a large body of Germans came along the same trench, evidently to counter-attack. As soon as they saw I was badly wounded they passed on, some of them stooping down to shake my hand as they passed, and reassuring me that they were 'Kamarade, Kamarade.' The trench was then occupied by German soldiers. One kindly disposed fellow came up and gave me his field-dressing, but when he saw I was helpless and unable to move, he applied the bandage himself. I was simply dying with thirst and could not get water as my water-bottle and equipment had been taken away from me. The soldier remained with me some time, and gave me two biscuits, but I was not inclined to eat. I lay in this position for two nights and two days; and when the Germans had cleared their own wounded I was lifted on to a stretcher and carried almost a mile to a dressing station. Here the German doctors were interested in my wounds and asked quite a lot of questions in fairly good English. I was placed in an ambulance and dumped outside a dressing station and on the road alongside numerous English and German wounded. My leg was set and placed in splints, with an iron frame at the sole of the foot and the whole leg bandaged from the hips to the sole. I felt much easier and was then placed on some straw at the side of the road and left alongside English soldiers and two English officers. I lay there for two days and one night. On the evening of the second day I was away. Here we were carried to the grounds of a large chateau and placed on straw. Some sister of a Red Cross society came around with hot coffee. We lay there all night, and the rain poured on us. I had a light blanket covering me, but like myself, was quite soaked. The leg of my trousers had been cut off to allow for splints and bandages; I had only one boot, one sock, and no cap, so you can imagine the misery of that night. The next day we were carried in ambulances some distance to a railway station and entrained in a form of hospital train and sent to another location in Germany."

[1] Approximately 60 years later Jim met this man at the end of Craigavon Bridge in Londonderry where the Old Comrades used to congregate on fine days for a chat.

[2] Names of Ulster towns were used as names of objectives which had to be attacked on July 1st.

Pte Lindsay Hall 15567
10th R. Inniskilling Fus.
4B Ward   208 Bed.
1st Eastern General Hospital.
Cambridge   Eng.

Tuesday.

My Dear Mother.

Just a few lines to let you
know that I got your two letters. The cigs
came all right, and they were not crushed for
a wonder. When I got Father's Telegram I
did not know who it was from, and I was
wondering what it was for. However when I opened it
I saw it all.

I sent you a letter a few days
ago, but I suppose you did not get it. I had not
got a stamp to put on it, so I put it into the
box without one, I am not sure if it went or
not, if it did I suppose you would have to put
2 on it.

I got wounded on Saturday afternoon
the first of July, It was in the Germans Lines, and
I was struck with a piece of shrapnel, just
above the knee. I was under the X Rays
on Saturday last, and I have just seen the
plate today. I see the piece of shrapnel

it has just missed the bone, so it is not too bad, I expect once the piece is out, it won't be long until I am discharged out of the hospital into a convalesent home, after a while there, I will get about 10 days leave, so I have something to look forward to .

I will never forget that morning the first of July when got then word "Up you go and the best of Luck," After an intense bombardment by our artillery we went over the top, and crossed over to the German lines, We were as cool as if we had been on parade, and went steadly over line after line, There was a machine gun on the left, in a strong German position, and it swept our advancing lines, I could see them boys, falling on my right and left, we did not stop but on we went. When we reached the German front line, we had no trouble cutting their barbed wene, there was none there, it had been completely blown away all that could be seen, was a few twisted iron spikes and splinters of wire lying in the bottom of shell holes, and all over the place. When we went into there front line, it could hardly be recognised, it was blown up everyway, There were some dug outs there with Germans in them

we threw bombs into them, and they came up, with
there hands held high in the air, saying "Mercy
Kamerade", we done for some of them, and the
rest were prisoners. Under cover of the french 75's
we pushed on again, the Artillery lifted from the 2nd
and played on the 3rd line, the German machine
gun still kept sweeping our ranks, catching our
boys. While this was going on the German Artillery
was playing havock with our supports and reserves
coming up behind. We passed over the second line
and went to the third line, we had a while there
while the 75's and Artillery kept banging away. The
noise was terrible, the shrapnel was bursting all
round us, high explosive shells was blowing the
ground all over us, tear shells was busting, and
made our eyes water something terrible. When we
reached our objective, we were under enflide fire
from both side, and in front of us, the wounded
were crying in agony, and a few chaps, lying
dead with head or legs blown off. Oh it was
terrible. The position was on the slope of a hill
slight hill, but we got there at a cost. We gathered
all our bombs together, for the Germans were
coming up on our left flank, up the trench
but we bombed them out. I was terrible thirsty
I never knew how dry I could be. Some chaps

took the water bottles off the dead men, and this partly relieved our thirst. I was lying in a but Shell hole at the side of the trench, The German was shelling us with all sort of shells. When I got struck in the knee with a piece of shrapnel, another struck the back of my equipment cutting the belt, and it glanced out of the entrenching tool, so that saved me, I tied up my leg with the field bandage, when ~~another~~ a lot of wounded were going back, and I joined them after a trying time we got back to our own lines, got our wounds ~~dressed and were~~ sent to a big hospital in France (I suppose I am still not allowed to give the name of place, ~~but this wont be censored~~) + here I am.

This is all at present hoping you are all well.

With Love From Your Loving Son.

Lindsay

Chapter 14
Return to Thiepval

Jim Donaghy:-

"I spent approximately ten days in a hospital and convalescence camp at Boulogne but I wanted to get back to the battalion and see my friends, those that were still there. A group of ten of us were told we could rejoin, but later we found we would have to temporarily join the 1st Battalion of the Inniskillings, as the remnants of the Tenth had been moved up towards Belgium. We were raging and protested strongly, but still we were sent to them. We were sent back to Thiepval, the exact spot we had attacked from on the morning of the 1st July. We spent our time doing working parties – collecting and bringing back the bodies of the dead for burial. Many had been lying there in all that hot weather for over a week, some lying where they had fallen. They were lying stretched on top of the sandbags just above the trench. Many were horribly mutilated. One big tall chap gave us problems as we carried his body on a stretcher as it was difficult to turn round the corners of the narrow winding trench. We had to lift the stretcher high above our heads in order to get him round the corners. Oh Lord! It was terrible."

Most of the men of the 10th Inniskillings killed on July 1st have no known graves as they had advanced so far their bodies were lying in no-man's-land. Over time they would be further mutilated by shell-fire or may have been buried or blown apart by the continual shelling. Their names are inscribed on the walls of the Thiepval Memorial to the missing among 73,357 listed as missing at the Somme. The Ulster Tower Memorial to the 36th Division was built near the site of the Schwaben Redoubt.

View of Thiepval battlefield, September 1916.

Photo: Imperial War Museum, Q1073

Chapter 15
Up to Belgium

After spending a week in the rear lines behind Thiepval, the 10th Inniskillings boarded a train on July 11th, at Conteville, which would take them fifty miles north to Berguette in preparation for duties on the front along the border with Belgium around Ypres. A thirteen mile route march through the night took the twenty two officers and 415 other ranks of the battalion to the village of Racquingham which they reached at 5.30am. In thirteen hours the men of 109 Brigade had marched twenty one miles with full kit, but they had enough energy and enthusiasm left to stage a little Orange Order procession through the village. The soldiers had found orange flowers growing along the roadside. They placed them in their caps and button-holes and were led by the flute bands of 109 Brigade.

Next day the Battalion marched to Acquin where they spent the week, making such an impact on the local inhabitants that later, when they heard the Ulstermen were returning to the area, they requested that the 10th Inniskillings should be billeted with them. After moving to Merkengham, the troops were transported up to within a few miles of the front by London omnibuses, which had been brought over to help speed up troop movements – always in one direction it seemed; towards the fighting.

The battalion arrived at Kortepyp camp, a few miles behind the lines, and after a few days of training and preparation moved to an old farm, called La Grande Manque Farm, which had been badly damaged by shelling.

On August 2nd, after a month's rest, the Derrys entered the front line for another seven day stint. This time they found the trenches somewhat different to the deep trenches of the Somme region. Here the trenches had been dug much shallower but the earth which had been removed from the trenches had been piled up to form 'breastworks.' Behind the front line lay Ploegsteert Wood, known to the men as 'Plug Street.' In this wood was a small hill, Hill 63, where Battalion Headquarters were located.

The area was quiet in comparison to other areas but a small continual casualty list mounted as the odd shell took its toll. Ploegsteert was notorious for its battles between the mortars of both sides. This made life for the infantry soldier extremely stressful and uncomfortable as each side tried to destroy the other's trenches, dug-outs and trench mortars.

Casualties were not solely caused by the enemy. On August 26th and 27th, the Battalion carried 420 cylinders of poisonous gas into the front line during their period in support, and then relieved 14th Rifles on August 28th. At 1.30am on August 31st the gas was released, followed four minutes later by a bombardment of heavy artillery on the German lines. The 14th Rifles made an attempt at a raid but were held up by the German barbed wire. During the night Pte. D. Burke was killed by a trench mortar. But an even more harrowing and morale sapping sight must have been that of Pte. Henry Rosborough who was gassed by the British gas and died the next day.

September 6th saw the battalion move a few miles north along the line to Cooker's Farm trenches. The town of Dranoutre was to the rear and to the front lay the dominant feature of the area, Wytchaete Ridge. At this part of the front the opposing lines were very close to each other and most operations being carried out in the British lines were under the watch of the enemy on the heights.

PLOEGSTEERT

On September 27th, 1916, the 10th Inniskillings moved to Wakefield Huts in the Ploegsteert sector of the line. They would remain in this area of Belgium until June 1917 and their stay would be an extremely active one.

On their return into the front line trenches on September 30th, the Derrys took over from the 14th Rifles. While in the rear lines they had been practising for a raid on a section of German trenches located opposite. This had been studied in meticulous detail based on intelligence and the latest aerial photography, and they had practised the raid repeatedly in specially constructed replica trenches.

At 10pm a raiding party of some seventy-eight men, (all volunteers) under the command of Lt. G. Webb and 2/Lts McCrea and McClenaghan set out from the Derrys' trenches. With blackened faces, steel helmets replaced with soft cap comforters and boots muffled, they quietly headed out into the darkness. They carried an assortment of conventional weapons; some had rifles, others pistols and a large number of soldiers carried only grenades. A few were armed with more unconventional weapons; trench knives and knobkerries to dispatch any sentries they may encounter in the quietest possible manner with the objective of concealing their presence from the enemy until the last possible minute. Three men from 150 Field Company Royal Engineers, accompanied the Inniskillings with the specialised task of positioning and detonating a new weapon…. a Bangalore torpedo. This was a long, thin pipe filled with high explosive and detonated by a time fuse and was designed to explode and clear a path through the German wire. This would be essential as it was wire which had caused the 14th Rifles such great problems in their raid the previous month. The key to the success of the operation was not just the previous intensive training based on the mock trenches, but also the need for a totally stealthy approach by all the men as they traversed no-man's-land. Once the torpedo was positioned and the fuse set by the engineers, everyone would take cover until it detonated. The slightest noise could have given away the position of the men as they approached the German trenches. No-man's-land was full of debris and shellholes which could have caused someone in this large patrol to trip or fall and the noise could have alerted the German sentries. Rockets and Verey lights would illuminate no-man's-land and if they had been spotted they would have been cut to ribbons by machine gun fire and artillery.

It was planned that the torpedo would be detonated at 10.10pm and on hearing the explosion in the Tenth's trenches the artillery would be contacted immediately by phone to put down a barrage around the predetermined section of the German line which was to be raided. As the patrol took cover from the anticipated blast of the torpedo… nothing happened … that is, except for a noisy click which was so loud it was heard back in the Inniskillings' trenches. Luckily there was no reaction from the Germans. Again the engineers went forward to rearm the fuse of the torpedo and after a nerve-racking 25 minutes waiting in no-man's-land the torpedo exploded with a deafening roar at 10.36pm. Almost immediately the screech of shells flying overhead was heard as the British artillery opened up on the German third line, and simultaneously trench mortars and machine guns attacked each flank. This basically caused a section of the German trench system to be cut off, preventing reinforcements from attacking the invading Inniskillings. The raiding party quickly jumped up and attacked the trench with shouts and roars as they threw dozens of grenades into the trench. Once they jumped into the German fortifications they met little resistance and found to their amazement that the Germans had abandoned their posts in a hurry, leaving their rifles with bayonets fixed and grenades arranged on the firesteps. It was reported that one section of the attack party found the remains of a German's legs with everything above the knees being blown away. It was believed that this was a sentry who had suffered the full blast from the torpedo.

 2/Lt McCrea started to search along the trench for a machine gun post which he had reckoned was in the vicinity and which he eventually found. With the help of a few volunteers, the captured gun was dismantled and brought over to the British lines while others went through the German trenches, blowing up all the dugouts and collecting as many German weapons as possible. One German was spotted sending up Verey Lights and flares to illuminate the area and also signal the German artillery for support by bombarding no-man's-land but Cpl. Adair and Pte. R. J. Brown fired shots and threw bombs at him killing him in the process. The patrol was then recalled to their own lines by a bugle call and weapons which could not be carried were abandoned in no-man's-land. Unfortunately, one of the Royal Engineers, L/Cpl Robert Thompson from Belfast was killed in the attack by a rifle grenade as they left the German lines. The members of the raiding party made several attempts to bring back his body, but they had difficulty getting it out of the trench and, as there were wounded to be helped back, his body had to be left behind.

Apart from the dead sapper, the raiding party had 14 other casualties of whom three were in a serious condition. On arrival back in their own lines the captured loot was examined and this included a heavy machine gun and its ammunition belts, eighteen rifles, a full German kit, two caps, a large quantity of stick grenades and other oddments including several food parcels, fresh from Germany, as well as a ladle!

Chapter 16
Gas! Gas!

The 1st Inniskillings went north on August 7th to the front along the Belgian border. Jim and some of his comrades from the Tenth who had been wounded on July 1st had to go with them. They felt that at least they were getting closer to their own Battalion and now they would be able to rejoin their comrades.

Jim Donaghy:-

"We were in trenches just a few hundred yards from the town of Ypres. When we weren't in the trenches we slept in the cellars of ruined houses in the town. I was in a cellar with John Burke from A Company. Every day we used to report to the Commanding Officer of the 1st Battalion and requested to be sent back to our Battalion, but again and again we were refused."

AUGUST 8TH, 1916

Jim Donaghy:-

"We had been warned that the Germans were going to mount a gas attack, but we didn't know when. We practised our gas drills regularly. In the quiet of the night we could hear the clanking of gas cylinders as they were brought up on a narrow gauge railway. Myself and George Leonard (also in the 10th Battalion but assigned temporarily to the 1st Battalion) were in the same Section. We were out one night on a wiring party and just as we were coming in I snagged my gas mask on the wire. We always wore our masks round our necks at the ready position in case of attack. I quickly got a replacement. Shortly after, around midnight, we heard the clanging of the gas alarms. Jerry had released the poisonous gas Phosgene. You could hear it hissing out of the cylinders. It

Pte George Leonard

was sweet smelling, like pear drops. We quickly fumbled on our gas masks and stood up on the firestep at the ready. Our Lewis guns opened up on the German line awaiting the attack through the gas. The Germans started to shell our trenches as well. We were ordered to keep firing during the attack and as I was shooting away George kept coming up to me. He was panicking and kept tugging at me, shouting, 'I'm choking Jim, I'm choking. Oh God Jim. What am I going to do? I canny breathe!' I set him down on the fire-step telling him, 'Take it easy you're only making yourself worse.'

I got on the fire-step and started firing again, but when I looked down he had got up and was stumbling along the trench. It was panic all around. Men were choking and vomiting with the gas. Next thing I knew, my rifle was jamming. With the heat of the rifle mixed with the gas the bolt had started to corrode and was covered in verdigris. I got a rag out of my pouch and cleaned it off as best I could and started firing again.

When the attack was over we couldn't find George anywhere. When it came to first light I was vomiting. There were lots of casualties. We found George lying dead at the bottom of the trench, just outside the dugout.

Soldiers wearing gas masks in a trench.

Photo: Imperial War Museum, Q60966.

Aerial photograph of a gas attack at Ypres.

Photo: Imperial War Museum, Q55066.

George was a volunteer, like most of the Derrys, but he always stood out and had been constantly commended for his fine soldierly appearance even by regular NCOs and officers. He was a nice wee chap.

In the morning at rollcall there were only three men still in the trenches from my Section. I was on sentry duty and looking through the periscope out into no-man's-land. As I looked, the landscape turned red – then green, then blue and all different colours. I told what I was seeing to my platoon officer and was ordered to report to the first aid post in the support trenches. I had to go by myself as no-one could be spared to escort me there as the Battalion had suffered so many casualties. Our communication trenches had been blocked by the shelling so I had to make my way back through the lines of a Scottish regiment holding a section of the trenches beside us. I must have collapsed because when I woke up I found I was being carried up to the first aid post over the shoulder of a sergeant from the King's Own Scottish Borderers. After some treatment there I was labelled and laid on the grass verge at the crossroads at Poperinghe. There were hundreds sitting and lying on the grass waiting on ambulances. They were all vomiting and choking. It was terrible! A priest from Strabane came round and took my name. He sent a fieldcard to my mother telling her I was wounded but OK. We were then taken by train to hospital."

On the night of August 9th/10th the 1st Inniskillings had seven officers killed and five wounded with eighty-one ranks killed and forty-three wounded. Almost all the casualties had been gassed with a few being killed by the shelling. Every one of the Battalion's many transport horses were gassed. Several others from the Derrys died that night. For the unfortunate 1st Inniskillings it was another bitter blow to a unit that had at least 450 killed at Gallipoli and 549 casualties six weeks before on July 1st.

Compared to what 1st Inniskillings had just endured, the Derrys, a few miles down the line in the Ploegsteert area, were having a much easier time.

Gas casualties

Chapter 17
Plug Street

Jim returned to the 10th Inniskillings in October 1916. It was an emotional reunion with comrades he had last seen on July 1st. He did not know who had been killed or, wounded or who had survived unscathed.

Jim Donaghy:-

"In fact, when I arrived at the Battalion, I hardly recognised it. It was full of new men, mainly from England. There was a large draft from Liverpool. Then I spotted some of the old faces.
We didn't refer to a friend as being killed or badly wounded. If someone was killed, 'He's gone west.' Someone who was badly wounded 'Got a Blighty.' We never really talked about what had happened on the 1st of July."

They may not have talked much about the events at the Somme, but it was always in their minds – the friends, the horrors. Whereas Jim had been in action again since July 1st with the 1st Battalion Inniskillings, the rest of the Tenth had been in the safety of the rear lines. On August 3rd they had moved up to the front line again to Ploegsteert Wood in Belgium – referred to as Plug Street by the soldiers.

Jim Donaghy:-

"Plug Street was all right as the trenches were in good order and dry, but it was 'hot' with the Germans continually shelling."

The troops were very tense after the actions of July 1st. After receiving such a punishment from artillery at Thiepval, the action of the enemy in this area proved to be more unnerving than normal with men running for cover on the approach of every shell, even those that would not cause damage in the immediate area. The position they were holding was called La Grande Manque which was an old farm and had been incorporated into the British defences. It had been severely damaged by shelling as had all the surrounding farm houses.

Major Macrory:-

"The effect of the sound of even the occasional shell was very curious on men who had escaped the hell of Thiepval and whom, one would have thought, had hardened to the worst that war could bring forth.
The reflex action of overstrained nerves was very evident when one saw brave men, who had so often faced and dared death, start to shudder almost involuntary at the distant sound of a shell exploding."

One of the artillery pieces most feared by the men was the German 'Minenwerfer.'

Jim Donaghy:-

"Minnies were big shells the size of an oil drum. You could see them on their way up and on their way down, slowly tumbling through the air. Sometimes you could see a trail of

"My Dream for years to come."A macabre postcard belonging to Capt. Glover Austin.
This nightmare would be a reality for many veterans.
Photo: Philip O'Doherty

Capt. Glover Austin and his wife.
(Owners of Austins of the Diamond, Londonderry,which was Ireland's first Department Store).
Photo: Philip O'Doherty

sparks coming out of them. If you spotted one, they were so slow that you could run up or down the trench away from it to try and escape the full effect of the blast. You couldn't always run as in places trenches may have been blocked or you were slowed down by men, mud or water. If you knew they were going to explode nearby, you put your head under a sandbag and hoped for the best. Boys, but were they powerful and when they exploded, they left a massive crater. If one exploded nearby, you could have been buried alive.

On one occasion, we spent a period of time in the front line trenches when we were being constantly bombarded by two big 'Minnies.' It turned out that the front line, for a change, was the safest place as Jerry didn't know the range of our trenches and the shells were falling too short or hitting the reserve trench well behind us.

I got three parcels just before Christmas, one from my mother and the others from an aunt and a friend of my mother's. As myself and two friends were carrying the parcels down the communication trench, Jerry was shelling like hell and we had to lie down three times and take cover as the shells fell around us."

A shell explodes above Ploegsteert Wood, April 20th, 1917 when the Derrys were at this location.
Photo: Imperial War Museum, Q2313

A SHORT QUIET INTERLUDE

In the Tenth's War Diary an entry for November 1st-4th contained a rare statement... "Nothing to report." The next week the War Diary commented on how quiet the tour was, as after another full week's stint in the front line, only three men were killed.

On November 11th the battalion left the front line and moved back to the rear at Wakefield Huts in battalion reserve for a break from the trenches. A special treat had been organised for November 15th when they marched to the town of Bailleul accompanied by the Divisional Band. On arrival, their firearms were piled in a field outside the town and then the men were marched to the cinema where the 36th Division "Follies" gave a great theatrical performance. A showing of some "excellent films" followed and although this may not rate as great amusement in today's entertainment and media rich society, the fun and pleasure generated by these performances and films would have the men chatting about them for a long time in the future.

A final week was spent in reserve which was most welcomed by the men as the weather had turned extremely cold and frosty. It would have been tough trying to stay warm or get a sleep in the trenches. The transition from the filth, danger and misery of the trench life to having the comfort and luxury of beds in huts and the additional indulgence of the Divisional baths further enhanced a most welcome respite. However, on November 17th the rest and relaxation was brought to an end as the battalion marched back into the front line, taking over from the 14th Rifles. The thought of going back into the line after the comparative safety and comfort of the rear lines must have been depressing, especially as their previous stint in this section of the front line had been fairly quiet. But, surprisingly, the Rifles reported that things were still fairly uneventful!

War Diary:-
> 'This is the quietest tour we have ever had in this part of the line (with only one man Pte J Devine being killed by a trench mortar). This is presumably on account of the Saxons having come into the line opposite us.'[1]

Remembering the Christmas Truce in 1914 when troops from both armies fraternised in no-man's–land, High Command didn't like things to get too comfortable for the soldiers on both sides as it was felt that there was an ever increasing possibility that they would end up just sitting facing each other and losing the will to fight. By now, the common soldier on both sides had realised that there were no winners in this war of stalemate and attrition.

On November 23rd High Command decided to stir things up and the Division's artillery was organised to put an incredibly devastating artillery barrage on the enemy's front line for no apparent tactical reason other than to put some aggression back into the line.

War Diary:-
> "This morning a bombardment of the enemy trenches in front of this sector was carried out by trench mortars. Our Stokes mortars fired over 1512 rounds and the medium trench mortars fired an additional 700 rounds, doing considerable damage to the enemy trenches with wood and sandbags being sent flying in all directions. The enemy's retaliation was weak and we had no casualties."

The bombardment had the desired effect as the next day the Germans responded with a very heavy night bombardment between 10.30 – 11.40pm on the 11th Inniskillings' line which was adjacent to the Tenth's trenches. The British guns replied with great vigour but so did the Germans, culminating in a retaliatory salvo of twelve 5.9" high explosive shrapnel shells on the Derrys' lines narrowly missing although there were no casualties. The line was now aggressive and violent again.

On December 21st the Battalion left Ploegsteert Wood and withdrew to Brigade reserve. When in the trenches at Ploegsteert, the Derrys were accommodated in the most unconventional billets they could have imagined: underground caves which had been excavated into Hill 63 by Australian miners. These were called the Catacombs and were so large that they could accommodate at least two battalions, giving good protection from artillery but they were cold and very wet in places. The men slept in bunk beds which lined the side of the underground passageways and were lit by electric lights. The battalion spent Christmas in the Catacombs.

An officer from the 10th Inniskillings
during gas training.
Photo: Captain McKenzie Collection

Jim Donaghy:-

"Just a few days before Christmas, Bobby Reid, myself and several others from the Battalion were sent to the rear for gas warfare training. The course had finished for Christmas and we had to walk back up to the Battalion in the front line, but managed to get a lift on one of the old London buses which had been brought over to transport troops. This was quite rare as most times we had to march from place to place. We had to get off early and make a detour, as the Germans were shelling the transport. On our way back to the Battalion we walked past a wee café but found that we were all short of money and could only scrape a few francs up between us. There was a card game in progress. Bobby went in with our money and won some of the games. With his winnings, we all had a few drinks before making our way back to the cold, wet catacombs. We arrived just in time for our Christmas dinner. It was served in a big cave and was a pretty good dinner of lamb, roast pork, potatoes and fruit, a welcome change from our normal rations."

Major Macrory:-

Anyone who can picture the catacombs of ancient Rome will get a fair idea of the gigantic Plug Street dugouts. Small engines drove dynamos, which lit the vast interiors with electric light. Rows upon rows of wooden bunks lined the passages and great glistening stalactites hung from the misty ceilings. Christmas dinner and festivities in such a place were made as cheerful as circumstances would permit and mind you it is not easy to feel really cheerful when one is trying to eat a bit of roast pig off a tin plate precariously balanced on the edge of one's bunk, the electric light winking dimly through a frosty mist and one's feet over the ankles in slimy water.

Things were far from jovial, but in every band of young men there are jokers and comedians who try to lift the spirits of their comrades. Soon signs started to appear outside dugouts and other areas held by the Derrys with the words, DON'T WORRY – SMILE!

This became the Battalion's motto. When things were tense and men apprehensive someone would break the silence with these words. Postcards were printed with the stronger version. SMILE, DAMN YOU! SMILE

A postcard sent home by Harry Wilson with the Tenth's motto.

Men did smile even though they had nothing to smile about; death was never far away. New Year 1917 was welcomed in with artillery action from both sides. The chance of a "Happy New Year" was soon shattered when two men, Pte Robert McCracken and Pte Andrew McFarland (who was attached to 109 Trench Mortar Battery) were killed near the trench barracade on the Ploegsteert – Messines Rd.

On January 4th a fighting patrol of 16 other ranks and 2 officers was sent out to try and intercept any German patrols that might be out in no-man's-land. During the patrol none were encountered, but tragically, one man, Pte John McLaughlin, was killed after being struck in the chest by a stray bullet. This incident was almost certainly the result of an accidental discharge of a weapon by another member of the patrol and must have been devastating for his comrade who had fired the fatal shot.

The weather was getting bitterly cold and a period of hard frost developed. Sheepskin "body warmers" which were worn over the soldiers' uniforms, had been issued to try to keep the soldiers a bit warmer, as they stood in the trenches with little physical activity to generate much needed body heat. There were a few coke braziers, but any sign of smoke or fire from a trench was an indication to the Germans that there was the possibility of a concentration of men in a particular section of trench warming themselves and a prime target for rifle grenades or trench mortars. After a period of relative inactivity by both sides, possibly due to the extremely cold weather making life even more difficult than normal, the shelling started again. On January 17th, Allied artillery shelled the enemy trenches from 4.50-5pm. What would have seemed to be a good morale boost to any new recruits in the line for the first time would have had the opposite effect on the older hands. The experienced trench warfare soldier knew that it made life harder for the front line troops on both sides as the enemy would usually retaliate shortly after they had been bombarded. In the German shelling which followed, 2/Lt T Swann was severely wounded in the stomach by shrapnel. Medics would later recount after the war that wounds to the stomach or intestines were almost certainly the most painful. Soldiers with head, chest or wounds to the limbs in the majority of occasions would be fairly composed, taking into consideration the dreadful nature of their wounds. However, injuries to the lower abdomen had men screaming in agony, especially those who had been severely injured by red-hot shrapnel, which had been blasted into them.

The artillery duels took a steady toll on nerves. On January 20th, enemy artillery was very active, but the events of this day would have another profound effect on Jim Donaghy's memory forever.

JANUARY 20TH, 1917

Jim Donaghy:-

"It was a bitter cold day. The Maoris, the natives from New Zealand, were on our right, located in a hollow with a little stream running through it. Jerry made a big raid on their position. I was in the Bombing Section and our post was to the very right of our trenches beside the Maoris. It consisted of several small dugouts in behind the front line. At the end of a three day stint here, A and B Companies were being relieved by C and D. An officer came up to me asking for information on the position we were holding which he was going to pass on to his men. My friend, wee Jack Cochrane, was a member of the new guard of D Company and he was staying in the dugout that I had been in for the previous three days. Before I left with my Company, Jack gave me chocolates and biscuits from a big parcel he had been sent from home. It was a special parcel, a present to him from his mother for his 20th Birthday. When my hands were full, he was still giving me things and filled my pockets with little luxuries from home. Later that day I was back in the front line trenches around 9pm and not long after, Jerry started a heavy bombardment of our lines. He was raiding us. We formed up once the bombardment eased to repel the forthcoming attack but put up such a good fight that he didn't get in to our lines. Just at the end of the bombardment, one of the last shells, a Minnie, hit the dugout that Jack was in. All that was left were several sandbags. I was sorry for Jack. He was a good friend, the chap that had signed up the same day as myself. A grand wee chap, so he was." [2]

The shell which killed Jack also killed Pte W. Caldwell and L/Cpl A. Leacock from D Coy and wounded another. The next day proved to be another fairly strenuous one for the Battalion and the shelling of their lines kept up.

On January 22nd, the Derrys were to be relieved from the front by 11th Inniskillings. The battalion must have been looking forward to this break as the last few days had been extremely nerve-racking for them. They were to be relieved at 2pm and many must have been watching the time ticking away. At 1.45pm just as the relief had started, without warning, the enemy artillery subjected the Derrys to the worst bombardment they had encountered since Thiepval. Shells were exploding right along the front line and the relief was instantly suspended with the commanding officer of the 11th Battalion placing them under the orders of the Commanding Officer of the Tenth, Col. Macrory. As the German bombardment got louder and grew in ferocity, the British artillery, which had now been contacted by phone, added to the noise with their counter barrage of 18 pounders. Unfortunately their shells seemed to have little effect on the enemy guns. Now the information was urgently relayed to the heavy artillery batteries which were located far behind the trenches and soon the screech of the heavy artillery shells going over the heads of the men in the direction of the Germans was adding to the terrifying crescendo. At 4pm, it looked as if the Germans were about to mount a major attack so half of the 11th Inniskillings were hastily sent to strengthen the front line. All of a sudden, along the line came the most dreadful of sounds, the banging of gongs signalling a gas attack. Gas masks were hurriedly fitted as both the 10th and 11th Inniskillings, 109 Trench Mortar Battery and members of the engineers waited with fixed bayonets for the Germans' attack. Luckily the gas attack didn't materialise as the wind carried it away from the Derrys' trenches but the shelling continued until 7.15pm, with the result that the men had to spend an extra few terrifying hours 'overtime' in the front line. They eventually left a very battered set of trenches, pocked with all types of shells and at 10.45pm made their way back to the Catacombs in brigade reserve for a well deserved rest. The battalion was extremely fortunate in suffering only two casualties in the bombardment.

As daylight broke the next morning the devastation of six hours of continual shelling was revealed with many trenches being destroyed. The ground was totally pockmarked by shell holes of varying sizes.

Col. Macrory wrote:-
"To look at the trenches one would have thought that hardly a man could have escaped and yet the men had escaped in some marvellous way with very few exceptions. Unfortunately the Germans had subjected the Division to our right to a worse experience and had finally raided in great strength through the south side of the wood. The long ghastly rows of dead bodies stretched out for burial next day revealed the heavy losses."

The battalion next to the Tenth had taken a terrible hammering and had numerous men killed and badly wounded with many of them having been gassed. The rows of dead laid out for burial next morning paid testimony to the fact that the Derrys once again had been 'The Lucky Tenth.' In the front line there was always plenty of work for the medical orderlies. The Derrys were fortunate in having two excellent men in charge – Captain Sammy Picken and Corporal Benn Hunter from Limavady.

(Above) Cpl. Benn Hunter M.M.
Photo: Benn Hunter

(Left) Capt Sam Pickem MC in Ploegsteert
Wood outside first aid post.
Photo: Capt McKenzie Collection

Benn was put in charge of the Battalion First Aid Post at the age of 18 and lost a leg during his duties.

Jim Donaghy:-

"Once the fighting started there wasn't a man in the Battalion that didn't know Benn. He talked quick and could be very short in his conversations as he had a tough job to do and didn't suffer fools or skivers. There was always a dugout for first aid and it was here that he was based. It was kitted out with medical supplies, bandages and stretchers and was handed over one unit to another. It was here also that the band members that doubled as stretcher bearers had their headquarters. If you had to get an injection, tablets or have a dressing changed up you went to Benn. He did a lot for the personal hygiene of the men and had showers erected for them coming out of the line whenever he could. There was many's a night that he never got lying down as he was tending wounded and dying. He won the Military Medal – and boys but he deserved it!"

February 15th, 1917

A strange incident occurred on February 15th when the battalion entered the front line for another stint. It was bitterly cold with the trenches and the surrounding countryside covered in snow and slush. At 5pm, a German single seater Halberstadt aircraft came down just behind the frontlines in the 10th Inniskillings' sector. The pilot was uninjured and surrendered to some men from C Company. It appeared on interrogation that he had been up testing the engine when he spotted a French Nieuport and a German Albatros fighter were locked in a dogfight when he went to assist the Albatros, but was hit by shrapnel at 10,000 ft from the British anti-aircraft guns and had to make a crash landing. He was a corporal and had been an instructor at various aviation schools. About an hour after the plane came down the German artillery started firing high explosive shells trying to hit the location where they thought the plane had come down to destroy it before it could be examined thoroughly by British airmen. Luckily few shells fell near it and on closer examination through binoculars, it was found that the plane was virtually intact with the exception of its broken wheels and a hole in the petrol tank. After dark a party of men left their trenches and pulled it out of the field and down the Ploegsteert to Messines road to near Hydepark Corner. The Royal Flying Corps sent a party during the night and took the plane away for a thorough inspection for signs of any new German aviation technology as it was at this period of the war that the Germans held the upper hand in air war.

Jim Donaghy

"When you were stuck in the trenches with little to do and had to keep your head down the aircraft overhead provided entertainment at times with duelling British, French and German planes in dogfights. Some of the German planes were painted in very bright colours with some even in bright red and at times we watched what we thought was the Red Baron and his Flying Circus. We would sit and look up at the planes and hear them shooting at each other and at times cheer the British fighters. It's only when the planes started to approach our lines at low level that we knew that we were what he was interested in and the shooting started from Lewis Guns, anti-aircraft guns and even rifles."

Two days later another rare incident happened showing the esteem which many airmen had for each other. At great risk to themselves from smallarms and anticraft fire, a German aircraft dropped a small bag weighed with sand and a long black, white and red streamer attached to draw attention to it. It fell in a shell hole and when it was recovered it was found to have a message stating that two British airmen had been shot down and captured of whom one was wounded but that they were both well.

Officers mess in Plug St Wood bunkers called "Limavady Lodge". Notice the roaring fire, the bottles on the table and the pictures of girls on the walls.

Photo: Capt McKenzie Collection

TRENCH RAID

Another large raid on the German trench opposite the Tenth's was carried out on the night of February 21st. A fighting patrol of 32 men, commanded by 2/Lt McKnight and 2/Lt Griffiths made its way into no-man's-land at 7.30pm in total darkness. Almost simultaneously, a heavy British artillery barrage opened up giving cover to the raiding party as the shelling caused the Germans to take cover from the high explosions. Disaster struck the patrol almost immediately when a German mortar shell landed, injuring six men with 2/Lt McKnight receiving a fatal wound to the head killing him instantly. He was a great loss to the battalion as he was a superb bombing officer and he and his men took part in many of the trench raids and were a fearless bunch. 2/Lt Griffiths was also wounded in the arm and the five others were only slightly wounded. At 7.45pm the artillery switched to a box barrage (which meant that as the exploding shells blocked the approaches on three sides, German reinforcements could not come to the assistance of the section of trench which was being attacked). Finally, the 12 stokes mortars of 109 Trench Mortar Battery opened up on the section of the German line which was to be attacked with a five minute hurricane bombardment. During this phase of the attack, the raiding party, which had been lying out in no-man's-land during the shelling, edged towards the German lines. They were armed with Bangalore torpedoes to blast pathways through the German barbed-wire entanglements but very surprisingly didn't have to use them, as the wire in no-mans land had been extremely easy to get through. Unfortunately, on reaching the enemy trenches, 2/Lt Griffiths found that the German front line trench had been filled with barbed-wire traps and entanglements and he was unable to make any progress with the raid and had to withdraw his men back to the British trench line.

On February 23rd the enemy decided to make a revenge raid but instead of a night assault decided to attack under the cover of first light and a thick mist. The Germans opened up with a heavy bombardment of trench mortars between 5.50am-6.30am and fired a great number of mortar rounds. About 6.15am a party of Germans were seen by No 13 platoon Lewis gun team under cover of the mist. The machine gun opened up at once firing repeatedly at what they had witnessed. A lot of shouting was heard and almost certainly the withering fire of the Lewis gun had beaten back the attack. During this time another hostile party had entered the trenches of the battalion situated on the right of the Tenth, but were very soon driven out in hand to hand combat leaving one dead German behind.

The Derrys left the Catacombs on February 25th, 1917, and went to the quiet of the rear lines at Bulford Camp to act as Divisional reserve for a month. This would give them a well deserved break from the front. Their places had been taken by 107 Brigade of the 36th Division. The enemy wasn't the only killer in the War. Winter spent in the cold, wet environment of the trenches, in conjunction with poisonous gas, poor food and a lack of waterproof clothing encouraged the human body to develop diseases such as chronic rheumatism, bronchitis and pneumonia. On the morning of their first day's rest, Lieutenant R. Crawley, during the course of inspecting a field for a Battalion parade, collapsed and died from a heart attack. He was buried with full military honours in the Bailleul cemetery. A group of forty men made up the firing party and four buglers from his Company played Last Post.

Lt. R. Crawley

The time at Bulford Camp consisted of training in the mornings but on the afternoon of March 1st Brigade sports were held in a spell of good weather and these events were very popular with soldiers cheering representatives of their battalion.

On March 9th while the rest of the battalion were digging trenches at Kemmel, L/Cpl. W. G. Irwin was sent home as he was under age having already spent two years with the battalion. This was another example of an underage soldier making so much of an impact that he had been promoted!

Trench digging continued for several days but entertainment was arranged for some afternoons to keep up morale. The 109 Brigade inter-platoon football competition was held on March 10th where the Derrys' champion footballers from D Coy platoon played the champion platoon of 9th Battalion but were narrowly defeated 2:1. On another afternoon the Divisional baths were at the mens' disposal, which were always a great luxury for anyone who fought in the squalor of trench warfare. Finally on March 18th the battalion was relieved by the ANZACs and moved further to the rear in the Meteren area where daily parades were carried out under company commanders. It was felt to be important to keep soldiers as occupied as possible and the parade was a way of making sure that kit was in good order and gave the men lots to keep them employed working on their uniforms, rifles and other equipment, ensuring that it was in good shape and in full working order. It also allowed good observation of the state of the officers and men and it was during this time that some men were sent home for a variety of reasons with Capt Fanning, 2/Lt Noble and 2/Lt Kevin "invalided to the UK." Also Pte. W. Gill proceeded to base as he was, "unfit to carry out the duties of an efficient soldier."

It was a regular occurrence for the battalion to march from one area to another. When this is observed in detail, it is amazing how fit and hardy these men were. Towards the latter end of March, the Tenth Inniskillings carried out some endurance marching and it should be noted that they were wearing heavy army boots and, although probably not carrying their full kit, they would still have had to carry a lot of their personal kit and of course their rifles. On March 20th they left the Meteren Area and marched to Morbecque taking up billets in the town. This was a total distance of ten miles. The next day they marched an incredible 18 miles in a snowstorm over road surfaces that were uneven, muddy and slippy! On 22nd they arrived in Acquin and throughout the march endured very bad weather with snow, hail and rain most of the way, marching a distance of ten miles. On their arrival when they were soaked through to the skin they had little in the way of drying their uniform for the next day or the luxury of a bath and were up early next morning practising for an attack.

A more relaxed time was spent between March 25th-31st with the men training hard for Brigade sports. In the most popular event, boxing, Cpl McClay from A Coy won the Lightweight championship with L/Cpl. Orr from B Coy runner up in the Featherweight competition. The battalion runners won the relay race and No. 5 Platoon were runners up in the musketry competition where they beat the 9th Battalion but were narrowly defeated by the 11th Battalion. Where other sports days back in civilian life may have had a novelty race, a grim event, which was also eagerly contested by the different battalions, was the stretcher-bearer race.

The Battalion returned to the trenches on April 14th, 1917 at Kemmel. The relief was carried out after dark as the lines were in direct view of the Germans in the Spanbroek Sector. Even small groups of men attracted artillery fire, never mind two battalions on the move. During this stint, the enemy was uncannily quiet. For the three days the Derrys manned this sector there was virtually none of the usual enemy activity. On April 18th as dusk was falling, a man was seen at around 7pm running from shell hole to shell hole. It was a German running towards the Derrys' trenches. A trench mortar NCO fired at him and the German was seen to be wounded. He turned and made his way back to his own lines. Before he had reached the safety of his own trench, some of the Battalion fired at him and he fell. After some deliberation, it was assumed that the German was giving himself up, so a patrol was sent out at 9.30pm to the spot where he had fallen, but he had disappeared.

The next day was also astonishingly quiet and, at 9pm, a patrol was sent out armed with what must have been the most unusual weapon carried by an Inniskilling Fusilier - bottles with messages in them inviting the Germans to give themselves up. The theory was that the man was possibly a fore runner for a party of Germans who wanted to surrender. The bottles were tossed into the German trench probably to the disgust of the patrol who would possibly have preferred them to be Mills bombs.

On April 20th, a German made his way across and surrendered to A Company. After being interrogated by an interpreter he said that eight of his comrades would come across if he could get a signal to them. He then left the British lines and tried to fetch his comrades but lost his way in the mayhem of no-man's-land and had to come back. He tried once more, but the Germans fired on him making his effort futile. That was the end of the war for him and as the Derrys were being relieved from the front line, Jerry was being sent to Brigade Headquarters. He would spend the next twenty months in safety as a prisoner of war.

Many of the ordinary ranks who stood out as 'officer material' were sent to Britain to officer cadet courses. On successful completion of these the candidate was commissioned as an officer. Sergeant Alfie Bogle was one of the leading NCOs in the Battalion right from its formation and in April he returned to the Battalion as a Second Lieutenant. The men under his command found him to be just as popular an officer as he had been a sergeant and treated him with the respect he had earned.

After their quiet stint, the Battalion spent its time out of the trenches doing working parties in preparation for a big attack. The enemy's aircraft were very active. Incredible though it seems, some of the local population still went about their business on the land just behind the trenches. The dangers however, were ever present for them as well.

Jim Donaghy:-
"In the mornings we used to watch in the distance an old farmer drive his little wagon up a track behind our lines. It was pulled by a horse and in front of it walked two cows that he was bringing in for milking. His dog walked beside him and it was a lovely peaceful scene. One morning, one of our aircraft flew low over our front lines and as usual Jerry opened up with anti-aircraft fire. He used to fire quite heavy shells at our planes and everyone used to get annoyed at our planes for causing these shells exploding in the air above our lines. On this occasion one of the shells was a dud and it didn't explode in the air. Instead it travelled on exploding to the rear, hitting the cart and killing the old man."

Nights could be a frenzy of activity in the front trenches. Men were on guard; there were night patrols to be carried out along with working parties repairing trenches that had been damaged by shelling during the day and, of course, the cursed wiring party.

Jim Donaghy:-

"One night Bobby Reid, myself and some others were out on a night patrol which was uneventful. We were in the process of taking off our gum-boots at the entrance of our dug-out. Bobby Taylor had gone down to collect rations from the reserve line. Tommy Parkhill was returning from a working party which had just finished mending a damaged section of trench and we were now assembled together outside the dugout waiting to go in. Parkhill was the first in and went over to the corner he normally slept in. All of a sudden he gave a big squeal as a huge rat ran over his hand. It was now perched up beside the only light we had in the dugout, a stump of a candle in a cut down jam tin. I stood to the side of the dugout, Taylor was behind me holding the sandbag of rations. It contained two little loaves, tins of jam, bully beef, tea and sugar and as the big rat made a bolt for the door, he hit it with the rations and completely mushed it. We were ripping at him – but we ate the rations anyway."

From April 20th to the Battle of Messines in June, the 10th Inniskillings experienced almost daily shelling and aircraft were particularly active on both sides. They soon realised that it was of the utmost importance to make sure that enemy aircraft were not allowed to fly over their trench lines as they always relayed what they had observed or photographed back to headquarters who informed the artillery of the targets to be bombarded. One plane gave such valuable information that the rear lines accommodation was so heavily and accurately shelled that the battalion had to leave the comfort of billets to sleep rough in a wood well away from all buildings. On another occasion, the day after a plane had a good look at the front line, a machine gun post where the gunners were sleeping in a large dugout was hit by carefully aimed gas shells. All the gunners were gassed or wounded but two men from A Coy went immediately to the gunners' aid and showed great gallantry in rescuing the gun crew. These men were Pte. T Gilmour who had repeatedly shown a good example in devotion to duty and Pte. R. F. Galway.

[1] The Saxon regiments normally preferred as little hassle as possible.
[2] Nearly 75 years later Jim Donaghy showed me the small well worn, sepia photograph of Jack Cochrane that he had kept as a cherished memento of a great friend. I copied the photograph, enlarged and enhanced the detail so that Jim's fading eyesight could see it clearly. When he looked at it, it was the only time through all my interviews that he was vexed.

Chapter 18
The Battle of Messines Ridge

On the flat, marshy terrain of Belgium, any feature which rose above the rest of the landscape proved of great military advantage to the side which held it. In most cases it was the Germans who held the high ground. Such was the case at the Messines and Wytschaete Ridges. These overlooked Ypres to the north and Ploegsteert Wood to the south, giving the Germans excellent observation posts. During daylight every movement of men, guns and supplies could be monitored and this information relayed to German artillery. The high ridges also offered good machine gun positions from which many of the front British trenches knew that they were constantly being watched, as did those in command. Any attack would be difficult to organise without the Germans watching the preparations, thus ruining the element of surprise.

The plan adopted by General Sir Herbert Plumer, who was in command, was of an unusual nature. The crux of the plan was to blow the Germans off the ridge using twenty-one mines, dug deep under the German strongpoints and trenches.

Jim Donaghy:-

"In different parts of the line, miners worked day and night. Sometimes the Germans dug out from their lines and blew up the tunnels our chaps were digging. There was many's a fierce battle underground. The miners were from coal mines in England. We had to help them in many of our working parties, passing sandbags, carrying props or getting rid of the earth that had been dug from the tunnels. On one occasion Sergeant Bobby Hamilton and Willie Davidson from Dungiven and myself had shot a few partridges in the rear lines. We asked the miners to cook them in their cookhouse for us. Boys but they were a lively bunch and full of fun!

It was lovely countryside and at this stage in the war, the land towards the rear lines was still in good order compared to other areas we had been at. We were doing three days in the front line and three in reserve. Most of our work in reserve was fusing grenades and other working parties in preparation for the attack. One evening we were making our way along Kingsway trench and were sheltered from view of the Germans as we were going downhill. Patches of wheat and corn were still growing in an area we called the Farm. As we rounded the corner, we spotted a cock and a hen pheasant as they ran into the corn. We had our rifles slung over our shoulders and they were loaded. As the Section surrounded them, I warned them to be careful as they might come out running or flying and to make sure not to fire in the direction of the huts, (these had just been built by the Derrys). When we flushed them out everyone opened fire. I shot one of them with my .303, just nicking it on the back of the neck. Lieutenant Middleton bought it from me for twenty francs, just enough for a good night in Dranoutre! The area around Messines was thick with game."

The artillery started their programme of shelling the enemy lines and strongpoints on May 31st and this continued day and night. The Ulster Division held a front line sector just over a

Bobby Reid and Jim Donaghy in the rear lines behind Messines.

Photo: Author

mile to the south of Wytschaete. They had the 16th Irish Division on their left. The divisional artillery was reinforced with more artillery pieces up to 15 inch calibre.

Jim Donaghy:-

"A week before the attack, I was transferred to the 109th Trench Mortar Battery as they were in need of NCOs. I was given a bit of instruction on the use of the gun. It was simple to operate. You dropped the mortar into the barrel and it hit the bottom. This detonated an explosive charge – a bit like a 12 bore cartridge and this propelled the mortar. A good gun team could have seven shells in the air before the first one hit the ground! They were ideal for hitting the German trenches and machine gun posts."

The 109 Trench Mortar Battery was a prestigious unit to be in after one of their officers, Captain E.N.F. Bell of the 9th Inniskillings, won the Victoria Cross on July 1st 1916. He had shot the gunner of a German machine gun which had pinned men down. He attacked three times throwing trench mortar bombs. When he ran out of bombs he started shooting at the enemy with a rifle as he stood on the parapet of their trench.

The trench mortar batteries had another name – 'The Suicide Clubs.' This was due to their habit of attracting fire from the enemy whenever they operated.

Jim Donaghy:-

"We came up and did our strafe nearly every afternoon. We varied the time and would blarge off up to one thousand rounds at times. We weren't too popular sometimes as the men manning the trenches beside us knew that there was a good chance that the Germans would retaliate; but we didn't care."

Newport Dugouts at Messines.

Photo: Captain McKenzie Collection

125

Jim Donaghy:-

"The lads in the Trench Mortar Battery were a great bunch from different units of the 109th Brigade. I got very friendly with four corporals from the 14th Rifles, all decent good-living chaps. We were all young NCOs compared to an old sergeant in the battery. We got on with him so well that we used to call him 'Father.' There were some real characters in it too. One wee chap from Coleraine loved the bottle. When the Orderly Officer was giving a tot of rum when we were coming in from working parties you would find him at the front and the back of the queue."

Training for the attack was thorough to say the least. A huge scale model of the front that they would have to attack through had been constructed at the rear, near Locre. It contained all the important features: strongpoints, topographical features, streams, woods, and was studied intensively by the officers and senior ranks.

At 5pm on June 5th the Derrys took part in a practice attack along with the rest of 109 Brigade in the Berthern area, returning to camp around 10.30pm. The Battalion then marched up to Wakefield Huts nearer the front line on June 6th, arriving at 8am. Once camp had been set up the rest of the afternoon was spent resting.

During the evening, they were issued with additional stores, bombs, wirecutters and – amongst other things blue and yellow flags which were the colours of the Derrys and were issued four to a platoon. These were to be displayed on rifles to indicate to senior officers and artillery observers the progress the Battalion was making.

Each individual checked his fighting kit which was later also inspected by his platoon commander: one hundred and twenty rounds of ammunition, two flares, gas masks, two Mills grenades, full water bottle, field dressing, mess tins, iron rations and one day's rations, two oranges, chocolate, candle, matches and solidified alcohol.

Men in the bombing section carried fifty rounds of ammunition in a bandolier and three grenades in each pouch if they were throwers. If they were carriers, they carried the same as the throwers but had twelve grenades.

The two men assigned to each Lewis gun carried revolvers as sidearms and a spare parts bag.

Haversacks and greatcoats were handed over to the quarter-master to ease the route march. As the Battalion marched up en route to the assembly trenches, the Germans shelled all round Kemmel Hill with heavy shrapnel. In the assembly trenches a hot meal was issued and it was here that the Derrys suffered their first casualties of the attack when a shell hit D Company's trench, killing one man and wounding several of their Lewis gun team.

But now the Tenth, along with the rest of 109 Brigade, were ready for their part in the attack. Jim, now in the Trench Mortar Battery, was ready for his.

"My gun's job was to knock out machine gun positions on untouched parts of the ridge. We knew we had to knock them out or else it could have turned into another 1st of July."

On June 7th, 1917, the attack on Messines ridge started. The mines containing one million pounds of ammonal explosives went off at 3.10am. The noise was so loud it was heard and felt in London. Immediately after the mines exploded, 11th Inniskillings and 14th Rifles attacked, closely following a creeping artillery barrage. They were supported by 9th and 10th Inniskillings.

Jim Donaghy:-

"It was beyond description. The noise and the flashes were terrific. It seemed as if the whole earth shook, just like an earthquake. You thought the earth was going to come up round you and collapse. The sky was filled with huge clouds of different coloured smoke."

Spanbroekmolen mine detonated fifteen seconds later than the rest and many 16th and 36th Division soldiers were killed by the tons of rubble falling to the ground as they were caught out in the open air after going over the top[1].

Jim Donaghy:-

"Once we had composed ourselves we fired away with the Stokes Mortar at the German machine gun posts.

A Stokes Mortar
Photo: Imperial War Museum, Q6405

I suppose in a way we thought it was going to be another 1st of July. That was until we saw the mines going off. The artillery and trench mortars knocked out the machine guns at an early stage. Before we got started, the Germans knocked out a lot of our artillery. There was a small ridge behind our trench. At the top there were some of the artillery's forward observers, spotting where their shots were falling and sending back information by phone to the guns. German shells killed some of them and they rolled down the bank into the trench beside us."

The first German line was taken by 109th Brigade with little resistance. There was more opposition at the second line but the third line put up a strong fight.

Jim Donaghy:-

"The prisoners started to come up to us in droves, shaking like mad, as we were advancing behind the infantry. There were hundreds of them and we waved them past us. They were taken to the rear by escorting parties."

The Tenth met stubborn resistance at the third line and were held up by machine-gun fire. They were helped by their comrades in the 9th Inniskillings. Once the infantry had taken the second line, several tanks pushed forward to the aid of the infantry. They were ideal for silencing machine-gun posts. One particular machine-gun position was holding the Derrys up in their advance, but wasn't spotted by the tank's commander. A sergeant from the Tenth tried to draw the machine-gun in question to the attention of the tank but to no avail. Then, while the tank was moving, he hauled himself on top of and hammered on it until he attracted the attention of one of the crew who engaged and destroyed the enemy position[2].

Jim Donaghy:-

"We were then sent up to a wood to give supporting fire to the Brigade. After we had been in this location for a few days, we were relieved and on the way back we saw the craters. They were massive."

Colonel Macrory described the scene of devastation in his diary as he walked over the battlefield the next day.

"It was the best day I have had in the war... It was the most marvellous sight. I went all over the battlefield yesterday, it is still littered with bodies and debris. The mine craters are wonderful. They are about 100 yds across and 30 yds deep... corpses all round, half buried, some flattened out like cardboard. Further on you find one of our men and a Bosch, both dead in a bayonet grip. Wytschaete is only a heap of bricks, nowhere more than a few feet high. The stench is horrible there as the enemy's dead (men and horses, results of our bombardment) have been lying about there for days. The whole country for 2 miles back is nothing but enormous shell holes and smashed trenches and dugouts, bloodstained and horrible fragments of humanity. Certainly this battle was the most marvellous and dreadful sight I have ever seen."

The remains of Wytschaete village, June 10th, 1917.
It was captured by the 36th Ulster and 16th Irish Divisions.

Photo: Imperial War Museum, Q5485.

The Battalion had casualties of four killed and one officer and 59 other ranks wounded. The Ulster Division captured 1,239 prisoners and many machine-guns and artillery pieces, all as a result of a careful and thoroughly planned attack, but also due to their bravery and courage.

The objective was achieved: the ridge had been taken and the high ground was no longer in German hands.

In a letter sent home to a friend of Sgt McCombe, who was killed in the battle, one of the Warrant Officers wrote:-

"The Ulster Division have behaved in a manner second to none. Our battalion has done fine work, indeed. The positions we took were thought to be impregnable, but with our artillery behind and our infantry leading we reached our objective with very few casualties. A German Brigade General, who was captured by one of the 10th, said the Irishmen came with such dash and gallantry that he was completely taken unawares, and he described the attack as one of the finest he had seen in his experience. When the mines went up one would have thought the earth had opened up, but this was only part of it. The next instant you could see the boys climbing over the parapet and rushing for their nearest opponent. Down the Germans went, for our boys had not much time to take prisoners. This was left to others for that duty. The boys are still in action, and have never lost an inch of the ground captured, although the enemy used his best troops against them in counter attacks. The Irish Division displayed great gallantry, and are thoroughly worthy of all that has been said about them. It was very sad about Sergeant McCombe. He was a fine soldier, and one that cannot well be replaced. It was when leading his platoon into action that he met his death. His officer had been wounded, and he at once rushed forward and took over command. Such deeds like these are worthy of the highest honour, because it happened at a time when we were being pressed. Such pluck and daring as shown by his fine example encouraged his men so much that they would have fought to the last man, and I think it can be truly said that battles are won by those who fall."

[1] Not all the mines blew up. Of the 21 only 19 exploded with another exploding when struck by lightning in 1955.

[2] This incident highlighted the need for communication between tanks and infantry and a system to communicate with tanks was implemented. Even today's tanks have a telephone at the rear so that infantry can communicate with the tank.

Photo:Imperial War Museum

Men of the 10th Inniskillings and 14th Rifles celebrate and show their souvenirs after the battle of Messines.

10th Inniskillings pretending to be surrendering Germans
with a variety of kit taken as souvenirs after Messines.

Men of the 10th Inniskillings show their souvenirs after the Battle of Messines.

Celebrations after the Battle of Messines.

MESSINES LINE ADVANCED

GREAT GUN ACTIVITY IN YPRES AND ST. QUENTIN SECTORS.

RAIDS AT VERMELLES AND ARMENTIERES.

ITALIANS ATTACK IN A STORM.

PASS, MOUNTAIN, AND 512 PRISONERS TAKEN.

Chapter 19
Home on Leave

Jim Donaghy:-

"Approximately a week after the Messines attack I was informed that I was going home on leave. I had applied for leave before but this was the first one that I had been granted in the two years since joining up.

No one knew that I was coming so when I arrived at my home they couldn't believe it and were jumping for joy."

Many of the people back in Britain had no idea of the real conditions on the Western Front. Many told their parents that things were exaggerated and weren't as bad as they were made out to be. Others gave a totally false impression of life in the trenches and made it out to be an heroic adventure.

Jim Donaghy:-

"When my relations asked me what it was like I told them the truth. They had a fair idea what it was like and grimly accepted it."

Being back home for the first time in two years was a most welcome change. Sleeping in a clean, dry bed, home cooking and the quiet, peaceful life in sleepy Drumahoe made the thought of going back to the front all the worse. All too soon leave was virtually over.

Jim Donaghy:-

"The day before I was to return to the front my aunt had organised a picnic up on Lisdillon Hill near our home. The weather was good and some of the family travelled in my uncle's wee car, but some of us went on bicycles. We had a good time but on the way home, as we were coming down the hill, the handlebars of the bicycle that I was riding caught against one of the little baskets on the bike and I was thrown on to the ground landing on my face. My cheek and temple were badly cut and I had hurt my knee. My uniform was damaged and I lost buttons off my tunic. When I reached home they bandaged me up and repaired my uniform.

Jim Donaghy's family home during the war at Faughan Bridge, Drumahoe (1991).

Photo: Author

I woke up the next morning stiff and sore but, while getting dressed, I found that I couldn't get my tunic on as there was a huge lump under my right arm on the ribs, presumably where the handlebars had dug into me. I travelled into Londonderry and reported to Ebrington Barracks for my joining instructions but the army doctor told me that I was too ill to return to active service due to the accident, and also, I had scabies! Scabies, just like lice and trenchfoot, was a common complaint for us in the trenches. I knew just before I came on leave that I had scabies but I didn't want a doctor to examine me as I would have spent a short time in hospital in France and lost my leave. The doctor rang the appropriate authorities informing them of what had happened and I was sent to hospital. I was there for approximately five weeks and during this time I was looked after by two young nurses that I had known very well before I joined up, so it was a fairly pleasant stay.

When I was well enough to return to Belgium I had a final trip out to my home. My relations and some friends saw me off from the station. It was hateful going back. When I reached the ferry, it was full of Belfast girls that worked in the munitions factories, returning to their jobs on the mainland and drunk young naval ratings full of high spirits, which made it worse."

Little did Jim realise how lucky he had been, or the horrors he had missed.

Londonderry around the time of the Great War.

Photo: David Bigger/McDonald Collection

Chapter 20
Passchendaele

There was a delay between the advance at Messines and the next attacks in the Ypres area, mainly due to the French units attached to the British not being ready in time. During this seven week period, the Germans had reinforced their lines using concrete pillboxes and thick belts of barbed wire.

General Plumer, who had painstakingly planned his attacks on the Wytschaete and Messines ridges, was replaced by Sir Hubert Gough. Gough set his objectives far into the enemy lines, without considering the terrain that the men would have to assault across. He expected units to take objectives several miles into enemy territory, territory that had been ploughed up by the action of 14,000 guns. This produced a landscape which resembled the surface of the moon, except that the craters had been filled with water as the shelling had destroyed the drainage system in an already marshy part of Belgium.

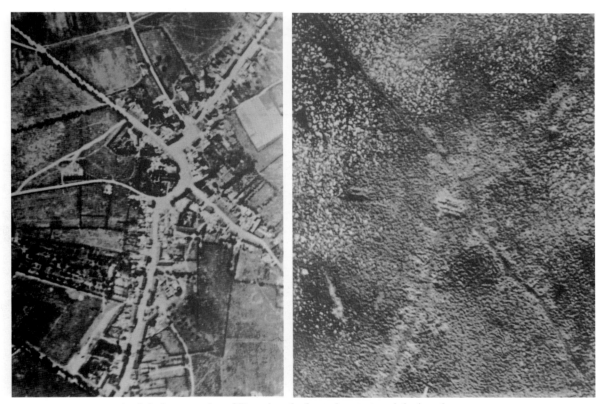

Aerial photographs of Passchendaele at the start and during the war.

Photo: Imperial War Museum, Q42918A

At 3.50am on July 31st, nine Divisions attacked. At the start things looked favourable and the British units advanced two miles into enemy territory. Unfortunately in the late afternoon, as the Germans were counter-attacking, it started to rain torrentially and this turned the ground into a quagmire. By the end of the day the British troops had been driven back to within five hundred yards of their original starting place.

Men of the Ulster Division bring supplies by mule up to the front line, July 31st 1917.

On August 2nd, the attack was suspended. It rained heavily until the 4th followed by bright sunshine on the 5th, but the land was still liquid mud and water-filled shell holes. On the night of August 7th, the 10th Inniskillings moved up to the front line on their way to the trenches in the Ypres salient. The Battalion had been in the rear lines for the previous six weeks. Now they were moving into a nightmare; the Ypres salient had always been a 'hot' area. To say that the breastworks were in a very poor condition after the heavy rain and continual enemy shelling was an understatement to say the least. There were no trenches as such. If traditional trenches were dug they just filled up with deep water and mud, and so the defensive structures had to be raised but they didn't afford the same level of protection as traditional trenches. Men had to quickly learn to keep their heads down at all times. The shelling was particularly intense by the Germans and was mostly of heavy calibre high explosive. The British guns were also firing in the opposite direction and the air was filled with the acrid smell of battle and the haunting, shrieking sound of artillery shells coming from different directions. Once again the 10th Inniskillings were going to have to endure hell... and Passchendaele would forever be remembered by all those who were there as synonymous with mud, suffering and death.

Men on the front line at Passchendaele

Photo: Imperial War Museum, E Aus 1146

At 1am, as the Battalion relieved the 15th Rifles from their stint in the front line, the enemy was very active and the Allied heavy artillery was retaliating. Moving into the front line was an arduous task carrying heavy kit through the deep mud and water filled shell holes. Suddenly, without warning, the Germans used shells containing their new secret weapon and one which would become the most feared weapon of the War – "mustard gas". This was in liquid form in the shell and was dispersed as a splattered spray as the shells impacted on the ground and was a particularly horrific weapon. Not only did it affect the lungs and eyes, but, unlike chlorine or phosgene gases which had been used before, the mustard gas made the skin come up in huge blisters, especially on sweaty, perspiring skin and the wet linings of the lungs. For phosgene and chlorine attacks, gas-masks were a fairly effective countermeasure if they were applied quickly and fitted properly. However, this was not the case with mustard gas as any exposed skin was affected. In this attack some men were heavily exposed to the chemical and Cpl. W. Adams, Pte. H. Burnside and Pte. J. Colhoun died shortly after with Pte H. Campbell and Pte J. Leighton dying later from their wounds in the most excruciating pain. To the rest of their comrades, who tried to give them assistance in the dark, the sight which they witnessed through the foggy eye-pieces of their gas masks must have been both dreadful and horrifying. Twenty other ranks were also wounded by the gas and many of these casualties would suffer daily for the rest of their lives, even some of those who would be alive over seventy years later.

The next few days saw more men of the Tenth gassed. The tension and anxiety of the men must have been indescribable as they scrabbled in the mud for cover, as the roar of every shell heading in their direction could have been the harbinger of its impending arrival.

The total casualties for August 8th, were seven men killed, twenty other ranks gassed and eighteen wounded. Most of the casualties came from B Company.

August 9th was a day of similar enemy action and the battalion had two killed, six gassed and fourteen wounded. Next day there was intense activity on both sides. It was the day of the attack. The Battalion watched several dogfights and two British planes were forced down.

Just as the Battalion was forming up for the attack, between 4 and 5am, the enemy anticipated their actions and subjected the packed trenches to a terrific bombardment. As a result, fifteen men were killed and many others badly wounded in the Derrys alone. One of the most popular officers in the Derrys was killed during the bombardment – Second Lieutenant Alfie Bogle, the great boxing champion.

Captain Patton, padre to the Derrys, wrote to Bogle's parents,

"We were given a difficult job to do last week, perhaps the most difficult we have ever had to do, and our fellows responded to the call as nobly as ever, though at terrible sacrifice to themselves. Alfie was killed in one of the heaviest bombardments of the War, leading his men in the front line."

2/Lt Alfie Bogle

Photo: Jack Bogle

August 11th was quieter in comparison. Colonel Macrory, who had left Major Knox in command during his absence, returned to the Battalion. Still the trenches held by the Battalion were under constant shellfire.

During the day a remarkable event took place. A private from the Liverpool Irish came out of no-man's-land and into the defences held by the Derrys. He had been wounded and had wandered through no-man's-land since the attack on August 2nd and had survived the constant shelling, heavy rains, gas attacks and his wounds. He obtained food from the kits of dead lying unburied in no-man's-land [1].

Later in the day Lt. J.W. Drennan was wounded and died a short time later. Colonel Macrory, on his first day back from leave, was shot in the thigh by a German sentry when he and his batman, Davy Donaghy, lost their way when reconnoitering the area. Colonel Macrory thought that all was lost as he couldn't make his way back to the British lines through the shambles of no-man's-land. Donaghy however dragged him back to the Derrys' trenches and for his bravery was later presented with a gold watch by Colonel Macrory who however, would never command the battalion again [2].

Major Macrory who was rescued by Cpl David Donaghy,
who was later awarded the Military Medal for his actions in rescuing another officer in March 1918.

Photos: Jim Donaghy

The Tenth was relieved on August 12th by the 15th Rifles. They marched back to Vlamertinghe camp to recuperate after a traumatic stint at the front and at the same time prepare for the attack on August 16th – the Battle of Langemarck at Passchendaele.

THE BATTLE OF LANGEMARCK

The battalion was in support of 9th Inniskillings and 14th Rifles during the attack. The 36th Division had been sent in to hold the line captured by the 55th Division as they had to be withdrawn after suffering numerous casualties. The Ulster Division had the unenviable task of holding a line with little or no shelter. Re-supplying the forward units was virtually impossible as the parties had to cross a quagmire of waterfilled shellholes. During this time they were subjected to gas and bombing attacks, artillery fire and a stream of accurate machine-gun bullets from the Germans in their pillboxes. The only thing the Ulstermen could do was to approach the pill boxes and try to post a bomb through the gunslit. The men of 109 Brigade paid dearly in lives, holding a line of shell holes, mud and water. The dead lay in the trenches and in no-man's-land, many decomposing as they couldn't be taken back through the quagmire for burial. Many had sunk into the mud and here and there limbs stuck out, covered in flies in the heat of summer. The stench was awful.

Jim's colleagues in the Trench Mortar Battery had an easier time as the trench mortars could not be brought forward in the attack since they were too heavy to be carried over the soft, muddy landscape. The men of the Battery would later pay dearly for the privilege.

At the end of the day, 10th Inniskillings had one officer killed with sixty-three other ranks either killed, wounded or missing.

For those who fought there, Passchendaele would never be forgotten.

[1] This incredible story is fact. The information was taken from the 10th Inniskillings' War Diary which was written up immediately after the event. It was deemed so noteworthy that it is in the official diary entry at a time when the battalion had lost so many of its own men.

[2] Once Colonel Macrory had recovered from his wounds, he was advised not to return to the Battalion. There are several theories, one being the fact that he had a confrontation with a senior staff officer. The Battalion had been in the front line at Passchendaele and as a result were exhausted and caked in mud. As they marched past the officer he informed Macrory that he would inspect the Battalion in two hours. The Colonel told him in no uncertain terms that it was out of the question but that he could inspect them once they had twelve hours rest. Another explanation for his failure to resume command was that at the time he was wounded Macrory, was in possession of sensitive and secret documents which, if captured, would have been valuable to the enemy. Possession of such documents in this sector of the battlefield was a court martial offence.

Lt J. W. Drennan died of wounds August 2nd 1917.

Photo: Philip O'Doherty

Corporal Willie Adams who died a horrific death from mustard gas poisoning, August 8th 1917. He was a brother of Corporal Davy Adams MM who was killed on July 1st 1916.

Photo: Author

Chapter 21
Trench Mortar Tragedy

Jim arrived back to the 36th Division after his period in hospital as the Ulstermen were just in the final stages of the action at Passchendaele. The landscape which his comrades had to attack across and hold was a shock to him. Old familiar faces from the Derrys were again missing, either dead or wounded. There was another tragedy yet in store for Jim.

Jim Donaghy:-

"When I got back, I found that nearly all my colleagues in the Trench Mortar Battery had been killed when one of the captured German dugouts they were in exploded (August 16th 1917). Over half of the Battery were killed, including most of the officers. The only survivor from the dugout was Lieutenant Norman Lowden. He had an altercation with the rest of the members of the Trench Mortar Battery and refused to stay in the dugout with them and had been outside. The dugout may have been booby-trapped or hit by a 'Minnie' but the effects of the explosion were so devastating that Lowden wouldn't sleep in a dugout after this[1]. The NCOs that I had been friends with from the 14th Rifles were also dead. Those lads from Belfast, you wouldn't have got a better bunch – all good living lads."

The Derrys had been relieved on August 17th by the 15th Rifles and were taken by buses to Winnezeele to recuperate after their tremendous efforts.

Jim Donaghy:-

"The division was to get some rest after Passchendaele. We were totally amazed they had us out at 7.00am with full kit doing manoeuvres day after day. Imagine, after all that fighting, and with the men exhausted, they had us doing manoeuvres!"

In September, Lieutenant Colonel A.K. Lord Farnham was given command of the Derrys as Colonel Macrory was in hospital with severe wounds to his leg. Lord Farnham had been in the North Irish Horse and was an Ulsterman from County Cavan.

Due to losses in the Trench Mortar Battery some of the Derrys were transferred to it. Second Lieutenant J.T.M. Bennett and five other ranks were detailed to it. As Colonel Macrory was no longer with the battalion, Davy Donaghy, the orderly who had saved him, found himself 'unemployed' and transferred to 109 Trench Mortar Battery[2].

A few days after the appointment of Lord Farnham as the new Colonel of the 10th Inniskillings the Derrys' first commanding officer Lieutenant Colonel, Ross Smyth, was killed back in Ireland.

Jim Donaghy:-

"Colonel Ross Smyth was killed in a driving accident at the end of Daly's Brae, outside Drumahoe, on his way home to Ardmore from his work in Ebrington Barracks. He had a great big pony and trap and was always driving about in it at full speed. He overturned it on the corner and was killed as a result."

Ross Smyth was fifty-five when he died. He was buried in Glendermott Parish Church at Altnagelvin with military honours and he and his son John are commemorated within the church by brass plaques.

On November 5th Sergeant Bobby Hamilton was promoted to Company Sergeant Major due to his excellent efforts within the Battalion, especially in action. A far cry from some other warrant officers in other units.

Jim Donaghy:-

> *"The quartermaster of the Trench Mortar Battery, Sergeant Major Kennedy, was a bit 'windy' and wouldn't come up near the trenches at all. On one occasion, I was in the trenches and my uniform was in a terrible state. It was so bad that one of my big toes was sticking out of the sole of my boot. As I was going on a course on gas warfare, I met Kennedy at the Headquarters of the Trench Mortar Battery. He wouldn't give me any new kit as it was too much bother for him. 'It'll do you rightly,' was all he would say. On my way out I met the second in command and I was so annoyed that I told him what had happened. He went in and gave Kennedy a good dressing down, so much so that he gave me a complete new uniform."*

[1] Lieutenant Norman Lowden was later killed in action on March 21st, 1918.
[2] David Donaghy would save the life of 2/Lt J.T.M. Bennett in March 1918 and was awarded the Military Medal.

Chapter 22
Battle of Cambrai November 20th-27th, 1917

After the Somme campaign, the Germans had withdrawn a few miles to the Hindenburg line in the spring of 1917. This was regarded by the enemy as being impregnable. Not only had it numerous underground bunkers which would be unaffected by artillery and the usual machine gun posts holding prime fields of fire, but it also had the most formidable belts of barbed wire, some as thick as fifty metres wide. These were so large that they would not have been affected by shelling, and attacking troops would have been held up in their advance to fall victims to the German machine guns. It was decided that the problem of the wire could be overcome with the use of tanks, which could pull the masses of wire along with them until they snapped, or crush them creating gaps for the infantry to attack through.

Jim Donaghy:-

"A few days before the attack a few of us were walking along when one of the section shouted, 'What the Hell's that down there?' We had a closer look and found that it was five or six tanks waiting until the day of the attack.

Cambrai was to be a surprise attack. Tanks were to be used in large numbers for the first time. There was to be no barrage before but instead there would be a hurricane bombardment by our Stokes Mortars and massed machine guns. I was sent up with a chap called Billy Mayne, from the 9th Inniskillings, and we were sent out to a position in front of the Battalion to cover the attack. At night we dug a narrow slit trench beside a sunken road for the gun with a wee dugout to give us some shelter as it was freezing cold. We were out there for days and many's a time I thought how dangerous it was. Not only were we out in no-man's-land but our trench was unsupported so a shell landing nearby could have caused the walls to have collapsed and buried you. There was no escape from it. Once you were out there, that was you during daylight hours. Working parties came up with ammunition and food at night. We dug holes in the bank at the side of the road for the hundreds of mortar rounds and camouflaged them. We had to be ready for the alarm sounding the attack. The attack was to start on the right as the other units had to come up in the line with us before our lines attacked.

The Germans were in strong positions, but our objective was to bombard the machine gun posts on a slag heap just as the Tenth went over the top followed by the 9th and 11th Inniskillings. The French had been building a canal, called the Canal du Nord, just before the war and this big mound had been made from the earth that had been excavated from the bed of the canal. The Germans had turned it into a fortress with barbed wire, trenches and machine gun posts. My gun's job was to knock out two machine gun positions on either side of the sunken road."

The attack was on November 20th, 1917. The 10th Inniskillings went into the attack with 27 officers and 430 other ranks. They advanced with the first wave of the attack, followed by 11th Inniskillings and then the 9th. The plan was to advance, not across open ground as in the past, but by fighting along, clearing and then advancing up along the German communication

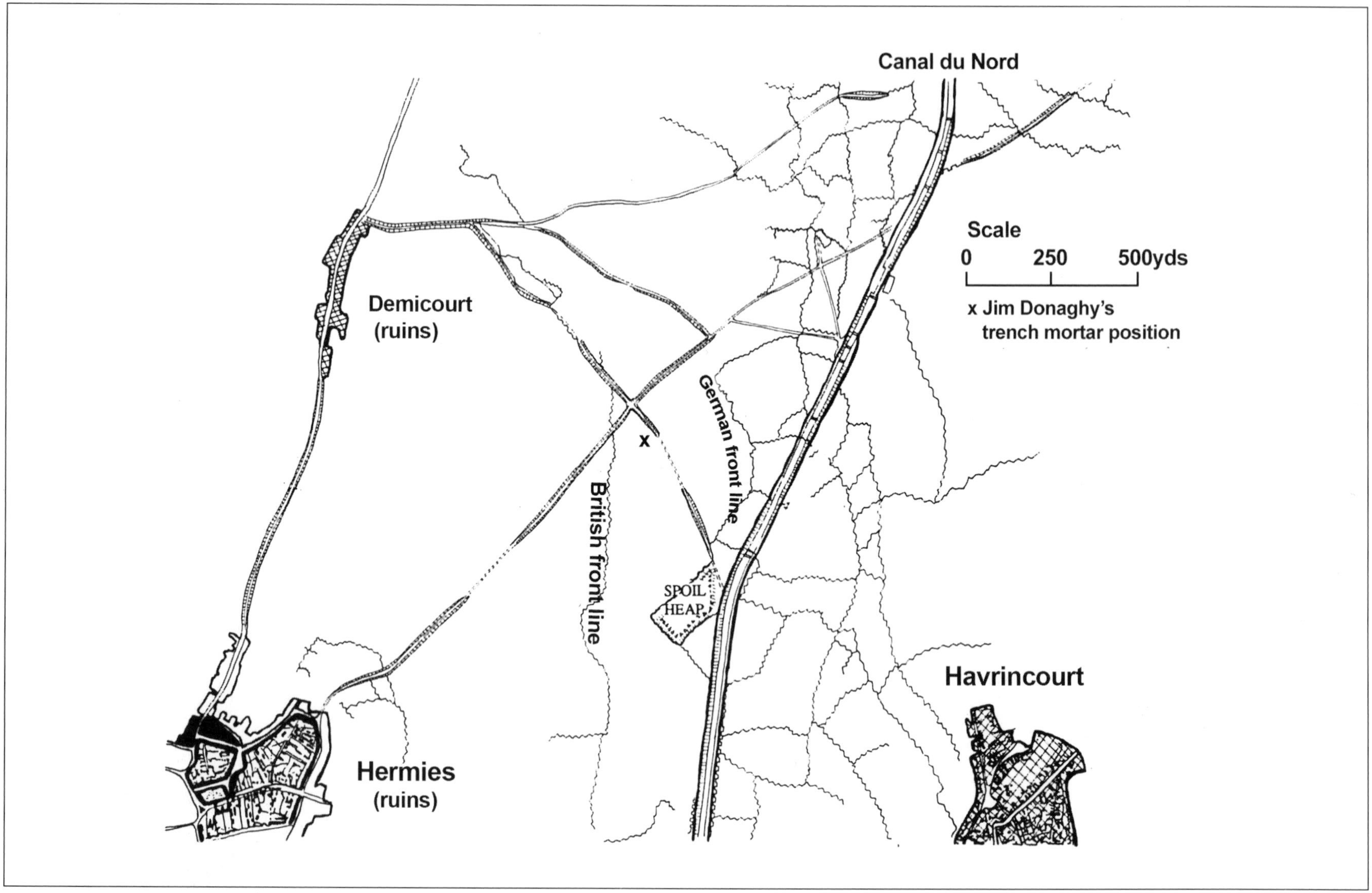

Map of the front-line area of 36th Division at Cambrai.

Canal du Nord

Scale

0   250   500yds

x Jim Donaghy's
trench mortar position

German front line

SPOIL HEAP

British front line

Havrincourt

Demicourt
(ruins)

Hermies
(ruins)

trenches, rather than through the trench lines. This would give greater protection from small-arms and artillery fire compared with a straight forward advance across open country. Another feature of the attack was that there was to be no set artillery bombardment in the lead up to the attack.

In the sector held by 109 Brigade, there were to be no tanks assigned. Instead their strategy involved the seizing of the spoil heap in front of the canal to use as an observation, machine gun and trench mortar position to cover the attack. The attack on the left flank, held by 109 Brigade, was to start two hours later than the attack to the north, using this to divert the enemy's attention. The essence of the attack would have to be speed.

On November 20th, 1917, three hundred and eighty one tanks, followed closely by infantry, attacked along a six mile front and, at 6.20am, one thousand guns opened up with an intense whirlwind bombardment on the German lines. In the sector held by the Derrys, the hurricane bombardment by the heavy artillery on the slag heap commenced instantaneously at 8.30am. The Trench Mortar Battery pounded the front trenches and machine gun posts and after four minutes, switched to other targets. The Derrys rushed the position and, after a short but fierce fight, captured it. The artillery started its programme of hitting pre-arranged targets on its advance up the German lines.

Jim Donaghy:-
> *"When the artillery started, we opened up with the trench mortars. Our gun was firing at the machine gun posts. We knocked out one quite quickly but the other took longer to disable."*

As dugouts were cleared they had signs saying 'Mopped Up' put at their entrances and a guard was left to take care of anyone emerging. (A lesson learned from July 1st 1916).

Inniskilling Fusiliers advancing over the German second line at Cambrai.

Photo: Imperial War Museum, Q3174

Battle of Cambrai, 1917. The spoil heap, which was composed of the earth removed from the Canal Du Nord during its construction can be seen in the distance. (German POWs are in the foreground)

Photo: Imperial War Museum, Q3781.

Inniskilling Fusiliers of 109 Brigade moving forward during the latter stages of the Battle of Cambrai

Photo: Imperial War Museum, Q3177.

A knocked-out British tank after the Battle of Cambrai

Photo: Imperial War Museum, Q56824.

Eventually, the Derrys took their objective at 9.30am in the middle of a blizzard after clearing over 1.5 miles of the front line trenches of the Hindenburg line.

Considering the gains of the morning, the battalion had very light casualties of one man killed, and one officer and forty five other ranks wounded.

Jim Donaghy:-

"Several parties returning told us that there were two machine gun posts just up the road (the ones we had knocked out) and the German machine-gunners were chained to their guns so they couldn't abandon their posts. They were all over six foot tall. We didn't get a chance to see them as we were hauling the guns along and I was carrying mortar rounds in a harness.

Towards the end of the battle of Cambrai, we moved up into a wood captured from Jerry. We were giving covering fire to attacking units and we held the wood for three days before being relieved by the Guards. That night there was the most awesome thunderstorm. We were exhausted and as the Trench Mortar Battery made its way back to reserve, the rain was lashing us and the lightning was flashing away. I had the job of carrying the big barrel of our trench mortar and I was terrified of it being struck by lightning. The rain was falling in torrents, making the ground we were crossing in the dark very slippery. Some of my mates had fallen into flooded shell holes. If it hadn't been for the other members of the battery seeing or hearing them and then going to their rescue, they would almost certainly have drowned.

On the way back to our ruined village, we came across a YMCA canteen which was a wee hut in a hollow, dug into a bank. You have no idea how glad we were to see it and get some shelter for a while from the rain. We were immediately given a cup of hot tea by the Reverend Corkey. He had been out in France before and had lost an arm. You were always glad to see the YMCA."

The Battle of Cambrai was heralded initially in Britain as a great victory by the ringing of church bells in London. Eventually, after a German counter attack ten days later, the battle ended in stalemate.

Jim Donaghy:-

"Shortly after the Cambrai attack we were sleeping in tents in reserve. It was bitterly cold and wet and there had been snow. I remember lying in my tent with a very bad fever. I must have went unconscious as the next thing I remembered was being carried on a stretcher into a train which took me to hospital."

Chapter 23
Trench Fever

Jim Donaghy:-

"I was sent to the American hospital and convalescence camp in the little seaside resort of Etretat, on the coast just north of Le Havre. The Americans had taken over the whole village and were using the hotel as a hospital. I was diagnosed as having Trench Fever[1]. This was similar to a very severe strain of influenza. They were doing tests on me and a group of other soldiers from different units as, at this stage, doctors didn't know the cause of the illness. I was in a room with three South Africans and a chap from Yorkshire. I spent Christmas here and was in hospital so long they made me an orderly in the canteen.

One day in early February I went into Le Havre for the evening. While I was there I bumped into my close friend Bobby Hamilton, the Company Sergeant Major of the 10th Inniskillings. We were both very surprised at this coincidental meeting and we went to a little café and chatted over a cup of coffee. I told him that I was here recovering from my trench fever and would be returning to the the Battalion any day now. Bobby informed me that he was waiting for the next boat. He also warned me that there was going to be a massive German attack and in the near future things were going to get very rough and that I should look after myself."

At the end of the evening Bobby and Jim said their farewells and wished each other the best of luck – and parted.

---

[1] It was discovered that Trench Fever was caused by the faeces of the body louse which plagued soldiers. So many men were incapacitated by the disease that it gave the authorities cause for concern.

A Fieldcard, usually sent after a battle which allowed a soldier the minimum information to be sent home informing family of his condition without having to wait for the censorship to which normal letters or cards were subject.

Photo: Author

Chapter 24
Snow and Shells

The 10th Inniskillings had a fairly inactive period after the battle of Cambrai, in comparison with the actions they had taken part in during the months before. Most of their time was spent in camps at the rear.

On November 29th, the Battalion travelled up to Beaumetz, several miles south-west of Arras and then marched to a camp at Guoy. On the 30th they travelled to Achiet-le-Petit from where they marched another fourteen miles before camping in tents. On December 1st, the Battalion moved to the outskirts of Bapaume where orders were received that the battalion was to return to the front line, this time at Havrincourt Wood, ten miles south-west of Cambrai.

On December 4th, the Battalion left Bertincourt for the front line. After they had their dinner the men were issued with their extra ammunition, Mills bombs and rifle grenades. Once in the trenches they relieved a unit of 29th Division and were in position by 7.30pm. The Battalion was billeted in ten deep-mined dugouts which were very cramped as they had to accommodate approximately 550 men and 30 officers.

Their stint was to have a lively start. The following morning the Germans put down such a heavy barrage that the Battalion 'stood to,' since they were sure there was going to be an attack. That night, the Derrys had to make their way along the trenches to relieve 2/8th Warwicks. It was fortunate that it was a clear frosty night, as the guide detailed to the Battalion got lost and traipsed them around the trenches before they found their location. After this fiasco, the troops must have been in poor spirits as it was 1.30am and the position they were taking over had been attacked during the afternoon and the trenches were in a poor state with much clearing up to be done. At 8am a message was received from Brigade Headquarters telling them that a prisoner had given information that a raid was to take place between 8 and 8.30am. At 8.20 a heavy bombardment to the right of the Derrys' position began falling mostly on the 9th Inniskillings' sector. This was fortunate for the Derrys as the front line trenches were only waist deep except for posts and there were no dugouts or shelter along the line. Only company headquarters had deep dugouts. 'Stand to' was ordered at 8.40am when reports came in that the Germans were attacking 9th Inniskillings. Things were getting desperate for them. They were running short of bombs so a company of 14th Rifles went to support them. It was a hectic morning with much bombing taking place. All available men at Battalion Headquarters were used to transport bombs up from the Brigade's munition dump. Men started digging in the front line to give themselves better cover. Around 2pm, a section from A Company was ordered to attack a German trench. After crossing open ground, they entered the trench and, although they found it strongly held, drove the Germans back until they ran short of bombs. The Germans counter-attacked, bombing them heavily. The Section made their way back to the Derrys' lines with two prisoners and although four of them had been wounded, they had killed a large number of Germans.

Shortly after this, an enemy machine gun post was in the process of surrendering Second Lieutenant Shearman. The six Germans operating in the position stood up with their hands in the air but, as Shearman and Corporal E. Blake DCM approached to accept the surrender, the Germans opened fire, hitting the officer in the shoulder. Corporal Blake managed to shoot two of them and the rest retreated. Blake then carried Shearman back to safety under very heavy fire. The attack eventually subsided and there was a lull in the fighting.

Cpl. E. Blake D.C.M

Photo: Royal Inniskilling Fusiliers Museum

On the night of December 7th, after a day of intense enemy shelling of the rear lines, a German rocket bomb killed three men of D Company just as they were about to be transferred to another trench[*1]. There were several reports that the Germans were about to launch massive raids on the stretch that the Derrys controlled but several artillery bombardments on their lines made sure they did nothing. During the German retaliatory bombardments, a shell burst on the Battalion ammunition dump at Havrincourt Wood and set a box of rifle ammunition on fire. The dump contained thousands of rounds of ammunition and about 1000 Mills bombs. A large number of men and mules were in the vicinity at the time and many would have been injured, except for the quick thinking and bravery of Corporal S. Donald who ran in and carried the burning box well away from the rest of the ammunition.

The Derrys left the trenches at Havrincourt and moved to the rear lines on December 9th in the early hours of the morning. Their journey took them through the old trench line at Trescault which was in a poor state of repair and with the continual rain they were up to their knees in places. As the battalion struggled and slid with their kit on their journey out of the trench system, a shell killed Second Lieutenant T. Hamilton and wounded three men. Major Knox, who was in command of the Battalion in the absence of Lord Farnham, described the relief journey as: 'One of the most tedious journeys after a relief ever experienced by this battalion.'

The Battalion, now out of the line, was involved in reorganising and cleaning up after the hardships of the previous weeks. Then it was back to working parties and moving from one location to another, travelling to Metz, Sorel and Rocquigny. There they were billeted in hutted camps which was fortunate as the weather was very cold and wet.

On December 16th, the Derrys travelled by train to Mondicourt where they then marched to the village of Halloy. During the afternoon the Battalion made its way through a severe snowstorm and arrived into the camp freezing cold, wet and tired to find that their billets were not ready. It was not until 10pm that they were billeted.

The next few days were spent resting and being subjected to billet and kit inspections. Still there was time on December 18th, for the Derrymen to celebrate the Shutting of the Gates with the burning of Lundy even though there was still a heavy fall of snow.

In the days coming up to Christmas, billets were prepared in festive spirit and on Christmas Eve it was mentioned in Battalion Orders that a further nineteen men from the battalion were to be awarded the Military Medal. On Christmas Day there were Services during the morning and Christmas Dinner was served to each Company by its officers with the Commanding Officer visiting each Company's Mess. During the afternoon it snowed heavily … a nice touch for the Festive Season but the next few days would be spent clearing deep snow from the roads. On January 1st the battalion was to make a long march but this had to be abandoned due to a heavy fall of snow on New Year's Eve. The next 12 days were spent undertaking kit inspections and shooting practice on rifle ranges. There was specialist rifle training for "indifferent shots" as well as gas drill and, of course, more work parties.

BACK IN THE LINE

The New Year had started off as a quiet and restful experience compared with the front line. However on January 13th, 1918, the battalion found itself marching

36th Ulster Division Christmas Card 1917.
Photo: Author

up the line, to relieve not another unit of the Ulster Division nor even indeed of the British Army, but rather a unit of the French Army, the 1st Battalion of the 119th French Regiment. They were holding a section of the front near Seracourt-le-Grand facing Essigny, three miles south of St. Quentin. It was a long 17 mile march on muddy roads and the men were tired as they trudged into the front line trenches. Much time was spent handing over the trenches with the French officers explaining the main features of their own and the enemy's line.

The Derrys found that the dugouts were good but, in the usual French tradition, the trenches themselves were in a bad state of repair and were very muddy. As the French had left an officer with each of the Tenth's companies and the French artillery was providing artillery support, several interpreters also remained.

Orders were given to carry out repair work of the trenches – but it was too little too late. At 6.20am on January 15th, the Germans opened up with a heavy bombardment. The French artillery replied with an excellent counter barrage. The action lasted for an hour and during that time two men were buried by collapsing trenches. When they were dug out they were understandably very shaken. One of these men was Pte. James Monteith[*2]. Only one other man was wounded but the shelling and torrential rain had made the French trenches deathtraps and most had fallen in. They were also impassable and rations could not be brought up to the front line trenches. They had to be carried across open country during the hours of darkness.

The next few days, and the time the battalion spent in support, was used to improve and repair the trenches and they were relatively quiet except for a short bombardment of fifty shells aimed at Battalion HQ.

The Battalion was relieved and marched to Fluqieres on January 29th. Baths had been set up, a most welcome feature for any man coming out of the line and time was spent in cleaning kit and resting. The Divisional band played at a football match between C and D Companies and an enjoyable and restful day was spent by the men of the Derrys. This was a pleasant setting to one of the worst orders the men of 10th Royal Inniskilling Fusiliers could have heard – they were to be disbanded.

[1] One of these men was Pte. W. Wilson (see Chapter 'Aftermath').
[2] James Monteith was the last surviving veteran of the 10th Inniskillings who fought in the battles after the Somme.

French troops watch the bands of the 9th, 10th & 11th Inniskillings at Ham. January 15th, 1918.

Photo: Imperial War Museum, Q10656

French troops watch the arrival of the 9th, 10th and 11th Inniskillings at Ham. The Inniskillings were to take over a section of the line south of the Somme from the French Army, January 15th 1918.

Chapter 25

Death of the Battalion

Towards the end of 1917, the incredible casualties combined with the decline in the number of new recruits, was affecting the fighting strength of the British Army. As a result, the infantry brigade structure was reorganised in February 1918. Under the new system, a brigade was reduced from four to three battalions, with the intention of allowing the original divisions to be maintained.

In February 1918 the 10th Inniskillings was disbanded under War Office orders along with their old comrades, 11th Inniskillings and 14th Rifles. The 1st and 2nd battalions were moved from the 29th and 32nd Divisions respectively to join 109 Brigade. The remnants of the Derrys, 52 officers and 685 other ranks, were dispersed to 1st, 2nd and 9th Inniskillings with a small number to 21st Entrenching Battalion. The 109 Brigade was now composed totally of Inniskilling battalions.

Lord Farnham was given command of 2nd Inniskillings. The 1st and 2nd Inniskillings, which were the regular battalions, were ordered to wear the colours of the 11th and 10th Inniskillings respectively as recognition of their courageous service throughout the War.

To many of the Derrys, disbandment was a terrible blow. Their thoughts went back to their days at Finner, the march of the Battalion through their home towns on their way to Randalstown and other memorable occasions when they were a proud band of men, untouched and naïve. The continual horrors, suffering and death had scarred the men mentally. Now the disbandment of their unit was the final indicator to them that the Derrys would never march through Londonderry or the County when the war was over. They were finished.

The 10th Inniskillings may have been disbanded but many of its men would die in their new units of 109 Brigade before the war was over.

Chapter 26
St. Quentin

Allied Intelligence Services reported a massing of German forces in the St. Quentin area of the line in March 1918. The area to be defended was a plateau to the south-west of the town. On March 18th, two German deserters came across to the Allies and stated that the attack was to be here as the British line was weak due mainly to lack of materials and manpower. The whole of the British Fifth Army was in a frenzy training, reinforcing and making emergency plans for the defence of substandard trenches.

Jim was released from hospital early in March and was sent south to join his new unit, 9th Royal Inniskilling Fusiliers.

Jim Donaghy:-

"I was sent to a big training camp a few miles outside Ham. There were men of various regiments and corps here and everything was being carried out with a sense of urgency. There were men being instructed how to shoot, bayonet and throw bombs. Many of these men had never been in the front line fighting before. There were drivers from the Army Service Corps, cooks and even medics! Basically anyone who could strengthen the weak Allied line during this impending attack. There were lots of men doing working parties and everyone was waiting for Jerry to start."

The 9th Inniskillings were in a part of the line with 1st and 2nd Inniskillings and 109 was known as the Inniskilling Brigade.

Jim Donaghy:-

"A group of us left the next day to march up to the front where the 9th Battalion was. We arrived as it was getting dark and got our pay almost immediately. Even the officers with our pay wanted to get rid of it before the attack. All night we were moved from dugout to dugout and got little sleep. When daylight broke we were moved along the front line. There was a big canal about half a mile behind us. We spent the whole day marching from one position to another. We would spend a short time there and then we would be marched miles to another location further along the front. This was to try and fool the German reconnaissance that there were more British troops in the front line than there really were. We spent two days doing this and we were very tired and in bad spirits. On the morning of the third day, the 21st of March 1918, the Germans started their attack."

Everything was favourable for the Germans. It was a foggy morning and when the German artillery opened up at 4.55am the British artillery could not find the location of the enemy's guns. Reconnaissance was impossible and the defenders were taken by surprise when the new lightly equipped shock troops quickly advanced through the fog.

The 1st and 2nd Inniskillings held on to their position, many to the last man. Remnants of them retired to other defensive positions. The 9th Inniskillings were fighting a rearguard action.

The Battalion stood its ground to let the rest of 36th Division escape. By night fall of March 22nd, the 1st and 2nd battalions had been destroyed holding their positions. The 9th Battalion alone had survived but had suffered many casualties.

"Seldom has the British army had to suffer such a period of intense anxiety as that from March 21st to April 5th 1918. The strategic position was painfully simple. If the enemy reached Amiens he held the key to the front lateral line of supply of the British army on the Western front, and that army would have to retire hurriedly south of the Somme, and would be fortunate if it were able to get away without grave loss of men and material. Then the enemy would be in possession of the French side of the English Channel, able to deny us the use of the Channel, to intensify his submarine warfare and, in effect, to besiege the British islands."
Sir Frank Fox

Jim Donaghy:-

"We were exhausted. We had no rest for about six days. We were holding a big sand quarry and were using it as a defensive position. The rest of the Allies were being forced back on either side. During the commotion of the battle a soldier shouted to me as he passed, 'Hey, Donaghy! Your pal's been killed!' I asked him who he was talking about and he told me it was Bobby Hamilton. I told him he was wrong as I knew Bobby was in England being commissioned. He shouted back that he had got a shell to himself.

Later I found out what he had said was true. Bobby had left the boat that night we had met in Le Havre with the other able bodied men going back to England. They had been sent up to the front to help repel the impending attack and had been killed in the process. Bobby was the bravest man I have ever met. The bravest man who ever stood in a pair of boots."

CSM Robert Hamilton was killed with the 9th Battalion on March 23rd, 1918. He was born in Dungiven, County Londonderry and was the first man in B Company of the Derrys to win the Military Medal, (December 1916). Later he was awarded the Distinguished Conduct Medal. Many felt he should have won the highest award, the Victoria Cross. His citation stated:-

"For conspicuous gallantry and devotion to duty. During an attack he captured an enemy machine-gun and three of its crew single handed. While holding the line during the following days he rendered valuable assistance in reorganising the company and getting forward supplies of bombs and ammunition, on several occasions under fire. His example and cheerfulness throughout were magnificent."
London Gazette March 28th, 1918.

CSM Hamilton was presented with the 10th Inniskillings' bullet riddled flag on the disbandment of the Battalion.

Jim Donaghy:-

"Bobby was a great friend of mine and was highly respected by all the men. Several times in the freezing cold conditions in the trenches he brought a big dixie of warm cocoa

up on his back for his men on duty. What other man of his rank would have done this for his men?"

Other men of the Derrys were making names for themselves with their new battalions. Another DCM won by the battalion was awarded in the same action to Lance Corporal Burke from Londonderry.

His citation reads:-

"For conspicuous gallantry and devotion to duty. He was in charge of a bombing section during an attack which captured thirty-five prisoners and killed a large number of the enemy. During another attack he cleared 200 yds of heavily held enemy trench, formed a block and repelled continued counterattacks. He showed splendid courage and leadership."

London Gazette March 28th, 1918.

CSM Robert Hamilton DCM, MM Killed in action, March 23rd, 1918, Aged 22.

Photo: Author

By now things were in a confused state as the remnants of the Inniskillings and many other units retired with the Germans hot on their heels.

Jim Donaghy:-

"We were at a crossroads called the 'Crucifix.' To one side was a graveyard and, as we had encountered in other places, the only thing standing was a large crucifix. We were regrouping. The men were from different English regiments, the 16th Irish Division and other units but they were all being rallied by the Colonel of the 9th Inniskillings. He was armed only with his blackthorn stick. Everyone was taking cover in a big dry drain. I didn't like the situation where we were. There were too many exhausted men packed into the trench and the Germans were closing in fast. I was very apprehensive and had a feeling we were about to get pasted by Jerry. Leading up from the drain was a small hill covered in a big orchard of apple trees. What we didn't know was that Jerry had spotted us and had moved a machine-gun to the flank of the drain where he could fire along the length of it from a height. I decided to seek cover somewhere outside the drain where it would be easier to make a break from the enemy if he had appeared. Just as I moved out, the machine gun opened fire into the drain and poured a hail of bullets into the men. The dry leaves and dirt in the bottom of it were flying everywhere and men were getting hit left, right and centre. The survivors quickly scrambled out of the drain and moved up the wood through the wood. I wasn't too keen to advance until I knew where we were going and took cover behind an apple tree. Another machine gun opened up. Bits of the tree were breaking off and more of us were hit. One chap's leg was badly shot up. It was just hanging on by a piece of skin. We moved up the hill, got him into an ambulance and pushed back even further.

We had now been holding the Germans at bay and moving steadily back for six days. We were withdrawn at last and marched five or six miles to the rear. The Battalion was sleeping on its feet. I walked into the man in front and cut my face on his steel helmet. We were met on the road by a fleet of lorries which transported half the battalion to a village. We were billeted in the school and had a rest at last."

Chapter 27
German Offensive, March 1918

Jim Donaghy:-

"Our rest was short lived. The next morning we were fell in outside the school and one of our officers was ordered with a party of men to go and give support to the Dublin Fusiliers who were holding the Germans back. Going up the line we passed a battery of French artillery firing like mad at the advancing enemy. The German artillery was firing back and we had four or five men killed. We finally found the Dublins and took cover in old disused trenches and were there for a whole day holding Jerry back. Our position was at a crossroads which had a big mound beside it. We could see that he had broken the line to our left and right and it was only the Dublin Fusiliers and the Inniskillings that were holding out. We were all mixed along the length of the trench and everyone was firing frantically. Jerry kept attacking repeatedly and things were getting desperate. We spent all night there fighting fiercely and by dawn we were running low on ammunition. There was one big ginger haired sergeant of the Dublin Fusiliers sniping on top of the parapet which was covered in bracken. He was camouflaged under a big Scotch thistle plant firing away at them. He caused a lot of damage to the advancing ammunition. I started to get apprehensive because of the situation and when I looked around me I couldn't see any other NCOs from the Inniskillings. I decided I would go for ammunition and at the same time see if I could find anyone from my Battalion. En route I saw some of them but I was surprised that I hadn't seen any officers for quite a while which was very strange. I collected some ammunition and ran back along the trench and handed some to the Dub Sergeant. As he turned away to load I heard a loud crack. He slumped down beside me in the trench dead, shot between the eyes, with his brains blown out.

Half an hour later a senior NCO came along and gave the order for us to move about a hundred yards down the trench. As we worked our way down we found it had been blocked by shellfire. We were told that we would have to get out of the trench and to fall back. This meant that we had to run back over open ground, exposed to the Germans' fire.

We all abandoned the trench. I left with a wee chap from the Dublins and we were running as fast as we could. The machine-gun fire was terrific. The bullets were buzzing round our heads like bees! He turned round to see if the Germans were close behind us, or what was happening when he fell suddenly. He had been shot through the mouth. I went back for him and started to give him first aid. A Captain ordered us back into the trench. I helped him into the trench where we were told to, 'move along smartly!' A Corporal took the injured man from me when a large group of Germans appeared above us on the parapet with fixed bayonets. Our position was over-run and we were ordered to throw down our rifles. The officers were separated from us and taken away. The Germans then started to strip equipment and clothing from us for themselves. Some men lost their greatcoats and other pieces that would be important for their comfort later. One of them snatched my blanket and wanted my coat and haversack. It was a battle, but I managed to hold on to them. Some thirty or forty of us were captured. We wondered what was in store as we were now prisoners of war."

The 9th Inniskillings faced the German attack on March 21st with 39 officers and 633 other ranks. On March 28th they came out with 16 officers and 169 other ranks. Many of the casualties had been members of the Tenth.

Cap badge of the Royal Dublin Fusiliers

Photo: Author

Photo: Imperial War Museum, Q5498

Machine-gunners of the Dublin Fusiliers, 16th Irish Division after Messines

Chapter 28
Working Behind German Lines

Many men were under the impression from reports they had heard that, once captured, the war was over for them. There would be no more living in the trenches, bombardments to endure, stand-tos, sentry duties and working parties. There would be shelter, food and no more danger of being killed or wounded. But this was 1918 and conditions had changed. Germany was enduring food and manpower shortages and was making an all-out effort to break the Allies.

Jim Donaghy:-

"After we were captured we were split into fours and used as stretcher bearers by the Germans. We had to ferry back the German wounded from the front and take them into the village of Ham. It was a holy terror. We hadn't had any substantial food in days and now we had nothing to eat. We could hardly stand as we were weak with hunger but we managed to get the odd biscuit. Any other food we got, we found or stole.

I teamed up with a chap from Ramelton in Donegal called Joe Buchanan. He was a member of the 9th Inniskillings. The first casualty we picked up was a big German sergeant. We hoisted him up and carried him for about ten minutes and when we looked, we found he was dead. We thought we were grand as now we hadn't anyone to carry for a while. As we were picking up our next casualty in the front lines there was a heavy Allied barrage. The shells were bursting all around us. The Germans were running round the place, diving for cover. We stood and laughed at them calling them all the names of the day. We didn't give two hoots about the shells, we just didn't care anymore.

The next German we had to carry was not as badly injured. He wanted us to take him a specific way, but we just took him along the route that we wanted to go. He was sitting up on the stretcher ordering us to do this and that. He was going crazy at us, we just laughed at him.

A few days later we were given the job of cleaning out French buildings for use as billets by the German soldiers. These Germans here were a bad lot. If you didn't get out of their way quick enough they would have knocked you to the ground and beat you up. A couple of chaps that I knew got terrible hammerings. On Easter Monday, I found an egg in one of the houses I was cleaning out! Boys did I enjoy that egg!

Later, Buchanan and myself were working beside the big canal at Ham. We decided we had had enough. We weren't going to do any more work for them so we hid all day under a flat bottomed boat which was on the bank. We thought about escaping but there was nowhere to go. When the prisoners went back to their billets at night we went back with them.

That evening was bitterly cold. I was sitting on the ruins of a shelled building when along came another prisoner who had been in the Trench Mortar Battery with me. He told me that our friend, Sergeant Murray, who had also been in the Trench Mortar

Battery had his leg taken off by a shell and had died later. I was most upset at this news. He was just an old farmer, not a soldier. He was so friendly and looked after us so well we used to call him 'Father.'

After all the casualties had been cleared, we were still kept in France. We were given the job of levelling ground for German airfields. Later when this task had been done, we had to drill wells for water. This was very hard labour and we were always very weak through the lack of proper food. The old engineer in charge of us was from Munich and wasn't a bad soul. He was half Russian and had a big black beard. He would frequently give us a hand with the boring, helping us to push the drill by hand as we walked round in a circle. He realised that we were weak and could hardly work.

We had a thirty minute walk to and from our work every day. One evening when we were walking back from a hard day's work, we met a German artillery battery. They were camping here for the night but we noticed two huts laid out for the officers. We sneaked into the huts and stole a big block of butter and a half of a loaf of bread. Joe Buchanan

A prisoner drawing meagre rations to be shared among four men.

Photo: Imperial War Museum, Q55249

and myself noticed the cooks dumping food. Immediately, we each grabbed a couple of old ammunition tins that were lying about and we filled them with the dumped food. It was spaghetti. We took it back to the camp and had a feed. We gave some of it to a chap from Belfast who was ill and very weak. He was glad of it.

Our standard rations as prisoners of war consisted of a small loaf the length of a man's hand. This was divided between five. You also got a watery potato soup made from mainly pig fat. If you found a potato in it the size of your thumb nail you were very, very fortunate. We made nettle broth to give us extra vitamins."

Although the men of 36th Ulster and 16th Irish Divisions fought in the trenches together and were friendly out of the line, now that the war for them was over, the old enmity resumed.

Jim Donaghy:-

"The camp we were billeted in was the ruins of a badly damaged chateau. The grounds were surrounded by a moat which had been fenced with high rolls of barbed wire. Inside the fence, huts had been built to house PoWs. This was also the headquarters for the Germans in the region.

The men of the 16th and 36th Divisions wouldn't sleep in the same accommodation, so as the men of the 36th Division were in the minority, myself and three others had to bivouac outdoors. We moved well away to a separate area. One Sunday, Joe Buchanan spotted a big staff car up at headquarters. He was interested in cars, so he went over for a look and started talking to the driver. During the conversation he noticed a wicker basket full of loaves on the back seat. When the German driver went into one of the buildings, Joe ran back for me and told me what he had seen. The two of us crawled into the back seat. During the process we were badly stung. We took two loaves each and carefully made our way back, making sure no-one had seen us. We then dug a shallow hole in the ground and buried the loaves in the clay.

We watched innocently from a distance as the driver got into the car and drove off down the road. A short time later we saw the same big black car drive up to the headquarters and again the driver got out and went into the building. We waited. All of a sudden six guards appeared with rifles and fixed bayonets. They tore over to the huts and roused the men of the 16th Division making them line up outside the huts and stand still. The guards were shouting and swearing, telling them that they would be shot. The huts were searched thoroughly including the men's few possessions but nothing was found. Later that night we sneaked back and dug up the loaves. Boys, but we had a great feed in our tents that night! Any bread left over we ground up and made a sort of porridge out of it."

Chapter 29
POW Germany

Jim Donaghy:-

"One day we were told that we were being moved to a new camp. They marched us to the railway and they put us into cattle trucks for the journey. We didn't know how far we were going, but it turned out to be Germany. The trucks were very cramped. You could just sit in a crouched position and no more. We travelled all night and the next morning, when the train eventually stopped at a station, several men in my truck were dead and others very ill. During all this time we hadn't been given as much as a drink or been allowed to stretch our legs or go to the toilet. We thought we had arrived at the camp and they allowed us to go to the latrine but we were marched back to the same train a short time later. Each prisoner was given a slice of black German bread and a hot drink that was supposed to be coffee, but tasted nothing like it. This was the first food in twenty-four hours. All prisoners boarded the train and we travelled for another day, again without as much as a drink. When we eventually arrived at the camp there were more dead in the truck and we were all in a poor state. We had arrived at a place called Stendyl.

It was here that the Red Cross registered us as prisoners of war and informed our families that we were alive. Big numbers were sown on to the backs of our clothes to identify us as prisoners. There was a rule that NCOs and above that who didn't want to work for the Germans didn't have to. Most of us out of principle wouldn't work for them so because of this we were given just enough food to keep us alive and no more.

Not only were there British prisoners here but also Russians and Italians. Most of the duties on the camp were carried out by the Russians. They had their own orchestra. Every one of its members had a big thick black beard. All that we had to do was parade in the morning and at night. Once we had signed a form stating that we had given our word not to escape, we were even allowed to go out of the camp and down to the town of Stendyl itself! We usually got a civil enough reception from the locals.

The German guards didn't like us very much but they hated the others, especially the Italians. They would beat and kick them for the slightest reason. On one occasion I got a severe beating. We were housed in a big hut holding twelve prisoners in triple bunk beds. Every morning there was a roll call. A whistle was blown and all prisoners had to parade outside their huts to be counted before breakfast. Four men in my hut were very ill with dysentery. As senior rank, I was responsible for ensuring that all men turned out, but this particular morning, two men were too ill to parade. I was trying to get them out (as I knew the Germans would be annoyed) when the guards came in and gave me a severe beating with a bayonet. My shoulder was injured and it still causes me pain seventy years later!

I was notified by the Red Cross that I would be getting a parcel and not long after this it arrived. It contained lots of things that made a starving prisoner's life a lot easier to bear: cigarettes, chocolate, biscuits, tea and cocoa, for example.

We were moved from Stendyl after a few weeks and were moved to a new camp at Gustro. This consisted of two barbed wire compounds on a big moor. It was covered in deep heather and was the Crown Prince's shooting estate. Below our camp was a convicts' camp. Boys but they were a bad lot!

At Gustro camp I found I wasn't getting parcels when the others were getting theirs. All the rest of the prisoners, except three that I knew of, got parcels regularly. I couldn't work out why.

Some of the privates and NCOs were working on farms for the Germans and they were treated quite well. Most of us still wouldn't work for them and as a result our rations got even worse."

A group of British POWs including several from the 10th Inniskillings.

Photo: William Wright

Chapter 30
Armistice

Jim Donaghy:-

"We knew the war was coming to an end and we used to chat regularly to one of the guards. He had lived in America before the war and spoke perfect English. He used to tell us of the meetings which had been leading up to the peace talks."

On November 11th, 1918 at 11am the guns on the Western Front fell silent. The war was over.

GERMANY SURRENDERS.

CESSATION OF HOSTILITIES.

ALLIED TERMS ACCEPTED.

HUMILIATING CONDITIONS.

AUSTRIA BREAKS ARMISTICE TREATY

BRITISH STORM MONS.

The Armistice Signed.

CESSATION OF HOSTILITIES.

All civil and military personnel at present employed on them shall remain.
5,000 locomotives, 150,000 waggons, and 5,000 motor lorries, in good working order, with all necessary spare parts and fittings,

Jim Donaghy:-

"Just after parade that evening a British RSM came out of the German headquarters. He calmly told us that the war was over. There was no cheering or shouting. We were all just glad it was over. The gates were opened and the only thing on our minds was to get home as quickly as possible.

The commanding officer of the camp was a hateful character. He could just be best described as a big Nazi. His second in command was a good officer in comparison. He heard us talking about forming up in parties and marching to Denmark to get out of Germany as quickly as possible, but he advised us not to go. He suggested we kept together and wait until the official people arrived to organise the return journey as no-one was sure yet as to what was happening in Germany.

We agreed that we would wait. Now we could do what we pleased. Five of us, a South African, a Dubliner, a chap from Yorkshire, a Canadian and myself spent our time going out at night to visit the little villages and hamlets near the camp. We would spot a spire in the distance and would decide to go there and investigate. We went to concerts, wee meeting places where the locals gathered for coffee and, of course, dances. We were always given a good reception by the locals, so good in fact that at times we didn't get back to 5am.

On one particular outing we went to a dance in the local village hall. There were very few men as they too had been away fighting in the war. We got friendly with one particular chap and his three sisters. They would give us coffee and we would dance with the girls or sit and chat.

One of the girls had a great conversation with the Scottish chap. She was asking him about Scotland and the singer Harry Lauder. It turned out that she knew more about Scotland than he did!

On the way home as we were walking down a little village lane in the early hours of the morning, one of the girls asked us where we had been at the front. We mentioned different places and as I named the place I had hated most, Mailly-Maillet, she burst into tears. Her brother had been killed there.

About a week after the Armistice, word was going round the camp that the Commandant had been stealing the Red Cross parcels that some of us hadn't been getting and selling them. He was caught at the railway station trying to escape to Denmark and was arrested. When the camp was searched we found four wagons full of stolen parcels. We went through them and I found so many parcels addressed to me that there was no more room under my bunk, and I could hardly get into bed. I really enjoyed those parcels.

One day when we were out walking we came across a house not far from the camp. One of our group wanted a drink of water so he knocked on the door. The woman asked us in and made us welcome. She lived in the house with her three children and her father. Her husband had been killed serving with the German army. They hadn't a lot as food was scarce. We went back the next day and gave her a poke of tea. She was delighted."

Jim and his friends realised that not only had they suffered and gained nothing from the war, but also the French and German families they had encountered over the last three years were in exactly the same situation.

To the Prisoners of War in Germany!

A PARTING WORD.

Gentlemen:

The war ended for you as soon as you became prisoners of war. But now it has ended for the whole world. A little while—and you will see your native land again, your homes, your loved ones, your friends. You will once more take up your accustomed work.

The fortune of war brought you as prisoners into our hands. You were freed, even against your will, from the fighting, from danger, from de... ...joys of peace could m... yours... there was no peace. Now peace is coming, and peace means liberty. When you are already reunited to your families, thousands of our countrymen will still be pining in far off prison-camps with hearts as hungry for home as yours.

You have suffered in confinement-as who would not? It was the fate of every prisoner in every prison-camp in the world to eat his heart out with longing, to chafe against loss of liberty, to suffer from homesickness, brooding, discouragement, blank despair. The days, the weeks, the weary years crept by, and there was no end in sight. There were many discomforts, irritations, misunderstandings.

Your situation has been a difficult one. Our own has been desperate. Our country blockaded, our civil population and army suffering from want of proper and sufficient food and materials, the enormous demands made upon our harassed land from every side-these and many other afflictions made it impossible to do all that we should have liked to do. Under the circumstances we did our best to lessen the hardships of your lot, to ensure your comfort, to provide you with pastime, employment, mental and bodily recreation. It is not likely that you will ever know how difficult our circumstances have been.

We know that errors have been committed and that there have been hardships for which the former system was to blame. There have been wrongs and evils on both sides. We hope that you will always think of t h a t-and be just.

You entered the old empire of Germany you leave the new Republic the newest and, as we hope to make it, the freest land in the world. We are sorry that you saw so little of what we were proud of in the former Germany-our arts, our sciences, our model cities, our theatres, schools, industries, our social institutions, as well as the beauties of our scenery and the real soul of our people, akin in so many things to your own.

But these things will remain part of the New Germany. Once the barriers of artificial hatred and misunderstanding have fallen, we hope that you will learn to know, in happier times, these grander features of the land whose unwilling guests you have been. A barbed wire enclosure is not the proper point of view from which to survey or judge a great nation.

The war has blinded all nations. But if a true and just peace will result in opening the eyes of the peoples to the fact that their interests are c o m m o n-that no difference in flags, governments, speech nor nationality can alter the great truth of the fraternity of all men, this war will not have been fought in vain. If the peoples at last realize that it is not each other who are their enemies, but the ruthless for... of Imperialism and Capitalism, of militarism of all sorts, of jingo... ...that sows hatred and suspicion, then this war will not have been fought in vain. Then peace will not be established in vain.

We hope that every one of you will go home carrying a message of good will, of conciliation, of enlightment. Let all men in our new epoch go forth as missionaries of the new evangel, as interpreters between nation and nation.

The valiant dead who once fought against each other have long been sleeping as comrades side by side in the same earth. May the living who once fought against each other labour as comrades side by side upon this selfsame earth.

That is the message with which we bid you farewell.

Three Cheers for Peace and Good Will

Hamburg, November 1918.

A leaflet given to Jim Donaghy by a German Officer as he left the POW camp.

Chapter 31
Going Home

Jim Donaghy:-

> *"We caught a train in Germany and it took us over the border into Denmark. We arrived at a port where we were to catch a boat back to Scotland. The place reminded me for all the world of Derry. It was a large town with steep streets, a bridge not unlike Craigavon, crossing a wide river just like the Foyle."*

The views of this Danish port, reminding him so much of Londonderry brought the dream to reality. He was now on his way home. The men wanted to get home as soon as possible, but they had to wait for most of the day for the boat.

> *"The officer in charge didn't want us to stray very far from the ship but we wanted to go in and see the town. As we had a long wait until the ship departed he allowed us to go. The Captain warned us to make sure to be back before 1am.*
>
> *It was Christmas Eve and we were made very welcome everywhere we went. Many of us looked the worse for wear – the time in the PoW camps had made its mark. People gave us coffee, cigarettes and other luxurious foods that we hadn't had in years. A group of us walked up to the top of a steep street window-shopping as we went. At the top there was a shop that sold dairy products and looking through the big shop window we stared at the blocks of butter the size of small televisions. In the camps as we were being starved of nutritious foods, our bodies craved certain things and one of these was real butter. We stared so much that the owner of the shop came out to us and invited us in. He gave us knives and laughingly encouraged us to cut chunks off the big blocks. We ate it just the way it was. It was beautiful. There was no food like this in a PoW camp!"*

All the men returned to the ship on time and it sailed at 1am on Christmas Morning 1918. All were in high spirits. They were on their way back to Britain and it was Christmas. The steamer slowly made its way along the fjord before entering the open sea. The smiles would not last long.

> *"On the journey across the North Sea we experienced the most terrific storm. Men were continuously being violently sick. We all thought we weren't going to make it. Imagine surviving the war, the hardships – and drowning on your way home."*

The men were relieved as the ship made its way into the shelter of the Firth of Forth before docking at Edinburgh.

> *"It was a cold miserable morning in Edinburgh. We were given lunch at the YMCA. After lunch we caught a train down to Yorkshire where we had to report to a camp for demobbing purposes. The old ragged uniform that I had worn continually for over the last nine months was replaced with two new ones. We hated this place. It was time wasting. We had spent enough time in the army, milling about in camps and we were itching to get home."*

COMING BACK TO DRUMAHOE

"I arrived in Larne on the ferry from Scotland and before I caught the train to Londonderry, I sent a telegram to my mother telling her I was on my way. When I arrived at the Waterside station, Londonderry, there was no one there to meet me so I started my long walk to Drumahoe. As I walked down Daly's Brae in my uniform, someone must have spotted me in the distance. The bell of Clarke's Mill at Drumahoe started to ring frantically as a signal to my mother that I was home[1]

When I got home the house was filled with my friends, relations and neighbours. They were overjoyed."

Jim was home – it was over at last.

[1] Mrs Hughes who lived at the mill had told Jim's mother that if she spotted him passing she would ring the bell.

A homecoming reception for POWs in Limavady Town Hall.

Photo: Author

Chapter 32
Remnants

Jim was lucky that he arrived home quickly and safely from the War. Although the Armistice had been signed some seven weeks before, the other members of the Ulster Division would spend additional months carrying out duties and following the withdrawing Germans into Germany. Much time was also wasted demobbing before they arrived home in small groups throughout 1919. Many of the men who had left with the 10th Inniskillings had been killed or badly wounded. Many were disabled with loss of limbs, deafness, blindness, lungs destroyed with poisonous gas, faces disfigured. For the remnants of the battalion who returned physically untouched, everything for them had also changed. The following give some varied examples.

A group of people, mainly relations, were waiting in the Railway station for the arrival of a group of demobbed Derrys. The mother and sister of a particular soldier were in the group waiting at the gate. The others greeted their loved ones and left the station. Eventually the platform was almost deserted. The man's sister went down the length of the train looking everywhere for him. She found him sitting in one of the carriages, bewildered – he didn't even know he was home!

He was never the same.

Lance Corporal Thomas Baird from Limavady was posted as missing after July 1st, 1916. His mother did not receive official word that her son had been killed until 1933, seventeen years after her son's death. She had waited for many months in the hope that in some way her son might have survived.

Cpl T Baird's grave at Thiepval
Photo: Author

Many homes in Ulster had the belongings of a missing son or father laid out for years on the faint chance that they would return one day.

Private Lindsay Hall (wounded on the 1st July) had won an engineering scholarship to University before the War, after coming first in all Ireland in engineering exams. When he returned, his place was no longer available.

Many men found on their return that they weren't reinstated in their jobs as had been promised before they enlisted. Of the ones who did, many found to their amazement and disgust that they were paid at 1914 rates, and the men who hadn't enlisted had been promoted during their absence.

Many of the veterans would not talk about the War when they came home, even until their dying day. Many didn't want to relive those horrific days. Others didn't want to talk to those who hadn't been there. After all, how could these people have any idea of the horrors and suffering they went through? Those who did talk found it difficult without, at some time, shedding a tear.

The Government had been eager to enlist men for the War. Now the War was over, attitudes had changed to the victims. Many of the thousands of wounded who, during the War, were treated as heroes found a cold reception in a Government office after the Armistice.

One of the older Sergeant-Majors, who had been extremely brave and well-respected in the Battalion, was spotted by Captain Moon during a visit to London after the War. The Warrant Officer was standing at the side of a busy street, a pathetic sight, selling matches.

The 10th Inniskillings formed an Old Comrades' Association several years after the war. Re-union dinners were always held on March 10th, the anniversary of their first major action – the terrible bombardment at Thiepval Wood. As one old comrade stated:

> *"We belong to an Association of men whose friendship for one another is cemented in suffering and bloodshed."*

A pact was drawn up between the members that as long as a member was alive and well, they would lay a wreath annually at the War Memorial in Londonderry on the Anniversary of the 1st of July.

On July 1st, 1990, Jim Donaghy was the last veteran to lay this wreath in memory of the men of the 10th Royal Inniskilling Fusiliers. On the same date, Leslie Bell laid a wreath at a remembrance service at the Ulster Tower at Thiepval.

Jim Donaghy, Harry Wilson & Tommy McClay at the War Memorial on the 1st July Anniversary 1982.

Photo: Londonderry Sentinel

Chapter 33
Reflections

When you write a book, you don't know if it will live up to your own and the buying public's expectations. A book's subject matter needs people to think it is worthwhile to open their wallets and spend their hard-earned cash.

During the writing of the first edition, I was passionate about researching through old documents, books and photographs. Those were the days before the Internet eased some of the burden, as now records are easily and instantly available in the comfort of your own home. Every additional piece of information that turned up was regarded as another part of the jigsaw. On the other hand, sometimes a labour of love can be too much for the average reader as the plethora of information breaks up a story, so I felt I had to leave some material out. My main intention, however, was to collate the last recollections of the veterans and hope that the story was a true reflection of what had happened.

On going to the printers to collect the first few copies, there was the excitement of seeing the finished article - the fruit of two years of intense research, interviewing, writing, finding a publisher and a myriad of other tasks. But this excitement was tinged with trepidation. The book had always been a race against time as I really wanted it to be finished and in print so that Jim Donaghy and Leslie Bell could see it.

Lesley Bell and Jim Donaghy meet for the first time since 1916 at the launch of the first edition in 1991.

Photo: Author

It was with the greatest delight that on the way back from the printers, I presented, albeit apprehensively, the first book to the late Benn Hunter from Limavady. Benn had been my first sponsor and his father was one of the two main medics in the battalion and had won the Military Medal for his efforts. I was surprised at Benn's reaction. On seeing his father's portrait in print, along with the comments of veterans recounting with admiration his harrowing work as a medic, his eyes filled with tears. Benn really appreciated that the story of the 10th Inniskillings was now in print and congratulated me for what I had done. I felt really humble.

The second copy was taken straight to Jim Donaghy. He read it in two days – a mammoth feat for his failing eyesight, but he too was delighted with the finished article. I hoped that the story hadn't altered in the transition from his spoken word to the printed page and I was both relieved and delighted when he said that it was 'a true account and a credit to the memory of the men of the battalion.' I was aware of the reason why he told me so many of those very personal stories recounting his friends and comrades - their achievements, their disappointments, their heartbreak. He had realised that, if these stories weren't recorded for posterity, they too, would die with the last men of the battalion.

However, once Jim and Leslie had given their endorsement to the factual credibility of the book, I didn't care what anyone else said, it was all immaterial; I had achieved what I had set out to do and they liked what they read.

Letters arrived from people in Canada, Australia, America, New Zealand and South Africa, who had read the book and were looking for more information or complimented me on my efforts. It was then that I realised the importance of the book in relation to family histories.

Chapter 34
The Forgotten Veteran

Well-known military historian and author, Richard Doherty, warned me that when the book would hit the shelves and articles appeared in the newspapers some people would ring and say, " If only you had asked me I could have …etc." He told me it happens all the time and some people seem to get a kick out of it as, although they saw the articles requesting additional material for the book in the first instance, they waited until the launch before coming forward. Sure enough the phone did ring and some letters did arrive exactly as Richard had said …but the biggest shock arrived on the day the book went to print.

On the day that the first edition of "*Three Cheers for the Derrys!*" went to the printers in 1990, I heard with disbelief from Robert Elliott, an English businessman and avid researcher with a passion for the 36th Ulster Division, that another member of the 10th Inniskillings was still alive. I was really disappointed about not having had the opportunity to interview him and include his story for posterity. What made it more incredible was that he had been living less than half a mile from Leslie Bell in Moneymore!

How could this have been? If the information was true, how come virtually no one had heard of this other veteran?

I made further enquiries and arranged to see him with Robert Elliott who came over especially from England. The veteran's name was James Monteith. I thought that he must have been in a confused or forgetful state if no one researching the Great War had been to see him.

James Monteith 1991

How wrong I was. He was absolutely delighted to see us and was so pleased to hear that a book was to be written about his battalion. He was clearly spoken and was so easy to listen to. He started off by telling us that he had spent the last thirty years of his life in a nursing home. They had been thirty, long, uncomfortable years due to illness and he was unable to lie in bed but sat, ate and slept in a chair in the same room all that time. With no close family and few visitors, it was a pitiful end to a life. I believe that one of the reasons why few knew about him was that, at the age of 94, he looked so fresh, too young to have fought in the Great War. He didn't seem to have too many visitors or anyone to talk to and on my first visit offered me his medals! He felt he had no one he wanted to leave them to. I explained to him that although I would have loved to have his medals, ethically I couldn't take them and he would have to leave them to someone else. These were his prized possessions but he was just so pleased to see someone who was genuinely interested in his memories and knew about his battalion. He recounted his memories with gusto and it just happened to coincide with Remembrance Day.

JAMES MONTEITH – HIS STORY

Born in Bonds Street, Londonderry, James Monteith enlisted in the 10th Royal Inniskilling Fusiliers in late 1915 at the age of 18, leaving his apprenticeship as a motor mechanic. His military career began at Finner Camp in Donegal, the training base for 109 Brigade of the 36th Ulster Division. His posting there happened to coincide with the Easter Rising of 1916.

He showed me a written order issued to him by a senior officer of the Ulster Division during the Easter Rising. He displayed it with pride to the few visitors he had, with a hearty laugh and would say,

> *"I must have been one of the first soldiers to go on a mission against the IRA. The order stated that due to IRA activity, I was to be despatch rider and cycle by myself to the post office in Bundoran from Finner Camp to collect the mail. There I was, 18 years old and by myself on a bicycle.... armed with a rifle loaded with six rounds of ammunition... and was terrified!"*

James was sent to France in July 1916, narrowly missing the Ulster Division's attack on July 1st at the Somme. The news of the carnage was not the most inspiring and morale boosting news for a raw teenage recruit. Even at the age of 94, his memory was still sharp and he talked emotionally about some of his experiences in the famous battles after the Somme - Messines Ridge, Passchendaele, Cambrai and St Quentin, where he fought as a machine gunner.

L/Cpl Diver (right) with his Lewis gun.

> *"I was trained on the Lewis gun as a machine gunner and when I joined the battalion, was teamed up with L/Cpl Tommy Diver from Rosemount. He was the gunner and I was the No. 2 with the job of loading the gun. Tommy was a great shot, no doubt about it, and had won the Military Medal. He was 18 too and as brave a man as I have ever met."*

James was Tommy's new assistant on the gun as his last had been a casualty on July 1st.

The Lewis gun was invented by an American just before the war and was manufactured in Birmingham. It was a fantastic machine gun and very popular with the British soldier as at 28lbs it was almost half the weight of the heavier Vickers machine gun, which was belt-fed and needed two men to operate it. The Lewis gun had a 47 round drum magazine, which fitted on top of the gun and could be carried and even fired by one man. Its nickname was the Belgian Rattlesnake as it had a rate of fire of 550 rounds of .303 rifle ammunition per minute. James had the job of carrying the drum magazines and ammunition, making sure the gun and magazines were loaded. He would also have acted as observer identifying additional targets for Tommy Diver to engage.

"Conditions in the trenches were terrible. We were living every hour of the day covered in lice and you spent a lot of time trying to burn them out of the seams of your shirts and uniform. I contracted scabies and was sent to the rear lines at Etaples for a sulphur bath. I had trench foot through standing for a long time up to the knees in the freezing cold water that frequently filled the trenches in winter. Soldiers lost toes or even their feet as they couldn't dry their feet out and also there were the effects of frostbite in freezing weather. Many-a-time we used to be on working parties in the front line carrying heavy "A" frames. These were used to reinforce the trenches and we carried them on our backs, slipping and sliding in the mud. It was a terrible life altogether. The food in the trenches was also very bad as most times the food was eaten straight from the can. It was mainly bully beef or tinned Maconochie Rations, which was an army stew. This was mainly poor cuts of meat, lard and vegetables. Instead of bread you got hard biscuits. We used to put the empty tins to good use and found that if you hung them on the wire in front of the trenches any approaching German patrol that touched the wire in the dark made the cans rattle like an alarm. When you did get cooked food it was transported up to the front in big billycans and most times was carried in on someone's back. By the time it got to you, it was usually just lukewarm, not hot. You sometimes got a quarter of a loaf of bread and with the cooked food it was a most welcome change as for years you were eating the same canned foods."

Soldier with hot rations in a dixie.

One of the duties most dreaded by a soldier was to be picked as part of a raiding party.

"Sometimes we had to go on raiding parties over to the German lines with orders to listen for information or bring back a prisoner for interrogation. I was picked for one and I'll tell you... I was scared stiff. I was always scared stiff... I wasn't brave at all... I was always frightened and scared. On the patrol we sneaked out in the dark and made our way over to the German lines and lay down at their wire listening. My heart was beating so fast you could have heard it. We found after a period of time that there were no Germans in that part of the trenches and I can tell you that on reaching our trenches again – the relief was unbelievable. Every man in the front line was scared but some knew how to hide their fear better than others."

"I can't remember anything nice about the War but at Christmas 1916, when we were in Belgium, I remember the Germans singing and playing melodeons in the trenches opposite us, only a short distance away. They must have brought a choir up to the front line to entertain the troops and they were singing Silent Night in German. The harmonies were beautiful but it was so sad to listen to when you were stuck in the cold, wet, filthy trenches with death all around you. If only people nowadays knew what conditions were really like in the trenches... they just don't know how lucky they are!"

"We were sent from the Tenth to the 109th Machine gun section for the Battle of Passchendaele in August 1917 and after it we returned to the battalion and our Lewis gun. During the battle we were assigned to a heavier Vickers machine gun, which was belt fed, clumsy and heavy. It was not manoeuvrable in the conditions and we were in a machine gun post with extra ammunition, and a case of Mills bombs on either side of me. We also had a periscope to check no-man's-land and this was our standard setup in most of our machine gun posts. However, Passchendaele was absolutely horrible. There were dead and dying lying in the mud. Mud was everywhere... deep, thick, mud and the dead were lying around as manure for the land. In fact... there was a place several miles behind the lines called Poperinghe and when the wind was blowing in the right direction you could have smelt the dead all that distance away. There were corpses lying among the dead horses. It was terrible! The bodies were as black as your boot. You know... when a body starts to putrefy it turns black. The dugout that I was in had the decomposing body of a young Scottish soldier lying at the entrance that you had to step over as you went out and in. There was nowhere to bury him. It was absolutely horrible!"

"As the war went on we didn't take much of an interest in the personal lives of our pals. Sometimes you didn't even know the name of the man next to you. There was no such thing as getting too friendly in the trenches. We became hardened as someone you were getting to know may be dead the next day and you would have thought about his family at home who didn't know the terrible news. I had to take home the personal effects of Lt. Alfie Bogle who was killed at Passenchdaele. When he was killed, his body was lying not far away from the trench in no-man's-land and that night some of his men went out and brought in his body. His pockets were emptied for personal effects to be sent home and as I was going home on leave, was given the job of giving his silver cigarette case to his father. I had to give this to him in his son's newsagents shop in Londonderry – not a pleasant thing to have to do."

James' best mate was now Tommy Diver. He couldn't help but get close to him as he spent most of his time with him and as a machine gun team their survival depended on each other - more than any other type of soldier.

"On the same leave I had a personal errand to do for Tommy. He had found a beautiful gold medallion in a wrecked house at Messines and he asked me to take this to his girlfriend who worked in a draper's shop in Londonderry."

Now James had got to know another part of Tommy's life and if anything happened to Tommy he knew that his girlfriend would be heartbroken and he would have to go and see her.

As comrades were killed, friends attended their burial - that is if their bodies were recovered.

"In 1917, at the graveside of one of my friends I knelt down and picked one of the wild poppies which were growing beside the grave. For some reason, I put the flower in between the pages of my pay book and used it as an act of remembrance long before it was adopted as the official remembrance symbol. I kept that dried poppy for years."

James explained that even the most mundane of sights or sounds could generate a violent response by the Germans and that great measures were taken to avoid this. James gave one such example:

"Sometimes the simplest thing seen or heard by the Germans could have resulted in them firing mortars. The worst were the Minnies as they fired a shell the size of an oil drum and the explosion absolutely wrecked the trenches. One of the funniest things I saw during the War was a mule coming up a wide communication trench pulling the cook cart behind it. To make sure the Germans didn't hear it, sandbags had been tied around its feet to muffle the sound but it looked hilarious with its thin legs and huge feet. If the Germans knew that the cook cart was there and men were around it getting their rations they would have shelled it."

With artillery and mortar shells being fired into the trenches on a daily basis, death was never far away.

"I must have been one of the few soldiers who fought in the four main battles after the Somme and didn't even get a scratch. But I did have some very narrow escapes. Once I had the trench blown in on top of me and another chap. We had to be dug out before we suffocated and even in the short time it took to get us out it seemed an eternity and we were badly shook up. I always believed that I had someone looking after me."

"I had the strangest thing happen to me. I was in the front line and was sitting behind a dugout with two men on either side of me. We were eating our rations and no one was talking. All of a sudden I heard a voice as clear as day say to me, 'Get up and go away.' I looked at the others but realised that they weren't talking. Again the voice spoke to me. Cagily, I stood up and walked down the trench and just as I went around the corner, out of the blue, a shell landed ... exactly where I had been sitting. When I ran back, the two others had been killed outright in the explosion ... it was the strangest thing ...I got the word!"

James' best friend, Lance Corporal Tommy Diver was killed beside him in action on September 29th 1918 - a mere six weeks before the end of the war. He was only 20 and has no known grave. James refused to talk about what happened. It was obvious that he just wanted to block out the memories of that day, as he would have been shoulder to shoulder with Tommy when he was killed. He was a superb Lewis gunner and was awarded the Ulster Division Certificate and the Military Medal for bravery on July 1st 1916. He was only 18 at the time and an underage soldier when he beat back the counter-attacking Germans as they tried to push the remnants of the Ulster Division off the German trenches they had paid for so dearly in the C line of the Schwaben Redoubt. His citation reads, "For conspicuous gallantry on July 1, 1916, in the Thiepval sector, when he brought his Lewis gun forward under very heavy fire and repelled an enemy attack." During this action his skilful use of the machine gun accounted for many attacking Germans and as he held them back this allowed more men to make it back to the safety of the Ulster Division's trenches. He had joined the 10th Inniskillings at 15 years of age, just a few weeks before his 16th birthday and, during the war, had also been gassed and wounded.

Cpl Tommy Diver MM UDC

However, at this stage of the war in September 1918, the 10th Inniskillings had been disbanded and some of the men had been assigned to other battalions of 109 Brigade of the Ulster Division. Tommy and James found themselves in the 2nd Inniskillings as Lewis gunners. The 109 Brigade, 36th Ulster Division now included the remnants of the 1st and 2nd Inniskillings who, throughout the war, had taken the most appalling losses. It was one of three British divisions put under the command of the King of Belgium for the battle. The Inniskillings were moved from Messines up to Ypres and during the attack of September 28th, which commenced in torrential rain, the Ulster Division was held in reserve. The attack was one of the most incredible since the war had dragged to the stalemate situation of the trenches as the attacking divisions broke right through the German lines of trenches into the open fields beyond, some

Photo: Dessie Harper

10th Inniskillings battalion machine-gun section with a Vickers belt-fed machine gun and 4 Lewis guns.
Other than the instructor and Capt G Austin the rest of the unit look very young.

Photo: Piers Henderson

A team of German machine gunners photographed in 1916. This unit looks equally young.

3.5 miles from their starting point. The next day the Ulster Division was ordered forward by train and they disembarked at the perilous location, Hellfire Corner. Unfortunately there was little artillery support, as guns could not be brought forward due to the state of the roads and the attack was losing momentum. It was recorded that even Lewis guns could not be brought forward to the places they were most needed. The soldiers were now advancing through open countryside but were being held up by belt-fed German machine guns, with their heavy rate of fire, hidden in the hedgerows and farm buildings. Lewis guns were urgently needed to engage these machine guns. Only a few guns did get up, including that of James Monteith and Tommy Diver and another Lewis gunner in the same battalion, L/Cpl Ernest Seaman who won the Victoria Cross on that day. His citation shows the ferocity and frenzy of the fighting in which they were an integral part.

L/Cpl ERNEST SEAMAN, VC, MM. 42364. 2nd Bn. Royal Inniskilling Fusiliers, aged 25. The London Gazette of November 15th, 1918, states: -

"For most conspicuous bravery and devotion to duty. When the right flank of his company was held up by a nest of enemy machine guns, he, with great courage and initiative, rushed forward under heavy fire with his Lewis gun and engaged the position single-handed, capturing two machine guns and twelve prisoners and killing one officer and two men. Later in the day he again rushed another enemy machine-gun position, capturing the gun under heavy fire. He was killed immediately after. His courage and dash were beyond all praise, and it was entirely due to the very gallant conduct of L/Cpl Seaman that his company was enabled to push forward to its objective and capture many prisoners."

Ernest Seaman VC and Tommy Diver MM were killed on the same day. James Monteith was there too in the same action. Seaman and Diver have no known graves, but their names are recorded on the massive memorial to the missing at Tyne Cot Cemetery in Belgium where 10,000 other soldiers are buried. Their names are recorded on the same panel of the memorial inscribed amongst 35,000 other names whose remains are lying in the surrounding countryside.

After the war, James worked as a postman in Londonderry and lived in the schoolhouse at Carnmoney near Eglinton Village.

"Although there were lots of girls, I never married. The war changed me totally. I could never strike up a long lasting relationship as my whole personality had changed. Back in 'Civvy Street' I found it hard to adapt to the mundane things again. Many of the things people spend so much of their time, money and effort on seemed to have little meaning now. I wouldn't have been easy to live with after the mental and physical torment we had come through."

" My hearing is now very poor – possibly due to the constant rattle of the Lewis and Vickers machine guns, never mind the constant explosions of shells and mortars. With me being in this nursing home and with no family, I feel I was the forgotten veteran."

James died on October 1, 1992 aged 95 and was buried in St Canice's church grounds in Eglinton. He was the last surviving veteran of the 10th Royal Inniskilling Fusiliers who had fought with the Ulster Division after the Battle of the Somme. It was the smallest funeral I was ever at with less than a dozen people attending it. Part of the proceeds of the first edition of this book went to buy James a fitting headstone with the inscription:-

"James Monteith, died Oct 1st 1992 aged 95. The last of the 10th Royal Inniskilling Fusiliers who fought with the 36th Ulster Division at the battles of Messines, Passchendaele, Cambrai and St Quentin."

Leslie Bell lived on to the right old age of 98 in Moneymore. He passed away on February 11th, 1996 and had a huge funeral that was fitting for the last of the 10th Royal Inniskilling Fusiliers.

A Derryman's Flanders Poppy

Mr. James Monteith, of 36, Strabane Old Road, Londonderry, has in his possession a Flanders poppy, which he plucked during the Great War. He has its blood-red leaves, now somewhat faded, carefully preserved in a New Testament.

Mr Monteith served as a runner with the 10th Battalion the Royal Inniskilling Fusiliers, and at the Battle of Passchendaele he was sent from Battalion Headquarters with a message to the front line. It was dusk at the time, and he lost his way. He wandered past the front line into No-man's-land on the Ypres Salient, and for seven hours he was lost there. During that time, with shells constantly coming across from the German lines, he covered a wide area striving to get back to the British lines, and wherever he went he was met with nothing but British dead, who had lain unburied for days. It was not until dawn that Mr. Monteith managed to find his way back to the British lines.

It was at Ypres where he picked up the poppy, which is now such a unique souvenir of an occasion so tragic. There must be few, if any, poppies in existence now, which grew on the Great War battlefields.

Taken from the Londonderry Sentinel, November 11, 1933.

Reproduced from research carried out by Trevor Temple.

Chapter 35
Homage

It was 1995 before I had the opportunity to visit the battlefields and war cemeteries for the first time. It was almost an act of homage to see the graves of those who were mentioned in the book and the places where they fought and so many of them died. I travelled with a small group of people in a minibus, which allowed us greater flexibility to visit where we wanted and spend as much time as we needed. One of the places I asked if we could include in our itinary was the site of the Cambrai battlefield where the 36th Division had attacked at the Canal du Nord. This was the place where Jim Donaghy and another chap from 109 Trench Mortar Battery called Billy Mayne were ordered out in a sap in no-man's-land with their Stokes mortar. (see Chapter 22) This was a very precarious position to be in. Once the attack started their job was to fire shells at the huge flat topped spoil heap that had been composed from the earth removed from the colossal canal during its construction. It had not been finished due to the war and had been turned into the most formidable German defences with the spoil heap overlooking and dominating the British trenches, with the big, empty canal channel behind. I realised that as it was such a big construction that there was a good chance that it would still be there over 75 years later and the bank along the canal would allow us access to it.

When we got to the canal we marvelled at its size and how it must have been a huge obstacle to the British attack. Then the great spoil heap, (or slag heap as the soldiers referred to it) came into our field of vision in the distance. We gained access to it through a farm gate, which led into a huge field where we were able to park our bus. I consulted the 1917 trench map I had with me which showed the exact positions of British and German trenches. We walked where the German trenches ran, along the bottom of the spoil heap, but we decided that we wanted to see the view from the top where the main German force would have been dug in with their machine guns and observation posts. As we struggled up the steep sides, now heavily overgrown with dense hawthorn, we started to come across unexploded shells and masses of empty machine gun bullet cases. Soon we started to find weird looking projectiles that looked like the rusty silencers from a car's exhaust system. It took me just a few seconds to recognise what they were... Stokes mortar shells! These unexploded high explosive mortars almost certainly were fired during the attack but there was no proof. What we discovered next was even more interesting. Some mortars had burst along one side and hadn't disintegrated in the usual way. They were the thermite rounds, another specialist weapon used in the attack.

The huge Canal du Nord at Cambrai in 1994. Back in 1917, the construction of the canal had been interrupted by the war and the Germans transformed the empty canal into a huge defensive position. The rock and soil, which had been extracted during its construction, was piled up in a great spoil heap that was also fortified by the Germans. It had a commanding position over the British lines.

Photo: Author

Author and some of the group at the bottom of the slag heap (position of front line German trench) at Cambrai with exploded and defused Stokes mortar rounds.
Warning: *Never touch any ordinance on a battlefield. It can be unstable and lethal.*

Photo: Author

They were designed to burst in the air above German positions showering them with reacting chemicals and molten metal burning at 3000°C. These were particularly fearsome mortars as they set fire to everything they made contact with and, once burning, were virtually impossible to put out. Even small particles coming in contact with human flesh left men in agony and usually had to be cut out with a knife before they burned deeper into the body. These were the same as Jim would have fired during the attack and, as there were only four Stokes mortars firing, there was a one in four chance that these shells had been fired by Jim Donaghy and Billy Mayne!

All of a sudden a French farmer arrived on the scene and was surprised to find a minibus load of Ulstermen on his land. He had never had visitors researching the war on his land before and after a conversation in poor French, he was delighted to have us visit and asked us if we wanted the unexploded 18-pounder shell for a souvenir. He then went to a rock and started to defuse it by banging its nose cone off which had us all running for cover, much to his delight! He explained that the land was still yielding a harvest of unexploded munitions 75 years after the battle. He was most happy to see us take away some of the defused scrap metal that our forefathers had left.

I had researched the exact position of Jim Donaghy and Billy Mayne's mortar from a copy of the original attack plan. With the aid of the map and the original sunken road, I was able to identify the features that had been fortified as the British front line. What also remained was a little Y junction on the sunken road and from this I could identify to within an accuracy of 20 metres, Jim and Billy's mortar position during the battle. It was an amazing experience to stand there and gaze at this huge fortification, almost like a pyramid with the top levelled off and witness the same view that they would have had during the Battle of Cambrai.

Author at the top of the slag heap overlooking the British lines.

But! Something... nothing short of incredible, was about to happen later that day.

One of the group asked the trip organiser if we could travel south in the direction of Ham to place a poppy cross on a soldier's grave for a family member. It was a fairly long journey just to place a cross on a grave as we had travelled to France already in the minibus and the prospect of another 60 mile round trip was not the most appealing. When we arrived at Savy British Cemetery, 6.5km west of St Quentin, we got out of the bus, glad to stretch our legs and proceeded to view some of the graves. Without seeming disrespectful, we had seen a huge number of graves in the previous days and weren't paying particular attention to the inscriptions on the headstones as much as we had been earlier in the trip. I decided to leave the cemetery and have a short walk. Next thing I knew, one of our party hurriedly came over to me and quietly said, "Gardiner, come over here, there's a grave which may be of interest to you."

I was astounded as it was the grave of Lt. Norman Lowden who had been Jim Donaghy's commanding officer in 109 Trench Mortar Battery. He had survived a huge explosion that had wiped out most of the men of the battery when Jim had been home on leave in 1917, but had been killed in the massive March 1918 German offensive. But then... the most incredible thing happened. As I turned away to leave the grave, another line of Inniskilling Fusilier headstones came into view and the first one I viewed was - William (Billy) Mayne! Yes, the same Billy Mayne that we had been talking about all morning when we visited the slagheap. Other men's graves from the battalion flanked him on each side. Think for a second if you will on the probability of this happening. That day we could have chosen to visit any one of hundreds of military cemeteries, viewed the names of hundreds of thousands of men on memorials or seen graves of hundreds of thousands of dead soldiers through France and Belgium and had now, through the most weird coincidence came face to face with the grave of a man we had all been talking about that very morning, hidden in a cemetery of nearly 900 headstones. The date of his death was March 21st, 1918, the day that the 1st and 2nd Battalions of the Inniskillings had been virtually wiped out and the 9th Battalion was the sole survivor. Jim Donaghy was serving with the 9th at this time and was captured some six days after they had fought a frantic rearguard action through this area, while trying to hold back the German advance.

I stood at Mayne's grave totally astounded, as did the rest of the group. Billy Mayne came from Sandholes near Cookstown, Co. Tyrone. He had lost two brothers on July 1st at the Somme.

An unreal experience. Coming across Billy Mayne's grave unexpectedly at Savy military cemetary near Ham.

Photo: Author

Going around different cemeteries is a very moving experience but many visitors cannot come to grips with the fact that these are not just rows of headstones but contain the remains of a soldier buried beneath. To most people their death is just surmised and anonymous. On visiting the beautiful little Authuille cemetery overlooking the River Ancre, I suddenly came across a row of 10th Inniskillings Fusiliers' graves. What made this such a moving experience was that every one had been mentioned to me by Jim Donaghy … they had all been his friends and he had told me the harrowing and emotional stories of how each of these young lads had died. Ernest (Eddie) Donnelly had been given first aid by Jim Donaghy during the battalion's baptism of fire on March 10th. I knew that Eddie's leg had been blown off and the last person he saw and talked to was Jim Donaghy as he struggling to give him first aid in the most impossible and terrifying of situations. Buried beside him was Jim Boyd whose mangled and unrecognisable corpse Jim had unwittingly been standing on as he gave Donnelly first aid. Next was George Stirling, a great friend of Jim's since childhood. He had been riddled with shrapnel and died in the utmost agony with medics doing all they could for him throughout the night in a front line dugout. On the other hand, Willie Graham, one of the most popular and jovial soldiers in the battalion, had the tiniest hole in the back of his skull where he had been hit by a tiny piece of shrapnel as he fooled about while washing his hair in front of his mates.

The memories of that trip will stay with me a lifetime.

Connaught Cemetery is located just outside Thiepval Wood where the Ulster Division emerged on July 1st. This would have been in no-man's land in 1916.

Photo: Author

Mill Road Cemetery located at the top of the slope on which the Schwaben redoubt was located. This was the location of some of the fiercest fighting on July 1st 1916. Graves are laid flat in some areas as the ground beneath is unstable due to subsidence in underground tunnels and dugouts.

Photo: Author

Remains of a German observation / machine gun post which still faces Thiepval Wood. This is one of the last visible remnants of the German trenches where the Ulster Division attacked on July 1st 1916.

Photo: Author

Chapter 36
The Final Marchpast

After the publication of the first edition of this book Jim Donaghy continued to recount his memories to me, many of which have been included in this updated edition. One of the most poignant was told to me just before he passed away.

On Saturday August 9th, 1919, which had been designated as Peace Day, a parade was organised in Belfast for those who had served in the Great War. The majority of the participants were from the Ulster Division and formed up in regiments for a march past at the City Hall. This was before any Remembrance Day had ever been held as the war had ended a mere nine months before and many soldiers had returned home less than seven months. This was the first time that a huge number of veterans from different units had met up.

Jim Donaghy
"As we hung about waiting for the start of the parade, we weren't sure what it was going to be like or even whether it was even a good idea considering all that had happened? We were filled with the memories of friends who hadn't come back and it was pretty emotional and people were fairly subdued as they waited formed up in ranks for the parade to march off. Then the band of the Irish Guards appeared and as soon as the Boom ...Boom ...Boom of the big bass drum started, we all straightened up as if on parade as the band struck up with the tune, "The British Grenadiers". Orders were shouted. Then as one - we changed from a crowd into the Ulster Division for the last time."

They were a different band of men from those who had left and as they marched past the City Hall in Belfast thousands cheered them. There were, however, many people crying in the crowds for their sons, husbands and fathers who hadn't made it home.

Jim Donaghy
"As we passed the City Hall, I saw out of the thousands of spectators, one pitiable woman run up to the review platform where the senior officer, Field Marshal French was standing and taking the salute. The wee woman looked as if she hadn't a penny and started to scream up to him out of her mind with grief. 'Where's my Johnny! Where's my wee Johnny! Where is he? Where did you leave him? Don't you know he was all that I had?' They then took her away."

For many it was a hard march mentally… but for a lot of others it was also physically hard, limping from war wounds or walking with the aid of sticks and prosthetic limbs where once muscular limbs had been. Some had to be escorted as they were blind but all had one thing in common: Pride. Pride that they had done their best and given their all.

The Ulster Division had done its best, with a record to equal the finest of the rest of the British Army or the British Empire. An integral part of its success was due to the 10th Service Battalion Royal Inniskilling Fusiliers or simply …. the Derrys.

"Three Cheers for the Derrys!"

Appendix

On Friday 30th June we received orders to march out of Forceville at 9.15pm en route for the Assembly trenches, which had been carefully reconnoitred and fixed upon beforehand. The start was made punctually by platoons at 100 yards distance going through Aveluy Wood, which was very dark. The Commanding Officer Lt.Col. Ross Smyth had the misfortune to slip and sprain his leg and had to be sent back in an ambulance. Command was then taken over by Major.F.S.N. Macrory. Some enemy shelling was experienced from this on but the battalion was fortunate in reaching its Assembly Trenches without casualties. By the time all Companies and Details were in position it was after 1am as the trenches were crowded and progress difficult and slow. Luckily the weather kept fine and the men were in good spirits. Final arrangements for the assault were now made and the four gaps in our wire entanglement (which had previously been cut) were inspected and labelled, with lookout men being posted close to them to direct all troops to their positions. The Brigade dispositions for the attack may now be provincially summarised. The 10th Bn. Royal Inniskilling Fusiliers occupied a front of approximately 200yds from the top of Inverness Avenue on the right to the top of Elgin Avenue on the left.

The objective was the German "C" Line from a point C (Omagh) exclusive - map reference R.20.a.7.4 on the left to a point R. 20.c.6.6 on the right. This included one strongpoint known as B.16 (Dungannon), which had to be consolidated when captured. As supports, the 14th Bn. Royal Irish Rifles whose orders were to assist in the holding of the "C" line. On our right were the 9th Bn. Royal Inniskilling Fusiliers with the 11th Bn. Royal Inniskilling Fusiliers in similar support. On our left was the 108th Brigade while in reserve was the 107th Brigade with orders to pass through us after the "C" line was taken and capture the German "D" line. The battalion dispositions were that "A" Coy should lead the attack on the right supported by 'C' Coy whilst "B" Coy led the attack on the left supported by "D" Coy. Each Coy carried picks, shovels, and a proportion of Royal Engineers consolidating material and had attached to it a machine gun and team from the 109th Brigade Machine Gun Coy as well as strong parties of bombers and "cleaners up" from the 14th Bn. Royal Irish Rifles. By 6am there was every probability of a bright sunny day. An issue of rum was served round to the men in the trenches. Our bombardment, which had been intense all night, now became terrific, the enemy retaliating with terrible vigour. By 7am the Stokes Trench mortars opened a hurricane bombardment on the enemy front trench with very great effect showers of earth and debris being thrown high into the air all along this trench. The uproar of the explosions coming from their side was now so great that it was difficult to make oneself heard, but our men preserved their usual cheerful and almost stolid demeanour through everything, grinning happily if one paused to speak to them.

A reference to the map will show that our advance had been made at an angle practically half-right to our front line trenches. The famous "sunken road" in No-man's-land" just in front of our line is however practically at a direct right angle to the line of advance and it had been carefully impressed on all ranks in order to keep to the true direction (of advance) the "sunken road" would be used as a preliminary forming up place for all our lines. This arrangement was well adhered to by our leading lines but in the excitement of the assault, some of the rear waves of men advanced straight out of our front trenches and at right angles to them. By this error these supporting waves reached the German lines much too far to the left which partly counts for the mixing up of the battalions that finally ensued.

A more serious error which occurred later was that the leading companies twice ignored the timetable of our artillery barrage and in consequence, through their eagerness to advance suffered heavy loss from our own artillery fire. It is unfair to blame anyone in particular for this regrettable incident as all the senior officers with these companies had fallen at the time and though all ranks knew the timetable they quite forgot about it in the impetuous ardour of their assault. It is unfortunately not the first time that this incident has happened through the course of the war and its liability is rendered greater by any special gallantry in the troops employed. At 7.15am on a beautiful summer morning the two leading companies began to move by platoons though the gaps in our wire into No-man's-land keeping flat in extended line with about 3 paces interval and in this formation crept cautiously up until the leading line was within 100yds of the German "A" line where it lay down to wait the signal for the assault. The three following similarly advanced and lying down at distances in rear of about 50yds successfully. Meantime the supporting Coys "C" & "D" moved forward through Thiepval Wood from their assembly trenches to the front line trenches just vacated by the leading companies where they prepared to move in lines of platoons in fours directly the advance was sounded.

At 7.30am sharply the hurricane bombardment of the Stokes mortars ceased and from our front trench came the regimental bugle call followed by the "Advance". Simultaneously Coy and Platoon leaders blew their whistles and the lines of men jumped up and advanced at a steady march towards the enemy trenches. The spectacle of these lines of men moving forward with rifle sloped and the morning sun glistening on their fixed bayonets, keeping their alignment and distance as well as if on a ceremonial parade. Unfaltering, unwavering – this spectacle was not only impressive, it was extraordinary. Hardly a man was seen to fall in this early stage of the advance. On our left the 108th Brigade had advanced slightly before the time but they had a longer distance to come so the total alignment was not affected. On our right the 9th Inniskillings were less fortunate than us and suffered as they advanced from enfilade machine gun fire coming from the Thiepval direction but never failed to preserve their alignment. Every credit is due to our artillery that had done all they had promised us in the matter of cutting the enemy's wire and levelling his front trenches. Not a single man of our Battalion had occasion as far as one can learn to use his wire cutters of which each Coy carried a supply. In the "A" line the leading Coys were reinforced by the two supporting Coys and our barrage having lifted, the men sped forward towards the "B" line having killed the few Germans who had so far appeared. The supporting Coys suffered more in the first part of the advance than the leading ones, the enfilading machine gun fire from Thiepval having increased in intensity. Enemy prisoners now began to come in, most of them having evidently been concealed in deep dugouts in the German support trench which runs close behind their front trench. They seemed for the most part dazed and bewildered by the fury of our bombardment and were only too glad to surrender and throw down their arms. They were sent back under escort to our trenches – about 16 prisoners to each escorting soldier. The first batches of these prisoners were so anxious to reach the shelter of our trenches that they outstripped their escorts in the dash across the open and meeting our reinforcing lines coming forward were bayoneted by them in the heat of the moment. Some reached our trenches and were there hunted by the few of our men remaining in our front line who were somewhat uncertain as to the true state of affairs. In "B" line which was captured with comparatively little opposition about 8am a considerable number of prisoners was taken and the dugouts were thoroughly bombed whilst waiting for the barrage to lift from the "C" line. It was here that 2/Lt. Spalding from "B" Coy was killed by a regrettable mistake. He had descended to bomb a dugout and was re-ascending when he was shot by a man of one of the rifle regiments who mistook him for a German. A start was next made towards "C" line. The advance was checked for a time owing to the right flank 9th R. Inniskilling Fusiliers being held up by enfilade machine gun fire from Thiepval. And during this check we also suffered a great many casualties from the same cause. On resuming our advance a section of our line pushed forward to repel and got gut up by our own artillery fire causing further casualties. Directly the barrage lifted from the 'C' line, our men pushed forward and captured the trench. This was about 9am. They found a large number of dead and wounded Germans in this line, which was at once consolidated by our troops. All available Lewis and Vickers Guns being placed in defensive positions.

By this time men from the supporting battalion (14th Royal Irish Rifles) were beginning to reinforce our men and shortly after the line was further stiffened by the arrival of some of the 107th Brigade. Our right companies were now largely distributed about the "Crucifix" which they assisted the 9th R. Inniskilling Fusiliers to consolidate. Portions of the left Coys were apparently at least 200yds too far to the left of their objective owing to having kept a wrong direction from the start as explained before. In fact by this time the men of our battalion were more or less intermingled with representatives with all other Brigades of the Ulster Division. It was extremely difficult to locate any position accurately owing to the battered condition of the trenches. Capt Miller ('D" Coy, had already been brought back to our lines severely wounded in the face with shrapnel. Capt Proctor, "C" Coy, was leading his men towards the Crucifix when his leg was shattered by shellfire and he lay in the trench for many hours, but it proved impossible to get him back owing to heavy fire. Eventually Capt Knox went forward with reinforcements about 5pm and carried him back as far as the "A" line where Capt Proctor died.

About noon Capt Robertson "B" Coy and Lt. Wilton "A" Coy were endeavouring to locate their position in "C" line with a map when they were simultaneously struck by rifle fire, the former being wounded in the chin and shoulder and the latter in the chest. Lt. Wilton was assisted back to our lines by one of our NCOs, Sgt. Porter ('B" Coy) who was endeavouring to get Capt. Robertson back when a bursting shell killed Porter and both fell. No news can since be obtained of Capt. Robertson. It will thus be seen that all four Company Commanders were killed or wounded during the morning but in spite of this the remaining officers and NCOs rallied and organized the men through the long and trying day. There could be no doubt that from noon onwards considerable confusion existed and contrary orders passed from one flank to another. At some time probably about noon some of our men in association with men of the 107th Brigade attacked and carried a portion of the German "D" line, which was held for some time till enemy artillery found the range and inflicted terrible loss on them. They then fell back to the "C" line and were again decimated by artillery fire. An order was given by the senior officer on the spot to retire some 10 or 20 yds in order to take up a position in a more sheltered trench. The order was taken wrongly and many men who had gallantly held positions rendered almost untenable by artillery and machine gun fire for hours undoubtedly got the impression that they were ordered to fall back on Thiepval Wood. A scattered stream of men began to arrive back in our front line, some wounded and all much exhausted by the terrible ordeal they had come through, the time then being about 5pm. At this juncture an urgent message was received at Battalion Headquarters from the right flank where Lt McClure of "C" Coy was in command of the remnants of our men and were still holding the Crucifix. Reinforcements, ammunition and bombs were all called for and perhaps the most important of all - water.

The stragglers were hastily rallied and sent forward to the Crucifix under Capt. Knox – some 30 men in all. Six four-gallon petrol tins full of water were also sent with a spare party. This party was severely shelled on its journey across no man's land and lost several. The survivors were unable to find Lt. McClure's party and handed the water over to men of different battalions in the "C" line. Capt. Knox and his party also failed to find Lt. McClure as great confusion reigned in that district, accentuated by terrible shelling and machine gun fire from Thiepval. Many casualties occurred and eventually late in the evening a retirement became inevitable. Our front trenches were now being manned from Eglin Avenue westward to the River Ancre by the 16th Royal Irish Rifles (Pioneers), 5th West Riding Regiment and the men of the 10th R. Inniskilling Fusiliers as they returned to our trenches were collected and sent back to their assembly trenches. A party was sent to Paisley Dump to draw rations and another party to Speyside for water and the men were made as comfortable as circumstances permitted. At 4pm on 2nd July the order was received to move the battalion back to Martinsart Wood and this was accomplished happily without further loss.

The bullet pierced New Testament and Iron Cross picked up by Stewart Moore from the soldier he shot during the opening minutes of the Charge of the Ulster Division on July 1st, 1916. There were no traces of blood on the Bible suggesting he was holding it as he emerged from the dugout.

Photo: Author

The names in the roll of those who served in the 10th Royal Inniskilling Fusiliers cannot give us a glimpse of their experiences and the horrors they endured in the trenches. Many men who survived the war came home marked by disability, disfigurement or were psychologically damaged. Quite a few died very young. The following few paragraphs shed some light on what these men and their families endured.

Some citations for award of the Ulster Division Certificate for Bravery.

Sergeant James Henry Jackson was awarded a Military Medal and Ulster Division Certificate for great gallantry and devotion to duty on July 1, 1916, in the Thiepval sector. On his platoon officer being wounded, on that occasion, he took charge of the platoon, and, although wounded in the lung, did most excellent work until the battalion was relieved. He was awarded a Bar to the Military Medal for gallantry in reorganising his platoon and repelling an attack during the battle of Messines on June 7, 1917. He took part in the fighting of the spring of 1918, and was last seen leading his platoon when the Germans then broke through the British lines. He was killed in action on March 22, 1918.

Lance-Corporal Robert Mitchell

For great devotion to duty on October 4, 1916, on the Spanbroek sector. When his Lewis gun team had been buried by a trench mortar, on that occasion, he dug them out, cleaned his gun, and continued to fire on No-man's-land until the end of the bombardment. He was also awarded the Military Medal. Robert Mitchell was reported missing on March 22, 1918, and was later discovered to be a prisoner of war in Germany.

Lance-Sergeant Edward Mills

For great devotion to duty in leading his platoon after his platoon officer had been killed on July 1, 1916 in the Thiepval sector. He showed great skill in organising a counter-attack, which drove the Germans out of a portion of their line, which they had retaken. He was later awarded the Military Medal.

RSM Andrew White

For great devotion to duty during a heavy German bombardment on March 10, 1916 in the Thiepval sector. He also showed great gallantry on May 10, when the Germans raided the battalion on our right. He did excellent work on July 1 when acting as Regimental-Sergeant-Major.

Lance-Sergeant Robert Hamilton (Later promoted to CSM)

For great gallantry in the attack of July 1, 1916 in the Thiepval sector. At about 7pm the Germans counter-attacked and his platoon officer being killed, he rallied the men round him and broke up the counter-attack. He led another counter-attack later in the evening.
(He would also be awarded the Military Medal and the Distinguished Conduct Medal and was killed in action in March 1918.)

Corporal Mark Lowther

For great devotion to duty on July 1, 1916 in the Thiepval sector when laying telephone wires under very heavy fire. Finding it impossible to keep the wire intact owing to shell fire he rejoined his company. He delivered several messages in person during the day and helped to carry up ammunition.

Private Robert Jeffrey
For great gallantry on October 4, 1916 in the Spanbroek sector during a bombardment of our line. When a shell buried the whole of his gun team he managed to get out and fire on No-man's-land until the end of the bombardment.

Sergeant Robert McCarter
For gallantry on July 1, 1916 in the Thiepval sector. He brought his Lewis gun forward under very heavy fire and repelled an enemy attack.

Sergeant Robert Thompson was awarded an Ulster Division certificate. On July 1, 1916, in the Thiepval sector he showed conspicuous gallantry in leading and reorganising his platoon, and consolidating the captured 'C' line against a German counter-attack. Although not detailed for the July 1 attack, Sergeant Thompson volunteered. He was afterwards reported missing, and subsequently was confirmed dead. A similar award went to his brother, **Richard Thompson**, for displaying great bravery in bombing the enemy in the German 'B' line, and rescuing a wounded officer under heavy fire. Richard Thompson emerged from the July advance without a scratch, but was wounded the following month and spent eight months in hospital. The Thompson brothers were exceptional in that eight of them would serve with the Armed Forces in the Great War – a record in Londonderry. Sadly, three were killed and two others were very seriously wounded with one losing a leg.

But incredibly, another family from the city, the Sinclairs, surpassed the Thompson family's terrible loss. **Corporal Andrew Sinclair** served in France for over three years, and was awarded the Military Medal for bravery in capturing an enemy machine gun on June 7, 1917, at Messines Ridge. He was the youngest of five brothers who responded to the call for volunteers at the start of the Great War. Unfortunately he died of wounds in September 1918. His brother Sergeant John Sinclair was killed at Passchendaele the previous

Four of the Sinclair brothers.

year with the 10th Inniskillings. In total four of the five brothers who joined up were killed with the surviving brother, Lance Corporal Richard Sinclair, who served in France, Gallipoli, and Egypt, being gassed in 1918.

Above:
The Ulster Division certificate awarded to Sgt. Robert McCarter. 'For gallantry on July 1st, 1916 in the Theipval Sector. He brought his Lewis Gun forward under very heavy fire and repelled an enemy attack.'

Right:
Sgt. Alex Campbell won the Military Medal. He is pictured here with his wife and another couple. They may have survived the war but almost certainly not unscathed. The soldier standing is displaying a wound stripe indicating he has been wounded once before.

Photo: Piers Henderson

200

Captain McKenzie and his wife relax during his leave.
He was a keen photographer and some of his photographs appear in this book.

Photo: Captain McKenzie Collection

10th Inniskilling Signal section at Randalstown.

Photo: Dessie Harper

Photo: Helen Colhoun

The Harriers, 10th Inniskilling Running Team at Finner Camp.

Breakfast Time at Finner Camp

Photo: Trevor Temple

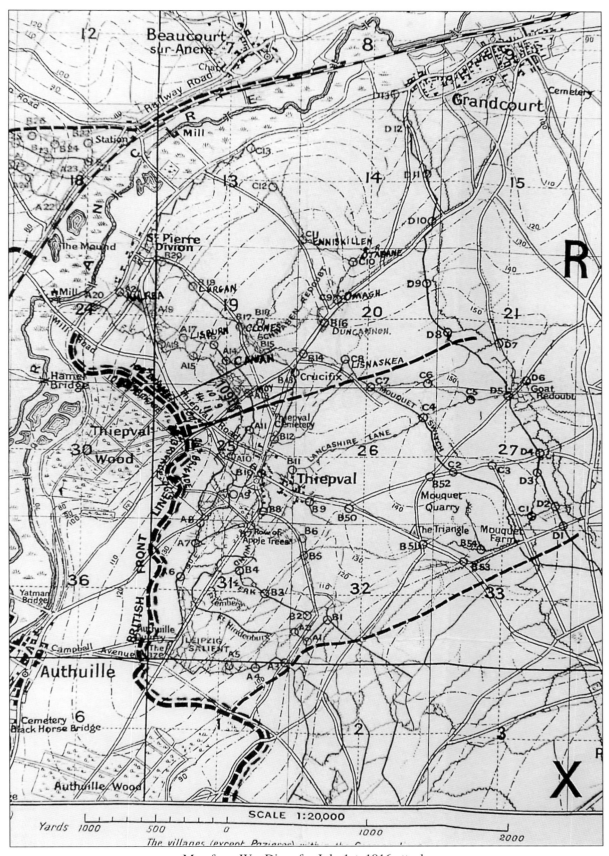

Map from War Diary for July 1st, 1916 attack.

Roll of Honour and list of those who served in the 10th Royal Inniskilling Fusiliers

During the course of my research, I came across the following names of soldiers who served in the 10th Royal Inniskilling Fusiliers. There is no official list available and therefore these names have been gleaned from various documents. Additions to the original list, which appeared in the first edition, have been made. Many of these names and numbers have been researched by Robert Elliott who has sifted through various sources of information, much of which has recently entered the public domain through the Internet, with the Medal Roll cards from the National Archives being particularly helpful. It is by no means a comprehensive list. Different official sources and other information can misquote numbers and names. We have tried to be as accurate as we can and apologise for any errors. Ranks shown are not necessarily those held at the termination of military service.

Much more information is available but, unfortunately, space does not permit its printing.

KIA = Killed in action	DOW = Died of wounds
MID = Mentioned In Despatches	DSO = Distinguished Service Order
CdeG = Croix de Guerre	MM = Military Medal
DCM = Distinguished Conduct Medal	UDC = Ulster Division Certificate for Bravery
MC = Military Cross	POW = Prisoner of War
M Mil = Medaille Militaire	Bar – meaning the recipient won the medal again.

The rolls contained in the final section are as follows:

The first list with the military service numbers ranging from 15264 to 16124 records the details of the original volunteers who signed up for Kitchener's or Carson's Army in September and October 1914. The second list consists of those who joined later. The third list contains the details of the officers.

Number	Surname	Forename	Rank	Awards	Info	Additional
15264	Adair	John	Cpl		4/10/16	KIA
15265	Adair	William	Pte			
15266	Adams	Andrew	Pte			
15267	Adams	John	Pte			
15268	Adams	William	L/Cpl			
15269	Adams	David	L/Cpl		1/7/16	KIA
15270	Adams	David C	Sgt	UDC MiD		
15271	Adams	Thomas	Sgt			
15272	Alcorn	Henry	Sgt			
15273	Alexander	John	Pte			
15274	Allen	George	Pte			
15275	Allen	Charles	Pte			
15276	Allen	John	Pte			
15277	Allen	Henry	CSM		1/7/16	KIA
15278	Anderson	Archibald	Pte			
15279	Allen	Robert N	Pte			
15280	Allander	John James	L/Cpl		1/7/16	KIA
15281	*					
15282	*					
15283	*					
15284	Anderson	William	L/Cpl		18/7/16	DOW
15285	Anderson	Alexander	Pte		16/8/17	KIA
15286	*					
15287	Anderson	James	Pte			
15288	Anderson	Robert	Pte			
15289	Armstrong	William	Pte		1/7/16	KIA
15290	Anderson	Robert	Pte		1/7/16	KIA
15291	Anderson	Robert	Pte			
15292	Anderson	William	Pte		12/8/17	KIA
15293	Anderson	Archibald	Pte		16/4/18	KIA
15294	Andrews	Herbert	L/Cpl			
15295	Arbuckle	Hubert	Sgt		2/9/18	KIA
15296	Arbuckle	Wesley	Pte			
15297	Atcheson	Daniel	L/Cpl			
15298	Atkinson	William	Pte			
15299	Atchinson	Matthew	Pte			
15300	Armour	Thomas	Pte			
15301	Austin	William	Pte			
15302	*					
15303	Bacon	Robert	L/Cpl		1/7/16	KIA
15304	Baird	William	Sgt	UDC		
15305	Bailey	Thomas	Sgt		1/7/16	KIA
15306	Bailey	Arthur	Pte			died 27/4/21
15307	Bailey	William	Pte			
15308	Barnett	William	Pte			
15309	Baxter	James	Pte			

Number	Surname	Forename	Rank	Awards	Info	Additional
15310	Barr	Robert	Cpl			
15311	*					
15312	Bates	Albert	Cpl			
15313	Bell	Robert J	L/Cpl			
15314	Bell	William	Sgt			
15315	Bell	Martin	Pte			
15316	Bell	Leslie	Pte			
15317	Bennett	Henry	Cpl			
15318	Black	David	Sgt		3/4/16	KIA
15319	**					
15320	Black	Robert	Pte			
15321	Black	George	Pte			
15322	Blackburn	James	Sgt			
15323	*					
15324	*					
15325	Boardman	John	Pte			
15326	Bogle	Albert	Sgt/Lt		10/8/17	KIA
15327	Bond	William J	Pte		30/9/18	KIA
15328	Boone	John Alex	Pte		9/7/16	DOW
15329	Bonnar	Herbert	Pte			
15330	Bovaird	Thomas	Pte			
15331	*					
15332	*					
15333	Boyd	Alexander	Pte		1/7/16	KIA
15334	Baird	William	Pte	UDC		
15335	Boyd	David	Pte			
15336	Boyd	George	Pte			
15337	Boyd	John	Sgt			
15338	Boyd	Robert	L/Cpl		1/7/16	KIA
15339	Boyd	Edmond	Pte			
15340	Boyd	Samuel	Pte			
15341	Boyd	James	Pte		10/3/16	KIA
15342	*					
15343	*					
15344	Bradley	Samuel	Cpl			
15345	Bradley	Samuel	Pte			
15346	Bradley	Samuel	Pte			
15347	*					
15348	*					
15349	Bracken	Thomas	CSM			
15350	Braid	William A	L/Cpl		10/3/16	KIA
15351	Brangham	John	Sgt	MM	29/3/18	KIA
15352	*					
15353	Brockerton	John	Pte			
15354	Brown	Henry	Pte			
15355	Brown	Thomas	Pte			
15356	Brown	John	Pte			

Number	Surname	Forename	Rank	Awards	Info	Additional
15357	Brown	Andrew	Pte			
15358	Brown	John	Pte			
15359	Brown	Matthew	Pte			
15360	Brown	Charles	Pte		22/3/18	KIA
15361	Brown	Andrew	Pte			
15362	Brown	John	Pte		2/7/16	DOW
15363	*					
15364	Burke	James	Cpl	DCM		
15365	Burke	Leslie	Pte			
15366	Burke	Sam	Pte			
15367	Burke	David	Pte		31/8/16	KIA
15368	Burns	Dysart	Pte			
15369	Burns	Joseph	Pte			
15370	*					
15371	Burns	Robert	Pte			
15372	Burnside	Joseph	Cpl			
15373	Burnside	Walter	Pte			
15374	*					
15375	Brown	A	Pte			
15376	Byers	Robert	A/WOII			
15377	Cairns	John	L/Cpl			
15378	Cairns	Robert	L/Cpl		1/7/16	KIA
15379	Caghill	Henry	Pte			
15380	Caldwell	Joseph	Pte			
15381	Caldwell	Herbert	Pte			
15382	Caldwell	Thomas	Pte			
15383	Cameron	Hector	Pte			
15384	Campbell	Robert. G	Pte	UDC		
15385	Campbell	Joseph	L/Cpl			
15386	Campbell	James. E	Pte		22/3/18	KIA
15387	Cagill	Henry. G	Pte			
15388	Campbell	John	Pte			
15389	*					
15390	Blair	R J	Pte			
15391	Campbell	Samuel	Pte			
15392	Campbell	Alex	A/Sgt	MM UDC		
15393	Campbell	John	Pte			
15394	Campbell	Robert	Cpl			
15395	Campbell	Samuel	Pte			
15396	Campbell	Ernest	A/Sgt			
15397	Campbell	Hugh. M	CSM/WOII			
15398	Campbell	Daniel. R	Sgt			
15399	Canning	Hugh	Pte			
15400	Canning	William	Pte			
15401	Canning	Thomas	Pte			
15402	Carney	Thomas	Pte			
15403	*					
15404	Cassells	James	Sgt			

Number	Surname	Forename	Rank	Awards	Info	Additional
15405	Cassidy	Robert	Pte			DOW-Home
15406	Cassidy	Samuel	Sgt			
15407	Clarke	Samuel	Pte			
15408	Campbell	James Fred	Pte			
15409	*					
15410	Clements	James	Pte			
15411	Clements	William	L/Cpl			
15412	Clyde	Alex	Pte			
15413	Cochrane	James	Pte			
15414	Cochrane	Thomas	Pte	UDC		
15415	Colhoun	Robert	Pte			
15416	Colhoun	John	Pte			
15417	Colhoun	James	Pte			
15418	Colhoun	Robert	Pte			
15419	Collins	Thomas	Pte			
15420	Connolly	Samuel	Pte			
15421	Connolly	Alfred	Pte			
15422	Connor	Joseph	Pte			
15423	Cooke	Robert	L/Cpl	MM	1/7/16	KIA
15424	Cooke	Hugh	Pte			
15425	*					
15426	*					
15427	Cowan	Robert	Pte			
15428	Cowan	Robert. S	Pte		1/7/16	KIA
15429	Cowan	Joseph	Pte			
15430	*					
15431	Cox	Thomas. W	RQMS - Lt			
15432	Cox	William	Sgt			
15433	*					
15434	Crockett	Walter	Pte		1/7/16	KIA
15435	Crockett	Charles. L	L/Cpl -Lt		28/4/16	KIA-Dublin
15436	Crockett	Thomas	Pte		9/8/16	DOW
15437	Crampsie	Thomas	Pte			
15438	Creelman	Joseph	Pte			
15439	Cresswell	Andrew	Sgt			
15440	Cresswell	Harry	Pte			
15441	Creswell	William. J	L/Cpl		5/12/17	KIA
15442	Cresswell	Samuel L	Pte			
15443	Cully	Andrew	Cpl			POW
15444	Cummings	Alexander	Cpl			
15445	*					
15446	Cunningham	William	Pte			
15447	Curry	John	Pte		1/7/16	KIA
15448	Currie	Andrew	Pte			
15449	Curtis	Ernest	Pte			
15450	Darragh	David	Pte			
15451	Davin	Arthur	Pte			POW

Number	Surname	Forename	Rank	Awards	Info	Additional
15452	Davidson	Robert	Pte		2/12/17	Died home
15453	Davidson	W J	Sgt			
15454	Deane	Hamilton	Pte		12/4/16	Died home
15455	Dempsey	Ephriam	Cpl			
15456	Devenny	James	Pte			
15457	Devenny	Neil	Pte			
15458	Devenny	Samuel	Pte			
15459	Diver	Thomas	L/Cpl	MM UDC	29/9/18	KIA
15460	Dickson	Thomas	Pte			
15461	Diffin	William	Pte			
15462	Doherty	James	Sgt			
15463	Doherty	Robert	L/Cpl			
15464	Doherty	William	Pte			
15465	Doherty	Albert	L/Sgt			
15466	Doherty	John	L/Cpl			
15467	Douglas	James McG	L/Cpl			
15468	Douglas	John A	Cpl			
15469	Dougherty	Joseph	Pte			
15470	Doherty	Richard	L/Cpl			
15471	Dougherty	Robert	Sgt			
15472	Donaghy	Samuel	Pte			
15473	Donaghy	William	Sgt			
15474	Donaghy	John	L/Cpl			
15475	Donaghy	David	Cpl	MM		
15476	Donald	Samuel	Cpl	MM		
15477	Donaldson	William	Pte			
15478	Donaldson	John	Pte			
15479	Donaldson	William G	Pte			
15480	Donnell	Thomas	Pte			
15481	Donnell	Charles J	Pte			
15482	Donnell	John	Pte		1/7/16	KIA
15483	Donnelly	Ernest	L/Cpl		10/3/16	KIA
15484	Doole	James	Pte			
15485	Douthart	Henry	Pte			
15486	Downs	John	Pte/Bugler		28/3/18	KIA
15487	Downs	Thomas	Pte			
15488	Duckett	William	Pte			
15489	Duddy	Alex	Pte			
15490	Duff	Thomas	Pte			
15491	Duncan	Andrew	Pte			
15492	Dunlop	William	Pte		1/7/16	KIA
15493	Dickson	John	Pte			
15494	Dymond	Robert	Pte	MM		POW
15495	Dinsmore	Andrew	Pte			
15496	Dysart	Hugh	Pte			
15497	Dysart	Robert	Pte			
15498	Edgar	John	Pte			
15499	Edgar	John	Pte			

Number	Surname	Forename	Rank	Awards	Info	Additional
15500	Edmundson	Samuel	Pte			
15501	Edmundson	John	Pte			
15502	Elder	Aaron	Pte			
15503	Elder	James	Pte			
15504	Elder	Robert	Pte			
15505	Elder	Samuel	Pte			
15506	Elder	William	Pte			
15507	Ellis	Phillip L	Sgt			
15508	Evans	J	Sgt			
15509	*					
15510	Evans	Harry	L/Cpl			
15511	Eyre	Charles	L/Cpl		1/7/16	KIA
15512	Ferguson	James	Pte			
15513	*					
15514	Ferris	Robert	Pte			
15515						
15516	Finlay	William	Pte			
15517	Finlay	Thomas	Pte	MM UDC	26/6/17	KIA
15518	Fleming	William	Cpl	MM		
15519	Ford	James	Pte			
15520	Frankland	William A	Pte			
15521	Frazer	David	Pte			
15522	Freeman	Robert	Pte		10/8/17	KIA
15523	French	James	Pte			
15524	Fulton	Alfred	Pte			
15525	Fulton	John J	Pte		22/3/18	KIA
15526	Fulton	Robert J	Pte			
15527	Fulton	James	Pte	UDC	2/10/18	DOW
15528	Fulton	David	Pte			
15529	Ferris	George	Sgt			
15530	Galbraith	John	WO2			
15531	Gallagher	John	L/Cpl	UDC MM		
15532	Gallagher	Robert	Pte		3/6/18	KIA
15533	Goligher	Thomas	Pte			
15534	Gamble	John	Pte			
15535	Gardiner	William	L/Cpl			
15536	*					
15537	Gardiner	Gilbert	Pte			
15538	Garvin	George	Pte	MM		
15539	Gibson	Thomas	Pte			
15540	Gilbert	Joseph	Cpl			
15541	Gillen	Dan	Sgt			
15542	Gillespie	Robert	Pte			
15543	Gilliland	David	Pte			
15544	Gilliland	James	L/Cpl		1/7/16	KIA
15545	Gilmour	William	Pte			
15546	Gilmour	Thomas	Pte		22/3/18	KIA
15547	*					

Number	Surname	Forename	Rank	Awards	Info	Additional
15548	*					
15549	Glenn	Richard	Pte			
15550	*					
15551	*					
15552	Gordon	John	Pte			
15553	Gough	Henry	Pte			
15554	*					
15555	Graham	Samuel	Pte			
15556	Graham	William	Pte		17/4/16	KIA
15557	Graham	Hugh	Sgt	M.Mil. UDC		
15558	*					
15559	Gray	James	Pte			
15560	*					
15561	Grumley	John	Pte			
15562	Grundle	James	Sgt		1/7/16	KIA
15563	Gurney	William	Pte			
15564	Gurney	Hugh	Pte			
15565	Given	Andrew	Sgt			
15566	Hull	John A	Pte		21/3/18	Died
15567	Hall	Lyndsay	Pte			
15568	*					
15569	Hamilton	Henry	Pte			
15570	Hamilton	Joseph	Pte			
15571	Hamilton	Charles	Pte			
15572	Hamilton	Robert	CSM	DCM MM.	22/3/18	KIA
15573	*					
15574	Hamilton	William	Pte		1/7/16	Died
15575	Hamilton	William	L/Cpl			
15576	Hamilton	William.B	Pte			
15577	Hamilton	George	Pte			
15578	Hamilton	John	L/Cpl		22/3/18	KIA
15579	Hawe	Samuel	Sgt			
15580	Harkness	Cecil	Pte			
15581	*					
15582	Harper	Hugh	Pte			
15583	Harper	Thomas	Sgt			
15584	Hall	Stuart	Cpl			
15585	Hall	William	Pte			
15586	Harper	James	L/Cpl		1/7/16	KIA
15587	Harper	Joseph	Pte			
15588	*					
15589	Harte	John	Pte	MM	22/3/18	DOW
15590	*					
15591	*					
15592	Hawe	John	Pte			
15593	*					
15594	Hay	William	Cpl			
15595	*					

Number	Surname	Forename	Rank	Awards	Info	Additional
15596	Hayward	William	Pte		8/7/16	Died
15597	Heaney	William	Pte			
15598	Henry	William	Pte			
15599	Henry	John	L/Cpl		1/7/16	KIA
15600	Henry	Thomas	Pte			
15601	Henderson	Samuel	Pte			
15602	Herdman	William G	Pte		22/2/18	DOW
15603	Hill	Andrew	Pte			
15604	Hogg	Matthew	Cpl		1/7/16	KIA
15605	Holmes	Robert	Pte			
15606	Holmes	William J	Pte			
15607	Horner	Robert	Pte			
15608	Hosier	Ernest E	Cpl		29/3/18	KIA
15609	Houston	Arthur	L/Cpl			
15610	Houston	Francis	Pte			
15611	*					
15612	Haslett	John	L/Cpl		1/7/16	KIA
15613	Hughes	George	Pte			
15614	Hughes	Henry	Pte			
15615	Hunter	John A	Pte			
15616	Hunter	Benn	Sgt	MM		
15617	Hunter	Fred J	Sgt			
15618	Hunter	Henry	Pte			
15619	Houston	George	L/Cpl		25/10/16	KIA
15620	*					
15621	Hutchinson	Albert	Pte			
15622	Hutchinson	Thomas	Cpl			
15623	*					
15624	Hutchinson	John	Pte		10/8/17	KIA
15625	Hutchinson	Albert	Pte			
15626	Hutchman	Alexander	CQMS			
15627	Hutchman	Frederick	Pte			
15628	Hutton	Millar	Pte		17/2/17	DOW
15629	Irwin	John	Dmr		12/9/16	KIA
15630	Irwin	Robert S	CSM	MM		
15631	Irwin	Fred	WO2	MM	16/8/17	KIA 9th Btn as Lt
15632	Jack	Albert	Pte			
15633	Jackson	William	L/Cpl			
15634	Jackson	James	Sgt	MM & Bar	22/3/18	KIA
15635	Jackson	William D	L/Cpl			
15636	James	Charles	Pte		1/7/16	KIA
15637	James	Gilbert	Pte			
15638	Jamieson	James A	Pte - 2/Lt			
15639	Jamieson	Thomas	Pte			
15640	Jamieson	James	Sgt	UDC		
15641	*					
15642	Jamieson	Charles	Pte			

Number	Surname	Forename	Rank	Awards	Info	Additional
15643	Jeffery	William				
15644	Jeffery	Robert	Pte	UDC		
15645	*					
15646	Kane	John	Pte		1/7/16	KIA
15647	Jordan	Duncan	Pte			
15648	Judd	David	C/Sgt			
15649	Kane	John	Pte			
15650	Kane	William	L/Cpl		2/5/16	DOW
15651	Kealey	Samuel	L/Cpl	MM		
15652	Kelly	Joseph	Pte			
15653	Kelly	Thomas	Pte		1/7/16	KIA
15654	Kelso	William	Pte			
15655	Kennedy	James	Pte		1/7/16	KIA
15656	Kennedy	Robert	Pte		14/10/18	KIA
15657	Kennedy	David	Pte			
15658	Kennedy	William R.G	Pte		1/7/16	KIA with MGC
15659	Kennedy	John W	Sgt			
15660	Kennedy	Caldwell	WO2			
15661	Kensdale	Roland J	RSM			
15662	Kerr	Heram	Cpl	UDC		
15663	Kerr	William	Pte			
15664	Keys	Thomas	Sgt			
15665	Murray	William	Pte			
15666	Kilgore	James	Sgt			
15667	Kilgore	John	Cpl			
15668	Kirkpatrick	David J	Pte			
15669	*					
15670	Kirby	Luke	CSM	MM CdeG		
15671	*					
15672	Knox	Robert	L/Cpl			
15673	Knox	Robert	Pte		29/3/18	KIA
15674	Laird	James	L/Cpl			
15675	Lamrock	Charles	Pte			
15676	Lavelle	William J	Cpl -2/Lt			
15677	Laverby	Robert	Pte			
15678	Laverty	William	Pte	CdeG		
15679	Law	Campbell	Pte			
15680	Lawrence	David	Pte			
15681	Lawrence	William	Pte			
15682	Lappin	John	Pte			
15683	Leacock	Alexander	L/Cpl		20/1/17	KIA
15684	Leake	Joseph	L/Cpl			
15685	no trace					
15686	*					
15687	Leighton	James	Pte		8/8/17	DOW
15688	Leitch	William A	Pte		29/9/18	KIA
15689	Letson	Arthur	Pte			

Number	Surname	Forename	Rank	Awards	Info	Additional
15690	*					
15691	Leslie	Hugh	Pte			
15692	Lyttle	John	Pte		1/7/16	KIA
15693	Logan	James	Pte			
15694	*					
15695	Logue	Joseph	Sgt			
15696	Logue	Hugh	Pte		22/3/18	KIA
15697	Logue	James	Pte			
15698	Long	William	Pte			
15699	Long	William	Pte			
15700	no trace					
15701	Loughrey	William	Pte			
15702	Loughrey	Robert	L/Cpl			
15703	Loughrey	Henry	Pte			
15704	Lowther	Mark	Pte	MM UDC	20/6/17	DOW
15705	Lowthers	Marcus	L/Cpl-2Lt			
15706	Lowrey	Fred	Pte			
15707	Logan	Andrew	Cpl			
15708	Love	John	Pte		19/11/16	KIA
15709	Loughead	John	Pte			
15710	*					
15711	Lyttle	William	Pte			
15712	Little	John	Pte			
15713	Molloy	Thomas	A/Sgt			
15714	Macauley	Robert	Pte			
15715	MacKey	Samuel	CQMS			
15716	*					
15717	Mars	John	L/Cpl			
15718	Martin	Robert	Pte			
15719	Martin	William	L/Cpl			
15720	Martin	William	Pte			
15721	Martin	William	Pte		1/7/16	KIA
15722	Monteith	Thomas	Pte			
15723	Martin	Israel	Pte			
15724	*					
15725	Matthews	John	Pte			
15726	Matthews	James	Sgt			
15727	Maultsaid	William	Pte			
15728	*					
15729	Millar	James	L/Cpl			
15730	Millar	John	Pte			
15731	Millar	William	Pte			
15732	Millar	W J	Pte			
15733	Millar	Knox	Pte			
15734	Millar	Thomas	Pte			
15735	Millar	G A	Pte			
15736	Millar	Alexander	L/Cpl		1/7/16	KIA
15737	Milligan	James	Pte			

Number	Surname	Forename	Rank	Awards	Info	Additional
15738	Millican	Frank	Pte			
15739	Milliken	George	Pte			
15740	Mills	Ernest P	Sgt	MM UDC		
15741	Mitchell	Alexander	Pte			
15742	Mitchell	Hugh	Pte			
15743	Mitchell	Joseph	Sgt			
15744	Mitchell	James	Pte		15/10/18	DOW
15745	*					
15746	Mitchell	Robert	Pte			
15747	Mitchell	Robert	L/Cpl	UDC		
15748	*					
15749	*					
15750	*					
15751	Montgomery	James	Pte—>WO2			
15752	Montgomery	John	Pte			
15753	Moon	James	Pte			
15754	*					
15755	Moore	Stuwart	A/Cpl			
15756	Milligan	William	Pte			
15757	Moore	Samuel W	Sgt			
15758	Moore	Major	Pte			
15759	Moore	Samuel	Pte			
15760	Moore	Mark	Sgt			
15761	Moore	John	Sgt			
15762	Moore	David	Cpl		28/03/1918	KIA
15763	Moore	Wilson	Pte			
15764	Moore	Robert	Pte			
15765	Moore	Hugh	Pte			
15766	Moore	William J	Pte	UDC		
15767	*					
15768	Mooney	William	Pte			
15769	*					
15770	*					
15771	*					
15772	Morrow	Archibald	Pte			
15773	Morrison	Thomas	A/Cpl			
15774	Morrison	James	Pte		1/7/16	KIA
15775	Morrison	Edward	Pte			
15776	Mullan	William	Pte			
15777	Mullan	William	Pte			
15778	Mullan	Arthur	L/Cpl			
15779	Mullholland	Samuel	Pte			
15780	Murphy	Thomas	Pte			
15781	Murphy	Albert	L/Cpl		1/7/16	KIA
15782	Murphy	James	Pte			
15783	Murphy	Thomas	Pte			
15784	*					
15785	*					

Number	Surname	Forename	Rank	Awards	Info	Additional
15786	*					
15787	McAfee	George	C/Sgt			
15788	McArthur	John	L/Sgt			
15789	McBride	David	Pte			
15790	McBride	James	Pte		1/7/16	KIA
15791	McCallion	Andrew	L/Cpl			
15792	McCallion	George	Pte			
15793	McCallion	William	Pte			
15794	McCandless	Thomas	Pte			
15795	McCandless	Robert	Pte			
15796	McCarter	Albert	Pte/Cpl		1/7/16	KIA
15797	McCarter	Alexander	Pte			
15798	McCarter	John	Pte			
15799	McCarter	Robert	C/Sgt	UDC		
15800	McCauley	William	Pte			
15801	McKay	James	Pte		10/8/17	KIA
15802	McClay	Thomas	Pte			
15803	McClay	Robert	Pte		1/7/16	KIA
15804	McClelland	Matthew	Pte			
15805	*					
15806	McClelland	James	Pte			
15807	McClelland	Joseph	Pte			
15808	McClements	William	Cpl	UDC		
15809	McCloskey	Samuel	Sgt			
15810	McCunn	Samuel	Pte			
15811	McCurry	Daniel	Pte			
15812	McConnell	Thomas. J	Pte			
15813	McCombe	Hugh	Sgt		7/6/17	KIA
15814	McCombe	William	L/Cpl			
15815	McCarron	Thomas	Pte			
15816	McCracken	Robert	Pte		1/1/17	KIA
15817	McDermott	John	Pte			
15818	McDermott	Charles	Pte			
15819	*					
15820	McDowell	John	Pte			
15821	McElguin	Hugh	Cpl			
15822	McFadden	James	Pte		28/4/17	KIA
15823	McFadden	James	Pte			
15824	McFadden	Charles	Cpl			
15825	McFadden	Robert	Pte		10/3/16	KIA
15826	McFadden	William	Cpl			
15827	*					
15828	McFall	William	Pte			
15829	McFall	Robert	L/Cpl		1/7/16	KIA
15830	McElwee	Archie	Pte			
15831	McFaul	William	Pte			
15832	McFarland	John	Pte			
15833	McFawn	William	Pte		16/8/17	KIA

Number	Surname	Forename	Rank	Awards	Info	Additional
15834	McGarvey	Thomas	Pte			
15835	McGarvey	William	C/Sgt			
15836	McGahey	William	WOII			
15837	*					
15838	McGahey	Charles	Pte			
15839	McGinley	William	Pte			
15840	McGinley	John	Cpl			
15841	McGrillis	Thomas	L/Cpl		29/12/16	Died Home
15842	McGuigan	William	Pte			
15843	McGinness	David	Pte			
15844	*					
15845	Magill	Malcolm	Pte	MM UDC		
15846	McGuinness	David	Pte			
15847	McGregor	John	L/Cpl		17/2/17	KIA
15848	McGregor	Samuel	Cpl		1/7/16	KIA
15849	McGowan	Donald	L/Cpl		1/7/16	KIA
15850	McGuire	David	L/Cpl		26/2/16	KIA
15851	McGrath	David	Pte		10/8/17	KIA
15852	McGrath	Robert	Pte			
15853	McGuigan	Thomas	Pte			
15854	Mahaffey	Robert	Pte			
15855	McIlhatton	George	L/Cpl			
15856	McIntyre	Samuel	Pte			
15857	*					
15858	McIntyre	James	L/Cpl	MM		
15859	McElroy	William	Sgt			
15860	Mackay	John Edward	Pte		1/7/16	
15861	Mackay	Samuel	Pte			
15862	McKay	Alexander	L/Cpl			
15863	McKay	John	Pte			
15864	*					
15865	*					
15866	McKeary	Robert	Pte			
15867	McKeown	Robert	L/Cpl			
15868	McKeegan	James	Pte		14/9/16	DOW home
15869	McKelvey	William	L/Cpl			
15870	Mackrell	John	Pte		1/7/16	KIA
15871	McLaughlin	William	Pte			
15872	McLaughlin	Robert	L/Cpl			
15873	McLaughlin	Joseph	Pte		5/1/17	DOW
15874	*					
15875	*					
15876	Loughlin	Daniel	Cpl	MM CdeG		
15877	McClean	David	Sgt			
15878	McLucas	Robert	Pte			
15879	McMenemy	John	Sgt		POW	
15880	McMorris	Arthur	Pte			
15881	McMillan	William	Cpl			

Number	Surname	Forename	Rank	Awards	Info	Additional
15882	McMullan	James	Pte		1/7/16	KIA
15883	McMullan	Hugh	Pte			
15884	McMath	Henry	Pte		1/7/16	KIA
15885	McManus	James	Pte			
15886	McNabb	Arthur	Pte			
15887	McNally	Charleton	Pte			
15888	McNally	David	Pte			
15889	*					
15890	McNulty	John	Cpl			
15891	McNaul	James	Cpl			
15892	McNerlin	John	Pte			
15893	McNeill	George	Pte			
15894	*					
15895	McNeill	Samuel	Pte			
15896	McNutt	Henry	Pte			
15897	McNutt	John	L/Cpl	MM		
15898	McPeak	William	Pte			
15899	Mawhinney	Edward	Pte			
15900	*					
15901	Neill	James	Pte		1/7/16	KIA
15902	Neill	Robert	Pte			
15903	Nevin	Daniel	Pte		23/3/18	KIA
15904	*					
15905	Neely	James	L/Cpl			
15906	Neely	Adam	Pte			
15907	*					
15908	Neely	Thomas	Pte		1/7/16	KIA
15909	Nicholl	William	Sgt	MM		
15910	Nicholl	William	Pte			
15911	Noble	Robert	Pte			
15912	Norton	John R	C/Sgt			
15913	*					
15914	Nutter	William	Pte			
15915	Orr	James	Pte			
15916	Orr	Robert	Pte		1/7/16	KIA
15917	Orr	David	Pte			
15918	Orr	Thomas	Pte			
15919	Orr	Thomas	Pte			
15920	Oliver	James	Pte			
15921	Oliver	Alexander	Pte			
15922	Oliver	Thomas	Pte			
15923	Overend	John	L/Cpl			
15924	Parkhill	Thomas	Sgt		22/3/18	KIA
15925	Parkhill	Robert	Pte		29/9/18	KIA
15926	*					
15927	Park	Samuel	Pte		25/3/16	DOW
15928	*					
15929	Patterson	Samuel	Pte			

Number	Surname	Forename	Rank	Awards	Info	Additional
15930	Patterson	Thomas	Pte		1/7/16	KIA
15931	Patterson	David	Pte		1/7/16	KIA
15932	Patman	Herbert	Pte			
15933	Paul	Arthur	Pte			
15934	Peoples	William	L/Cpl			
15935	*					
15936	Peoples	George	Pte			
15937	*					
15938	Biggeart	John	Pte			
15939	Platt	David	Pte			
15940	Platt	Daniel	Pte			
15941	Platt	Samuel	Cpl			
15942	*					
15943	Pickering	Thomas	L/Cpl			
15944	Pollock	William	L/Cpl		28/4/18	KIA
15945	Pollock	Samuel C	Pte			
15946	Pomeroy	James	Pte			
15947	Purcell	Charles	Pte			
15948	Porter	James	Sgt		1/7/16	KIA
15949	*					
15950	Quigley	Adam	Pte			
15951	Quigley	John James	Pte			
15952	Quigley	John James	Pte		21/3/18	KIA
15953	Quigley	Robert	Pte			
15954	Quigley	William	Pte			
15955	Rafferty	Samuel	Pte			
15956	Rafferty	Thomas	Pte			
15957	Rankin	John A	Sgt			
15958	*					
15959	Rankin	Robert	Pte		10/3/16	DOW
15960	Rankin	Thomas	Pte			
15961	*					
15962	Rankin	Thomas	L/Cpl			
15963	*					
15964	*					
15965	Reid	Robert	L/Cpl			
15966	Reid	Arthur	Pte			
15967	Reilly	James	Pte			
15968	Richmond	Robert	Pte			
15969	Richmond	Samuel	Pte		21/11/18	Died
15970	Reilly	Harry James	L/Cpl		1/7/16	KIA
15971	Ritchie	William	Pte		1/7/16	KIA
15972	Robinson	James	Pte			
15973	Robinson	James	Pte			
15974	Robinson	John	Pte			
15975	*					
15976	Robinson	Robert	L/Cpl			
15977	Rodden	James	Cpl			

Number	Surname	Forename	Rank	Awards	Info	Additional
15978	Rodden	Robert	Pte			
15979	Rodgers	John	Pte			
15980	Rodgers	Henry	Pte			
15981	Rosborough	Henry	Pte		1/9/16	KIA
15982	Ross	William	Pte			
15983	Ross	David	Pte			
15984	Ross	Hedley W	L/Cpl			
15985	*					
15986	Roulston	James	Sgt	MM	5/10/18	DOW
15987	Roulston	Samuel J	Pte			
15988	Russell	Robert	L/Cpl		1/7/16	KIA
15989	Rutherford	Fred	Pte			
15990	Rutherford	John R. S.	Pte			
15991	Rutherford	Joseph	Pte			
15992	Rutherford	Robert	Pte			
15993	Shields	Fred	Sgt			
15994	*					
15995	Shields	William	Pte		5/8/16	KIA
15996	Shields	William	Pte	MM	13/5/18	KIA
15997	Shanks	William	L/Cpl	MM	21/3/18	KIA
15998	Shaw	Samuel	Sgt			
15999	Simms	William	Pte		26/3/18	KIA
16000	Simms	George	Pte		10/3/16	KIA
16001	Simms	George	Pte			
16002	Simpson	John	Pte		1/7/16	KIA
16003	Simpson	Robert	Pte			
16004	Simpson	Hugh	Pte			
16005	Simpson	William	Pte			
16006	Simpson	James	Pte		16/8/18	KIA R.Ir.R
16007	Simpson	Samuel	Pte			
16008	Scott	Joseph	L/Cpl		1/7/16	KIA
16009	Scott	J J	Cpl			
16010	Scott	Edmund	CSM/WOII		MiD	
16011	Spence	Daniel	Sgt			
16012	Sinclair	Andrew	Cpl	MM	13/9/18	DOW
16013	Sinclair	John	L/Sgt		10/8/17	KIA
16014	Sloan	William M	Sgt			
16015	Smy	Herbert	Pte			
16016	Smyth	Daniel	Pte			
16017	Smyth	James	Pte		1/7/16	KIA
16018	Smyth	James	Pte		1/7/16	KIA
16019	Smyth	Samuel	Sgt		15/8/15	KIA
Gallipoli						
16020	Smyth	Samuel	Pte			
16021	Smyth	James	Pte			
16022	Smyth	Robert	Pte			
16023	Smyth	Robert	Pte			
16024	*					

Number	Surname	Forename	Rank	Awards	Info	Additional
16025	Speer	Joseph	Sgt	MM		
16026	Speer	Robert	Pte			
16027	Spooner	William	Sgt			
16028	Spratt	William	Pte			
16029	Starrett	Robert	Pte			
16030	Starrett	William	Pte			
16031	Starrett	Samuel	Pte			
16032	*					
16033	Sommerville	Robert	Pte		1/7/16	KIA
16034	Stevenson	John	Pte		11/8/17	KIA
16035	Stevenson	James	Pte			
16036	Stevenson	William	Pte			
16037	Stewart	John	Pte			
16038	Stewart	William	L/Cpl			
16039	Stewart	William	Pte			
16040	Stirling	George	Pte		10/3/16	KIA
16041	Strawbridge	James	Pte			
16042	*					
16043	Synnott	William	CQMS			
16044	Taggart	David	CQMS			
16045	Tate	William M	Pte			
16046	*					
16047	Tait	Henry	Pte			
16048	Taylor	Matthew	L/Cpl			
16049	*					
16050	Teasey	William	Pte			
16051	Templeton	William	Pte		16/8/17	KIA
16052	Templeton	William	Pte			
16053	Thompson	Robert	L/Sgt		1/7/16	KIA
16054	Thompson	William J	L/Cpl-2Lt		26/3/18	KIA
16055	*					
16056	Thompson	Richard Gale	Cpl			
16057	Thompson	Samuel	Pte			
16058	Thornton	William	L/Cpl		10/7/16	DOW
16059	Tosh	William	Pte		16/8/17	KIA
16060	Trainer	William	Pte			
16061	Turkington	Pierce	Sgt			
16062	Turner	William	Sgt			
16063	Usher	David	Pte			
16064	Walker	David	Pte			
16065	*					
16066	Walker	David	Pte		1/7/16	KIA
16067	Walker	John	Pte	UDC		
16068	Walker	John	Pte			
16069	Waddell	Robert	Sgt			
16070	Waddell	Thomas	Pte			
16071	Wallace	Joseph W	Cpl			
16072	Wallace	Joseph	Pte		1/7/16	KIA

Number	Surname	Forename	Rank	Awards	Info	Additional
16073	Walls	James	Pte			
16074	Walsh	James	Pte			
16075	Watt	Frederick	Pte		1/7/16	KIA
16076	Watt	Samuel	Sgt	MiD		
16077	Watt	William	Pte			
16078	Watton	John	L/Cpl			
16079	Watton	John	Cpl			
16080	*					
16081	Walker	John	Pte			
16082	Watson	James	Pte		23/6/17	KIA
16083	Watson	James	Cpl			
16084	Wray	Robert J	Pte			
16085	Watters	James	Pte			
16086	Warke	Matthew	Pte			
16087	Warke	Henry	Pte			
16088	Weir	George	Pte			
16089	White	Robert J	Pte			
16090	White	Samuel	Pte			
16091	*					
16092	Whyte	Robert	Pte			
16093	White	Andrew	CSM/WOII		MMMC	
16094	White	John	Pte		7/12/17	KIA
16095	Whyte	Fredrick S	A/Sgt			
16096	Whiteside	Joseph	Pte			
16097	Wilkinson	John	Pte			
16098	Williamson	Joseph	L/Cpl			
16099	Williamson	Lewis	Pte			
16100	Wilkie	James	Pte			
16101	Wilson	James H	Sgt			
16102	Wilson	William	Pte			
16103	Wilson	William J	Sgt		POW	
16104	Wilson	John	Sgt		1/7/16	KIA
16105	Winton	Matthew	Pte			
16106	*					
16107	Wisener	James	Pte		1/7/16	KIA
16108	Wisener	William	Pte			
16109	Woodend	John	Pte		4/10/16	KIA
16110	*					
16111	*					
16112	Woods	Robert	L/Sgt			
16113	Wilmot	John	Pte			
16114	Wray	Henry	Pte			
16115	Wylie	Albert	Sgt			
16116	Wright	John S	L/Sgt		1/7/16	KIA
16117	Wright	Thomas	Pte			
16118	*					
16119	Wright	George	Pte		1/7/16	KIA
16120	Wray	James	Pte			

Number	Surname	Forename	Rank	Awards	Info	Additional
16121	Wray	Thomas	Cpl		1/7/16	KIA
16122	Wylie	John	Pte			
16123	Wilton	John	Sgt	UDC		
16124	Young	Robert	Pte			

Details of the men who enlisted for the 10th Inniskillings after November 1914.

Number	Surname	Forename	Rank	Awards	Info	Additional
27059	Adair	Edward	Pte		1/7/16	KIA
40635	Adams	William	Cpl		8/8/17	KIA
23497	Agnew	Robert	Pte			
24676	Aitken	Lewis	Pte		1/7/16	KIA
19110	Allen	Joseph	Pte		30/9/18	DOW
20954	Allen	Robert	Pte		1/7/16	KIA
24274	Allen	Samuel	Pte			
19855	Allen	Samuel John	Pte			
25251	Allison	George	Pte		10/9/16	KIA
21191	Anderson	Robert	Pte			
23294	Anderson	William	Pte	MM	1/7/16	KIA
19705	Anderson	William	Pte			
29324	Anderson	William J	Pte		16/8/17	KIA
23393	Andrews	Mathew	Pte			
19081	Armstrong	Samuel A	Pte			
29900	Ashfield	Hugh	Pte		11/8/17	DOW
21185	Bailey	Robert	Pte			
23628	Baird	Thomas	L/Cpl		1/7/16	KIA
19500	Barr	William	Pte			
21242	Barr	William	Pte		1/7/16	KIA
40637	Beattie	William	Pte		16/8/17	DOW
27015	Beggs	William	Pte			
-	Bell	William	Pte			
42080	Bennett	William	L/Cpl			
-	Black	Joseph	Pte			
19547	Blair	Daniel	Pte			
19857	Blair	James	Pte			
24768	Blake	Edward	Cpl	DCM		
19082	Boardman	Samuel	Pte			
27166	Boyd	Andrew	Pte		7/12/17	KIA
27382	Boyd	Christy	Pte	MM		
20939	Boyd	George	Pte			
23161	Boyd	John	Pte			
19526	Boyd	John J	Pte			
19534	Boyd	Thomas	Pte			
20007	Branagh	Robert	CSM	WOII		
28118	Brolly	John	Pte			
23471	Brown	Daniel	Pte		26/6/17	DOW
27461	Brown	Daniel	Pte		29/3/18	KIA
22345	Brown	Robert	Pte		1/7/16	KIA
21025	Brown	Robert J	Pte			

Number	Surname	Forename	Rank	Awards	Info	Additional
21056	Brown	W.C.	Pte			
21189	Brown	Patrick	Pte			
30818	Browning	Frederick C	Pte		16/8/17	KIA
21057	Brownlow	Robert	Pte			
23162	Burns	Michael	Pte			
27871	Burnside	Henry	Pte		8/8/17	KIA
23200	Byers	John	Pte		1/7/16	KIA
21062	Cahoon	Allen	Pte			
19135	Cahoon	Thomas	Pte			
20782	Caldwell	Herbert	Pte			
19783	Caldwell	Stewart	Pte			
19134	Caldwell	William	Pte		20/1/17	KIA
28074	Campbell	Brown	Pte			
19518	Campbell	Hugh	Pte		8/8/17	KIA
19859	Campbell	James	Pte		15/10/18	Died-POW
-	Campbell	John	Pte			
19860	Campbell	Samuel	Pte		2/1/17	DOW
19047	Campbell	Thomas R	L/Cpl			
27512	Campbell	Thomas	Pte			
28741	Campbell	Thomas	L/Cpl		13/7/18	Died home
19701	Campbell	William	Pte			
21192	Campbell	William	Pte		11/8/17	KIA
23165	Cassidy	H	L/Cpl	MinD		
19084	Cassidy	James	Pte		9/8/17	KIA
27133	Clyde	William	Pte		1/7/16	KIA
-	Cochrane	Francis	Pte			
22978	Cochrane	John	Pte		20/1/17	KIA
19527	Colhoun	James	Pte		8/8/17	DOW
19704	Colhoun	Thomas	Pte			
26425	Colhoun	William	Cpl			
20002	Colhoun	William	L/Cpl			
23652	Collins	Robert	Pte		9/5/16	DOW
20936	Connor	James	Pte			
21063	Convery	Thomas	Pte		1/7/16	KIA
19549	Cooke	J	Cpl	UDC		
43522	Cooper	Arthur E	Pte		25/8/17	DOW
30817	Cooper	Harry	Pte			
24187	Cox	Sidney	Cpl			
20001	Craig	Robert	Pte			
27372	Craig	Samuel	Pte		28/6/16	DOW
19558	Creelman	Robert	Pte			
22907	Creswell	John	Pte		11/8/17	KIA
23166	Crossley	Allen E	Pte			
23291	Curry	Joseph	Pte			
21186	Curry	Thomas	L/Cpl		25/3/16	KIA
25627	Curry	Thomas	Pte			
24270	Dallas	William G	Pte			
29283	Davis	Andrew	Pte			

Number	Surname	Forename	Rank	Awards	Info	Additional
19559	Dempsey	James	Pte		20/11/16	Died
24904	Devennie	James	Pte	UDC		
19542	Devine	John	Pte		24/11/16	DOW
25525	Devine	William J	Pte		1/7/16	KIA
21210	Dickson	David	Pte		1/7/16	KIA
19560	Dinnen	William	Pte		1/7/16	DIED
21075	Dinsmore	James	Pte			
26371	Dinsmore	Samuel	Pte			
19113	Dixon	John	Pte			
19049	Doey	Samuel	Pte			
23292	Donaghy	James	Cpl			
20380	Dornan	David	Pte		22/3/18	DOW
19084	Dornan	Stephen	Pte			
21863	Douglas	James	L/Cpl			
19085	Douglas	James	Pte			
19137	Douthart	John	L/Cpl			
22947	Downs	John	Pte		1/7/16	KIA
24777	Downs	Samuel	Pte			
23739	Downs	Thomas	Pte		1/7/16	KIA
23203	Duff	John	Pte			
19774	Duncan	Robert	Pte			
20380	Durnan	David	Pte		22/3/18	Died
19787	Dysart	John	Pte			
19086	Edgar	John	Pte			
43547	Edridge	Henry J	Pte		13/11/17	KIA
19051	Edmundson	Robert	Pte			
30821	Egan	Henry	L/Cpl			
20861	Ellis	Ernest H	L/Cpl			
23830	Ellis	William	Pte		1/7/16	KIA
19504	Ellison	William	Pte		1/7/16	KIA
23902	Espey	John	Pte			
42267	Espie	Samuel	L/Cpl			
19138	Ewing	William	Pte		7/6/17	KIA
19139	Faith	James	Pte		26/6/17	KIA
23951	Fannon	John	Pte		22/3/18	KIA 1st Btn
-	Ferguson	Herbert	Pte			
23150	Ferguson	Robert	Pte			
24265	Fillis	William	Pte	MM UDC	21/3/18	KIA
14745	Flackes	William	Cpl			
-	Ford	Robert	Pte			
23205	Forsythe	George	Pte		1/7/16	KIA
24192	Fullerton	John	Pte			
26000	Fulton	Alexander	Pte		13/8/17	DOW
27056	Fulton	William	Pte			
18318	Gallagher	Robert	Pte			
19561	Galway	Robert	Pte			
40643	Galway	Fergus	Pte			
23018	Gamble	James	Pte			

Number	Surname	Forename	Rank	Awards	Info	Additional
19562	Gaston	Robert	Pte			
21076	Gault	David	Pte		21/3/18	DOW 1st Bn
21064	Gault	Henry	Pte			
21077	Gault	Kennedy	Pte		1/7/16	KIA
21078	Gault	Robert	Pte			
19143	Gibson	Thomas	Pte			
21195	Gibson	William	Pte			
22359	Gilchrist	William	Pte			
20384	Gill	Walter	Pte			
29451	Gilmour	John	Pte		30/3/17	Died
19144	Gilmour	Robert	Pte		1/7/16	KIA
19865	Glass	George A	Pte			
25653	Glass	John A	Pte			
29571	Godfrey	James	Pte			
21196	Golligher	William	Pte			
19531	Goodman	John W	Pte			
2179	Gough	James G	Pte			
-	Gourley	Samuel	Pte			
23949	Gray	John	Pte		26/7/16	DOW-Home
19536	Gray	William	Pte		1/7/16	KIA
23484	Greer	William	Cpl		16/10/16	KIA
20381	Greer	William	Pte		1/7/16	DOW
19769	Grissam	James	Pte			
19053	Grundle	Richard	Pte			
28522	Guthrie	William	Pte		4/5/17	DOW
19519	Hamilton	James	Pte			
23171	Hamilton	James	Pte		5/2/17	KIA
23431	Hammond	John	Pte		1/7/16	KIA
28130	Hanlon	Archibald	Cpl			
-	Hanna	James	Pte			
8934	Hannon	Thomas	Sgt			
19117	Harbinson	Robert	Pte	UDC		
21070	Harper	David	Pte		16/8/17	KIA
27010	Harpur	Ernest	Pte		1/7/16	KIA
19095	Hassan	Mathew	Pte	MM		
24150	Harriday	Thomas	Pte		9/8/16	KIA
-	Hattrick	Alexander	Pte			
27599	Hayes	James	Pte		2/7/16	DOW
27591	Henderson	Thomas	Pte			
16995	Hiffe	William	CSM		3/11/16	Died at sea
25499	Holmes	David	Pte			
25467	Holmes	Samuel	Pte			
29610	Houston	Thomas	Pte			
-	Howard	James	Pte			
29646	Hughes	James	Pte		14/8/17	KIA
19054	Hunter	Alexander	Pte			
24463	Irvine	Robert	Pte			
19056	Irwin	Edward	L/Cpl		1/7/16	KIA

Number	Surname	Forename	Rank	Awards	Info	Additional
19057	Irwin	Samuel				
23421	Irwin	William G	Pte			
20520	Jack	Alexander	Pte			
-	Jack	Stewart	Pte			
19059	Jackson	James	Pte	UDC		
22349	Jackson	Joseph	Pte		1/7/16	KIA
25018	Jackson	William	Pte		1/7/16	KIA
19778	Jamison	James	Pte			
27694	Johnston	George	Pte			
19868	Johnston	John	Pte		1/7/16	KIA
23394	Jordon	Samuel	Pte			
9956	Joyce	Norman	L/Cpl	MM		
27250	Kelly	Robert	Pte			
25237	Kelly	William T	Pte			
29300	Kenny	William H	Sgt	MM		
22350	Keys	Thomas	Pte			
22362	Kilpatrick	Joseph	Pte			
21198	King	William	Pte			
19869	Kitson	Charles M	L/Cpl			
19090	Knox	James	Pte	UDC		
19094	Knox	William	Pte			
23177	Kyle	Samuel	Pte		29/3/18	KIA
19870	Kyle	Thomas	Pte		9/11/16	KIA
26373	Lafferty	Alex	Pte			
19064	Lamb	Samuel J	Pte			
23813	Lappin	William	Pte			
19060	Lee	James	Pte		1/7/16	KIA
27306	Lee	William	Pte		1/7/16	KIA
28607	Leonard	David	Pte			
19062	Leonard	George	Pte		9/8/16	KIA 1st Btn
43532	Lewis	Ernest	Pte		10/8/17	DOW
24868	Livingstone	Samuel	Pte			
43553	Little	Mark	Pte		11/8/17	KIA
19510	Logan	John	Pte			
19679	Logue	James	Pte			
19511	Logue	John	Pte		1/7/16	KIA
26958	Logue	John	Pte			
22502	Long	Edward	A/Sgt			
26725	Loughrey	William	Pte			
21211	Lowry	Stewart	Pte			
19512	Lumsden	John	L/Cpl			
21199	Lynch	David J	Pte			
19848	Lynd	William	Cpl			
19871	Lyttle	John	A/Sgt			
19775	Lyttle	Robert	Pte		1/7/16	KIA
20949	Macauley	Samuel	Pte			
20134	Mackey	Andrew J	Pte			
24954	Madden	Andrew	Pte			

Number	Surname	Forename	Rank	Awards	Info	Additional
24675	Madden	George	Pte		10/8/17	KIA
27233	Mann	Robert	Pte			
-	Maguire	Robert	Pte			
21079	Marshall	John	Pte			
40651	Martin	Alexander	Pte		20/11/17	KIA
19513	Martin	Daniel	Pte	UDC		
19120	Martin	David	Pte			
28406	Martin	Leslie	Pte		22/3/18	KIA 1st Btn
22339	Martin	Samuel	Pte			
43561	May	Archibald	Pte		16/12/17	DOW
43533	Mays	Frederick R	Pte			
19159	Meharg	Richard	Pte			
26726	Melville	William	Pte		1/7/16	KIA
16177	Mernor	Edward	A/WO1			
21074	Michael	William	Pte			
19096	Millar	Thomas	Pte			
26691	Millican	Samuel	A/Sgt			
26384	Mills	Robert	Pte			
24761	Mitchell	James	L/Cpl		1/7/16	KIA
19535	Mitchell	John	Pte		1/7/16	KIA
19514	Mitchell	Joseph	Pte			
20816	Mitchell	Thomas	Pte			
21266	Mitchell	William	Pte			
19124	Montgomery	Robert	A/WOII	MM+ Bar		
22364	Montgomery	Robert	Pte			
19125	Montgomery	Samuel	Pte		1/7/16	KIA
26764	Monteith	James J	Pte			
22336	Mooney	Robert	Pte		1/7/16	KIA
20385	Moore	Alfred	Pte			
19882	Moore	Bertie	Pte	MM UDC		
18971	Moore	George D	Sgt			
24273	Moore	Henderson	Pte		10/3/16	KIA
19071	Moore	Thomas	Pte			
21068	Moore	William J	Pte			
23733	Moorehead	Samuel	Pte			
19544	Morrison	George	Pte		1/7/16	KIA
20379	Morrison	Samuel	Pte			
28599	Morrison	Joseph D	L/Cpl		29/3/18	KIA 9th Btn
21060	Mundell	Duncan	Pte		20/2/16	KIA
23184	Murdock	James	Pte			
29342	Murray	Herbert	Pte			
29263	McAleer	Joseph	Pte			
19780	McAllister	William	Pte		1/7/16	KIA
24955	McAuley	Hugh B	Pte		16/8/17	KIA
24067	McCarron	Thomas	L/Cpl		1/7/16	KIA
19846	McCarter	William	Pte			
19875	McCauley	John.D	Pte		1/7/16	KIA
19669	McCauley	Samuel	Pte		1/7/16	KIA

Number	Surname	Forename	Rank	Awards	Info	Additional
19163	McClarnon	Thomas	L/Cpl			
19693	McClay	John	Pte		1/7/16	KIA
21202	McClay	William	Cpl	MM	22/3/18	KIA
24024	McClay	William	Pte		1/7/16	KIA
19550	McClean	Joseph	Pte			
26738	McClements	William	Pte			
29938	McClintock	James	Pte		16/8/17	KIA
25524	McConachie	Alexander	Pte			
14703	McConnell	Joseph	Pte		7/12/17	KIA
22368	McCracken	Joseph	Pte			
19154	McCracken	William	Pte			
41202	McCreight	George	RSM		11/8/17	KIA
22912	McCrossan	George	Pte		16/8/17	DOW
20941	McCurry	John	L/Cpl			
26996	McDermott	John	Pte			
19515	McDonald	Joseph	Pte			
19155	McDonald	Robert	Pte		1/7/16	KIA
20003	McElroy	William	Pte			
24267	McElwee	Albert	Pte			
26915	McFarland	Andrew	Pte		1/1/17	KIA
29797	McFarland	John J	Pte		9/5/17	DOW
20951	McFaul	Thomas	Pte			
10959	McGahey	James	Pte		16/7/16	DOW Prisoner
24271	McGall	Joseph	Pte		1/7/16	KIA
23644	McGonigle	Samuel	Cpl	MM		
19157	McGowan	Angus	Pte	MM		
21201	McGowan	David	Pte		16/8/17	KIA
19689	McGowan	Thomas	Pte		11/8/17	KIA
23186	McGrath	James	Pte			
19122	McGrath	John	Pte		1/7/16	KIA
30692	McGrotty	John	Pte			
20136	McGuire	George C	Pte			
29178	McGukin	Archer	Cpl			
19161	McIlfatrick	Stewart	Pte			
19878	McIlroy	Thomas	L/Cpl	MM		
21073	McIlwrath	Robert	Pte	MiD		
19065	McIntyre	William	Pte		10/8/17	KIA
23424	McKinney	Daniel J	Pte			
22341	McKinney	Moses	Pte			
19516	McLaughlin	Alexander	L/Cpl		29/9/18	DOW
29794	McLaughlin	Alexander	Pte		9/5/17	KIA
21741	McLaughlin	John	Pte			
22329	McMichael	John	Pte			
27192	McMullan	Robert	Pte		3/7/16	DOW
28180	McNabb	John	Pte			
19066	McNaughton	James	Pte			
28398	McNerlin	Hugh	Pte			

Number	Surname	Forename	Rank	Awards	Info	Additional
28399	McNerlin	William J	Sgt			
27587	McQuilken	Alexander	L/Cpl			
19672	McQuilken	John	Pte			
19881	McSeveney	Robert	Pte			
19101	Nelson	James	Pte			
30815	Newton	Walter	Cpl			
19681	Nicholl	Thomas	Pte			
26918	Nixon	Thomas	Pte		10/8/17	KIA
23812	Noble	Alexander	Pte			
21081	Norris	John	Pte		1/7/16	KIA
21364	North	Edward G	Pte			
19884	O'Neill	Robert	Pte			
21190	Orr	Reuben	Pte		1/7/16	KIA
23120	Orr	Samuel	Pte		10/8/17	KIA
27691	Parke	William A	Pte			
19102	Parkhill	Mathew	Pte		8/8/17	KIA
22353	Parkinson	John	Pte			
21203	Patterson	James	Pte			
21923	Patterson	Robert	Pte		28/3/18	DOW
19707	Patterson	William	Pte			
19127	Patton	Joseph	Pte			
23809	Payne	William	Pte			
20219	Peacock	Francis	Pte		1/7/16	KIA
19885	Peacock	William	Pte			
19525	Peoples	James	Pte			
21214	Pickering	Robert	Pte			
43555	Pite	William	Pte		16/8/17	KIA
28661	Porter	Archibald	Pte			
20383	Purdy	Thomas	Pte		21/3/18	KIA
23992	Purvis	William	Pte			
19699	Quigley	John	Pte		1/7/16	KIA
25522	Rankin	Thomas	Pte			
20938	Reid	Thomas	Pte			
22620	Reilly	James	Pte		10/8/17	KIA
27692	Rice	William	Pte		1/7/16	KIA
40662	Robinson	Arthur	Pte			
19545	Rodgers	Charles	Pte			
27318	Roulston	John	Pte		28/6/16	DOW
19572	Rowe	Robert J	Pte		1/7/16	KIA
27251	Scott	Gordon	Cpl			
24686	Scott	James L	Pte		1/7/16	KIA
21245	Scott	Samuel	L/Cpl		1/7/16	KIA
29341	Shaw	Joseph W	Sgt		16/8/17	KIA
19886	Sherrard	Edward	Pte			
23953	Sherrard	William	Pte			
25496	Sheppard	John	Pte			
26055	Shields	John	Pte			
21242	Shields	Robert	Pte		9/8/17	KIA

Number	Surname	Forename	Rank	Awards	Info	Additional
21212	Simpson	Robert	Cpl			
20378	Simpson	Samuel	Pte			
19670	Sinclair	James	Pte			
19074	Sinclair	Samuel	Pte		5/12/17	KIA
19075	Smith	Thomas	L/Cpl		1/7/16	KIA
26336	Smyth	William	Pte			
24901	South	Richard	Pte			
27954	Steele	Andrew	Pte			
19076	Sterling	William	Pte			
22843	Stevenson	George	Pte		1/7/16	KIA
23227	Stevenson	Joseph	Pte			
20958	Stewart	Adam	Pte		1/7/16	KIA
29332	Stewart	George	Sgt		10/8/17	KIA
29444	Stewart	Joseph	Pte -Lt			
25924	Swann	Samuel	Pte			
19888	Swann	William J	L/Cpl		1/7/16	KIA
19107	Taggart	Robert	Pte		1/7/16	KIA
40667	Talbot	James	Pte		7/6/17	KIA
43578	Tassell	Edward V	Pte		27/3/18	DOW
19706	Taylor	Robert	Pte	UDC		
43558	Tayman	Albert J	Pte		16/8/17	KIA
19129	Templeton	William	Pte			
19688	Thompson	William	Pte			
24141	Troy	John	Pte			
29188	Turbett	Samuel	L/Cpl			
20418	Turner	William	Pte			
42666	Waldren	Thomas H	CSM			
21086	Walker	Joseph	Pte			
19691	Walker	Robert	Pte			
27885	Walker	Samuel	Pte			
23681	Walker	Thomas	Pte			
22833	Wallace	George	Pte			
19553	Walsh	Edward	Pte			
21098	Warke	Joseph	Pte		1/7/16	KIA
20419	Warke	Robert	Pte			
19889	Watton	James	Pte		7/12/17	KIA
19130	Watton	Thomas	Pte			
19890	Watton	William	Pte			
25628	Whiteside	Robert	Pte			
24771	Williams	James	Pte		16/8/17	DOW
19773	Williamson	William J	Pte			
27385	Wilmot	James	Sgt	MM		
21208	Wilson	George	Pte			
23248	Wilson	James	Pte		24/6/17	KIA
43538	Wilson	William	Pte		7/12/17	KIA
28491	Wilton	David	Pte			
28045	Winton	Thomas	Pte		7/6/17	KIA
19173	Woodend	Arthur	Pte			

Number	Surname	Forename	Rank	Awards	Info	Additional
23567	Woodend	Thomas	Pte		30/9/16	KIA
25337	Woods	John A	Pte			
19690	Woods	Robert	Pte			
23216	Workman	William	Pte		10/8/17	KIA
22344	Wright	Joseph	Pte			
19554	Wright	Mathew	Pte			

OFFICERS

	Surname	Forename	Rank	Awards	Info	Additional
	Allom	Hugh M	Lt			
	Austin	Glover E	Capt			
	Barnett	J Bolton	2/Lt			
	Barton	Edward H	Major			
	Beale	Oscar Child	2 Lt		4/10/16	KIA
	Bennett	John TM	2 Lt	MC		
	Bogle	Albert	2 Lt		10/8/17	KIA
	Borcherds		2 Lt			
	Boyd	F.D.	Capt			
	Boyle	Robert M	Capt	MC		POW
	Brown	T	2 Lt			
	Brunt	John Jarvis	2 Lt		24/3/18	KIA
	Brush	G.H.	Major			
	Caskey		2 Lt			
	Chambers	E.H.	2 Lt			
	Chillingworth	Hugh F	2 Lt			
	Chinnick	John Noble	2 Lt			
	Cinnamond	Francis	2 Lt		13/11/18	Died POW
	Cooke	A.F.	Capt			
	Cox	Thomas W	Lt			
	Crawley	Eric	Lt		26/2/17	Died
	Cronin		2 Lt			
	Darling	George	2 Lt			
	Davidson		2 Lt			
	Donnellan	John Nolan	2 Lt			
	Douglas	James	Lt			
	Douglas	James	2 Lt			
	Drennan	James W	Lt		12/8/17	DOW
	Fanning	Robert	2 Lt	MC		
	Foy	J	2 Lt			
	Gaussen	William Ash	2 Lt			
	Glass	R.W.	Capt			
	Griffiths	William C	Lt		27/10/18	KIA
	Hamilton	Thomas	2 Lt		8/12/17	KIA
	Hessey	W.F.	Brig-Gen	DSO + Bar		
	Hughes	Robert C	Capt			
	Irwin	Robert	Lt	MC		
	Jameson	J	Capt			
	Jameison	Herbert W	Lt			

Surname	Forename	Rank	Awards	Info	Additional
Johnston	W.P.	Capt			
Keogh		2 Lt			
Kemp	Albert	2 Lt		1/7/16	KIA
Kendal	G.G.	Lt			
Kevin	C.K	2 Lt			
King.	Richard G.S	Chaplain	CF III Class		
Kitson	Charles M	2 Lt	MM		
Knox	R.S.	Lt/Col	DSO + 2 Bars		
Knox	W.H.	2 Lt			
Lindsay	Henry N	Lt			
MacKenzie	Kenneth A	2 Lt			
Maconachie	William	Capt			
Macrory	Francis	Lt/Col	DSO		
Mark	S.M.H.	Capt	MiD		
May	T.W.	2 Lt			
Miller	J.T.E.	Capt			
Mitchell	James	2 Lt	MC		
Montgomery	John Moore	2 Lt			
Moon	William J K	Capt	MC		
Morrison	Thomas D	2 Lt			
McCaw	John M	Lt	MC		
McClatchie	Edward Alex	2 Lt			
McCleave	J. N	2 Lt			
McClure	Ernest	Lt		1/7/16	KIA
McConnell	R.B	2 Lt	MC		
McCracken	Ben B	2 Lt		23/8/17	DOW
McCrae	Thomas	Lt	MC		
McKnight	Thomas	2 Lt	MC	21/2/17	KIA
McMechan	James	Capt	MC.		
Neill	Robert G	2 Lt			
Nelson	W	Capt	MC		
Nesbitt	Athol Nelson	2 Lt			
Noble	H.D.F.	Lt			
Parker	A. T. P.	2 Lt			
Parkhouse	John Foster	2 Lt			
Paton	J.G	Rev. Capt	MC+2 Bars		
Patterson	Arthur H	2 Lt	MC		
Phillips	E.M.	2 Lt			
Picken	Samuel	Capt	MC		
Picken	Paul Harley	Lt			
Plowman	G.H.	2 Lt			
Price	William	2 Lt			
Proctor	James C	Capt		1/7/16	KIA
Richards	S.E.	2 Lt			
Richardson	Arthur G	2 Lt			
Richardson	H.F.	Major			
Ritter	J.L.	Capt			
Robertson	Maxwell A	Capt		1/7/16	KIA

Surname	Forename	Rank	Awards	Info	Additional
Senington	Frank W	2 Lt			
Shannon	W.J.	2 Lt	POW		
Shareley	E	2 Lt			
Shaw	Robert	Lt	OBE		
Shearman	E.G.J	2 Lt			
Smale	P.W.	2 Lt			
Smartt	R.B.N	2 Lt			
Smyth-Ross	Acheson	Lt/Col		27/9/17	Died Home
Smyth-Waring		Major			
Spalding	Albert	2 Lt		1/7/16	KIA
Spears	Harold T	2 Lt		16/8/17	KIA
Starr	A.J.	2 Lt			
Stevens	W.A.	Lt			
Stronge	Norman C	Capt	MC		
Swann	T.G.	2 Lt			
Taylor	C	2 Lt			
Toker	R.E.	Capt			
Trench	F.C.B.	Major			
Turner	C.J.M.	2 Lt			
Wakley	A.W.	2 Lt			
Warke	Robert J	2 Lt			
Watson	Guy	2 Lt			
Webb	George H	Capt			
Wherry	J.H.	2 Lt			
White	L.C.W.	2 Lt			
Williams	F.C.	2 Lt			
Wilton	J. McElmunn	Capt	MC		

A group of girls at the commemoration of the Battle of the Somme at the Londonderry War Memorial, 1928. The girls are wearing their fathers' medals.

Photo: David Bigger/McDonald Collection

Acknowledgements

I am extremely grateful to the following people and organisations for their help in making this book possible:

Jim Donaghy MBE for sharing his most personal memories and instilling the idea for the book in the first place. His wife Josie, for listening patiently to us night after night. Leslie Bell for giving me the privilege of hearing his recollections first hand and James Monteith, who may have considered himself to be the forgotten veteran at the time, but now his memories are recorded for future generations.

Eamonn Deane of Holywell Trust for his support throughout both editions and the staff of 'Yes!' Publications especially Fionnuala Deane, Eugene Duffy and Jacqueline McColgan. Also Trevor Temple for help with proof reading and allowing me to use some of his research from the Diamond War Memorial Project. Thanks also to Richard Doherty for his careful and thorough proof reading.

A special word of thanks goes to Robert Elliott who worked fastidiously on updating the roll of those who served in the Battalion. His meticulous cross-referencing from a wide variety of sources has produced a list containing the details of almost all of the original 10th Inniskillings. This has filled in many of the blanks from the first edition's roll. Robert has been a constant source of support throughout the second edition and I am indebted to him for all his help.

Paul Clark from UTV who kindly wrote the foreword to the second edition and thought these recollections worthy to be used in some of his Remembrance Day programmes.

I am extremely grateful to Norman Torrens for the loan of the film which he made many years ago of veteran Harry Wilson when he too realised that the recollections of these veterans were precious and needed recording for posterity.

My thanks are also due to the people who kindly helped me with my research by supplying photographs and other information. They are too many to mention individually but special thanks to Ross McKenzie for copying images from Captain McKenzie's photo album. Also to Jean Scott for the use of her father's papers and photographs.

I would like to thank the original sponsors of the first edition and the many friends I made during the writing of this book.

I fully appreciate the years of support, encouragement and tolerance afforded to me from my wife Lesley who has over the years urged me to reprint a second edition.

Finally, to all of you who thought that the memory of the men who fought and died with the 36th Ulster Division should not be forgotten.

HE whom this scroll commemorates
was numbered among those who,
at the call of King and Country, left all
that was dear to them, endured hardness,
faced danger, and finally passed out of
the sight of men by the path of duty
and self-sacrifice, giving up their own
lives that others might live in freedom.

Let those who come after see to it
that his name be not forgotten.

Pte. John Gray
Royal Inniskilling Fusiliers